NAVIGATION WORKBOOK
1210 Tr

DAVID BURCH LARRY BRANDT

STARPATH
www.starpathpublications.com

Copyright © 2014, Starpath Publications

All rights reserved. No part of this book may be reproduced or transmitted in any form or by any means, electronic or mechanical, including photocopying, recording, or any information storage or retrieval system, without permission in writing from the author.

ISBN 978-0-914025-44-3

Published by

Starpath Publications

3050 NW 63rd Street, Seattle, WA 98107

Manufactured in the United States of America

www.starpathpublications.com

Table of Contents

INTRODUCTION v
    Scope v
    Chart 1210 Tr v
    Terminology v
    Magnetic Variation v
    Tides and Currents v
    Tools of the Trade vi
    For more Help vi

EXERCISES 1
    CHAPTER 1 – THE ROLE OF NAVIGATION 1
    CHAPTER 2 – NAUTICAL CHARTS AND CHART READING 3
    CHAPTER 3 – OTHER NAVIGATION AIDS 6
    CHAPTER 4 – COMPASS USE 9
    CHAPTER 5 – DEAD RECKONING 11
    CHAPTER 6 – PILOTING 13
    CHAPTER 7 – ELECTRONIC NAVIGATION 15
    CHAPTER 8 – TIDES AND CURRENTS 17
    CHAPTER 9 – NAVIGATION IN CURRENTS 19
    CHAPTER 10 – NAVIGATION RULES 21
    CHAPTER 11 – NAVIGATION PLANNING AND PRACTICE 31
    CHAPTER 12 – IN DEPTH… 35

RESOURCES 37
    Tide Tables 38
    Current Tables 42
    Current Sailing Resources 48
    Light List 49
    Light List Luminous Range Diagram 56
    Light List Characteristics of Lights 57
    Local Notice to Mariners 58
    Excerpts from NOAA Chart Catalog No. 1 64

US Coast Pilot Vol. 2, Chapter 5 66
Coast Pilot Chapter 5 Index 74
Coast Pilot Climate Data (Appendix B) 75
Coast Pilot Marine Weather Statistics (Appendix B) 76

ANSWERS 77
    CHAPTER 1 – THE ROLE OF NAVIGATION 77
    CHAPTER 2 – NAUTICAL CHARTS AND CHART READING 77
    CHAPTER 3 – OTHER NAVIGATION AIDS 79
    CHAPTER 4 – COMPASS USE 81
    CHAPTER 5 – DEAD RECKONING 82
    CHAPTER 6 – PILOTING 83
    CHAPTER 7 – ELECTRONIC NAVIGATION 85
    CHAPTER 8 – TIDES AND CURRENTS 85
    CHAPTER 9 – NAVIGATION IN CURRENTS 87
    CHAPTER 10 – NAVIGATION RULES 89
    CHAPTER 11 – NAVIGATION PLANNING AND PRACTICE 91
    CHAPTER 12 – IN DEPTH... 95

APPENDIX 97
    A1. Using Electronic Charts 97
    A2. Interpolation 98
    A3. Sources for 1210 Tr Printed Charts 100

INTRODUCTION

Scope

These exercises are designed to help small-craft navigators hone their skills in both routine and special circumstances. They are practical exercises in chart reading and plotting, position fixing, dead reckoning, compass work, and the use of special publications such as Chart Catalogs, *Tide Tables*, *Current Tables*, *Light Lists*, Notices to Mariners, *Chart No. 1*, *Navigation Rules*, and *U.S. Coast Pilots*.

These exercises can be incorporated into an ongoing navigation course or used by individuals on their own. This book along with a text book of choice would then make up a self-study course. The chapters of this workbook correlate with those of the book *Inland and Coastal Navigation, 2nd edition* by David Burch, but other books can also provide the necessary background.

The level of these exercises is about that required in the USCG Masters license exam for 100 GT, which in turn is about the same as that used in coastal navigation certification exams from the U.S. Sailing Association, American Sailing Association, Royal Yachting Association, and the Canadian Yachting Association.

Chart 1210 Tr

The exercises in this book that require a chart use NOAA chart 1210 Tr, Martha's Vineyard to Block Island including Western Approach to Cape Cod Canal. This is one of several NOAA training charts. This one is frozen in time to about 1990, but is otherwise similar to the standard navigation chart of this region (No. 13218), which is updated weekly, as are all NOAA charts now that they are all Print on Demand (POD). For training exercises, it is best to use the training chart version 1210 Tr, so all details match the exercises.

The 1210 Tr is available at most NOAA chart dealers and from several online outlets (see Appendix A3.). This is the most popular of all training charts, used by most navigation schools in the US. Consequently it has been bulk printed by commercial companies and is available for less cost than the POD version.

Except for this paper chart that must be purchased separately, all other resource materials are provided in the Resources section, which includes excerpts for all publications needed.

You can also work the exercises with an electronic version of 1210 Tr, and for that solution we have an extended discussion in Appendix A1, which includes a source for the echart. We encourage mariners to solve the charting exercises using both paper charts and electronic charts. Also provided are a few tips on the use of ECS (electronic charting system) for solving navigation problems.

Terminology

All references to miles are nautical miles. Sometimes this is stated as miles other places as "nmi." One nautical mile is about 6,000 ft. (Exact is 1 nmi = 1852m = (1852x100/2.54)/12 ft, which is about 6076.115 ft.)

General phrases like "north of" or "due east of," etc, always refers to true directions, unless otherwise specified. Wind directions are labeled by the source of the wind, i.e. north wind flows from north to south, sea breeze blows from the sea toward the land. Wind waves and currents, on the other hand, are labeled with the true direction they flow toward. (Swells, as opposed to wind waves, are labeled by the direction they come from.)

Magnetic Variation

The magnetic variation on the 1210 Tr chart (frozen in 1990) covers magnetic variations that vary from 15.0 W to 15.5 W. To simplify the exercises, however, we use a fixed value of 15.0 W for all locations of the chart, and for all exercises.

Tides and Currents

Because the design of the NOAA *Tide Tables* and *Tidal Current Tables* have changed to some extent since the time of the 1210 Tr chart, we have chosen to use more modern values for the related exercises. Tide and current data provided are from 2011.

Tools of the Trade

These are the basic plotting tools used in marine navigation. There are many alternatives, but these are the most common by far, worldwide, on all vessels.

Dividers

Dividers are used to measure the distance between two points, and also to help align parallel rulers or plotters. There are several styles. Shown here is a type of "speed bow." You can interchange one of the points with a pencil lead for drawing circles of position or other arcs.

A "bow" is a tool that will hold its point separation once set, and it is set by a rotating knob in the center of the tool—as opposed to conventional dividers which are just pulled open or squeezed closed. A "speed bow" is one that you can pull open or close by hand without having to use the center knob. In other words, you can override the fine control of the center knob by firmly pulling or pushing on the legs themselves.

This particular model has become the dividers of choice for the vast majority of professional navigators worldwide because of its ease of use and accuracy. This economic model is called (appropriately) "ultra light dividers."

Parallel Rulers

This is a tool that lets you draw one line parallel to another, some distance away from it. To use it, align one edge of the rulers with the base line, and then holding down that side of the tool, move the other side to the location of the new line. If the new location cannot be reached in one step, then you walk the rulers across the page to the destination.

It takes a bit of practice to manipulate these without slipping, but after some practice it is quite easy. There are numerous styles and sizes of these. A simple design, in clear plastic with small cork anti-slip pads, 15 inches long is a popular and functional option.

Weems Plotter

An alternative to parallel rulers is a rolling tool called a parallel plotter, or more specifically, the Weems parallel plotter, named after its inventor. These are designed to roll without sliding, which they generally do fairly well, with little practice. Unfortunately, rolling plotters do not work well near the edges of charts or over folds in the chart. A solution is always also carry parallel rulers underway and use the Weems plotter whenever possible, but immediately switch to parallel rulers if need be. On a large chart table (or kitchen table) many navigators find this tool faster and easier to use than parallel rulers.

Triangles

The most accurate chart plotting is often done with two matching navigation triangles. They take a bit more practice to master, but the larger protractor scale and more positive positioning does enhance the accuracy. They are popular with professional mariners.

Three-Arm Protractor

Other applications are possible, but the main function of this tool is to plot a fix from two horizontal sextant angles, which is faster than the compass and ruler plotting.

For more Help

Check starpath.com/1210tr for news and resources related to this book as well as contact with the authors. Comments and suggestions will be much appreciated and addressed promptly. Training aids are available as well as links to navigation schools and navigation certification associations around the world that offer basic and advanced training in marine navigation. Links to local classes from US Power Squadrons and USCG Auxiliary are also provided.

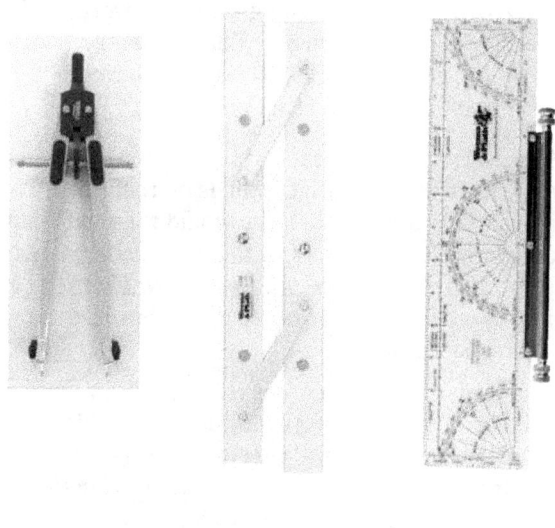

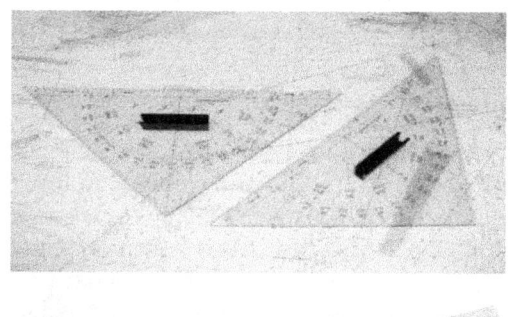

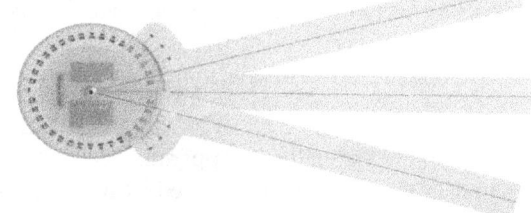

Plotting tools. *Dividers, parallel rulers, Weems Plotter, triangles, 3-arm protractor*

EXERCISES

CHAPTER 1 – THE ROLE OF NAVIGATION

These questions are usually addressed in early chapters of a navigation text. Some are terminology, some philosophy.

1-1. The art of dead reckoning navigation lies in...

(A) Determining a best estimate for your position based on logbook records of course, distance and time.
(B) Determining your exact position based on course, distance and time.
(C) Estimating your position based on bearings to at least two known landmarks.
(D) Estimating your position based on identifying a buoy that you have just passed.

1-2. Piloting is the art of navigating a vessel...

(A) By reference to GPS courses and fixes.
(B) By reference to nearby landmarks and buoys.
(C) In heavy waves when the vessel may become airborne.
(D) By following other vessels of similar size and draft.

1-3. Choose from the following the one INCORRECT statement concerning The Navigation Rules:

(A) The Rules apply to stand-up-paddle boards.
(B) The Rules do not apply to kayaks, rowboats or jet skis.
(C) The Rules apply to submarines.
(D) The Rules apply to seaplanes when landing on the water or taking off from the water.

1-4. The numerical value of the direction to an object from your viewing location is called the...

(A) True bearing, if the value is read from the binnacle compass of your vessel.
(B) Relative bearing, if the value is referenced to Magnetic North.
(C) Magnetic bearing, if the value is referenced to the outer ring of a chart's compass rose.
(D) Magnetic bearing, if the value is referenced to Magnetic North.

1-5. Arguably the most important book in navigation is...

(A) Bowditch's *New Practical American Navigator*.
(B) The *Navigation Rules*.
(C) *Chapman Piloting and Seamanship*.
(D) Latest editions of the *Tide Tables* and *Tidal Current Tables*.

1-6. When your vessel's accurate position at a particular time has been determined by some form of piloting or by electronic navigation using GPS or radar, and noted on a navigation chart, it is said to be...

(A) An estimated position (EP).
(B) An updated DR.
(C) A fix.
(D) A position forecast.

1-7. What is the approximate length of a nautical mile in feet that is very valuable for every navigator to know?

1-8. What is the most important reason for learning traditional navigation skills?

(A) Check the GPS.
(B) To use if the GPS receiver or display electronics fail.
(C) To use if the GPS signal is not available at our location.
(D) Good seamanship calls for us to be prepared to navigate in any condition.

1-9. A *small craft* is characterized by...

(A) Overall length under 65 ft.
(B) Maximum speed of 7 kts regardless of length.
(C) There is no single definition; it depends on the circumstances.
(D) Any shallow-draft vessel under 100 ft long.

1-10. Translate this into landsman language without using the word log: "We logged 20 miles according to the log, which I logged into the log."

1-11. Give at least one reason why the main challenge of modern navigation training is learning route planning and not position finding.

1-12. Which statement is true?

(A) For safe navigation I need the latest nautical charts.
(B) For safe navigation I need nautical charts and at least 3 books.
(C) A well designed electronic charting system can meet all of my needs for safe navigation.
(D) All statements are true.

1-13. Concerning the practical application of GPS compared to basic knowledge of piloting skills, give a few examples of where this thought might apply: "It is far more important to know for certain where you are not, than to know precisely where you are."

1-14. Looking ahead to some basics, looking at a chart or the special publication called Light List, (A) What is the color of even numbered buoys? (B) What is the color of odd numbered buoys?

1-15. Looking clear across the ocean, how do the British pronounce buoy?

CHAPTER 2 – NAUTICAL CHARTS AND CHART READING

These exercises require some version of Chart No 1. A full version of this and other publications are online (starpath.com/navpubs). An older version is printed on the reverse side of 1210 Tr. It could be helpful to skim through the Coast Pilot excerpts in the Resources section to become more familiar with the chart. Use the Light List or Coast Pilot Indexes from the Resources section to locate aids, marks or regions as needed. Use magnetic variation of 15.0° W for all locations on this chart, for all questions in this book. It will be very instructive to download a full copy of the latest Light List and read the Introduction (about 20 pages).

2-1. Concerning the 1210 Tr training chart... (A) What is the latest revision date of this chart? (B) What is the title of the chart? (C) What map projection is used for this chart? (D) What scale is the chart? (E) Are soundings in feet, fathoms, or meters? (F) What is the chart datum (reference level) for soundings? (G) What is the chart datum (reference level) for elevations? (H) What are the precise Lat and Lon boundaries (ie top and bottom Lats; right and left Lons)? (I) What is the precise height and width of the chart in nautical miles? (J) Around the edges of the chart is the notice "LORAN-C OVERPRINTED." What does this indicate? (K) What modern chart is the nearest to same coverage as 1210 Tr?

2-2. Aligned north-south along longitude 71° 24' is a series of seven White and Orange buoys. What is the purpose of these buoys?

2-3. South of Martha's Vineyard's Gay Head there is an island called "Nomans Land". This island lies within a rectangle labeled "Prohibited Area." Does Note A tell us what the restrictions are for this area? If yes, what are the restrictions? If not, where would one find the applicable restrictions?

2-4. What is the land mass appearing in the southwest corner of the chart?

2-5. What is the name of the reef off the west end of Cuttyhunk Island?

2-6. What is the name of the shoal, approximately 5 miles in length, which runs along the south part of Vineyard Sound, extending westward from the right edge of the chart?

2-7. What is the name of the point where the Massachusetts/Rhode Island state border meets the sea?

2-8. What is the identification of the radio tower located a little more than a mile east of Newport, Rhode Island?

2-9. Immediately west and south of the Brenton Reef Buoy there is a depth contour line. What depth does this line represent?

2-10. Why are no soundings given in Narragansett Bay?

2-11. There are three compass roses depicted on the chart. Per each compass rose, what year was the magnetic variation surveyed?

2-12. As of the year of magnetic survey (and as depicted on each rose), what was the maximum difference in variation between the three roses?

2-13. As of the year of survey, what was the predicted annual change in Variation at each rose location?

2-14. What is the name of the channel that forms the first leg of the south entrance to the Cape Cod Canal?

2-15. What is the name of the next channel leg entering the Canal?

2-16. What is the name of the ledge about a mile south of Sakonnet Point?

2-17. What is the name of the ledge about a mile south and slightly east of Warren Point?

12-18. Running from near the tower at Gooseberry Neck across to the west end of Cuttyhunk Island is a dotted line that is labeled. How is this line labeled?

2-19. What is the significance of this line?

2-20. Nashawena Island has a prominent landmark charted. What is it?

2-21. In Vineyard Sound there are areas marked with a circled E and a circled F. What are these, and why do you think they are there?

2-22. Running south southeast from New Bedford are two parallel dotted lines marked Note C. What do these lines indicate?

2-23. There is a Caution notice near the west edge of the chart, approx. Lat 41° 32' N, Lon 71° 30' W. To what does this notice refer?

2-24. How many locations of unexploded depth charges can you find on the chart?

2-25. What is the name of the island just NE of Cuttyhunk and NW of Nashawena?

2-26. What is the name of the point that forms the southern shore of West Falmouth Harbor?

2-27. What charted fixture is located on the west end of Wings Neck, just east of the entrance to Cape Cod Canal?

2-28. Some major navigation aids on the chart such as the Buzzards Light are depicted as having radio beacons, a technology now out of use. Referring to the *Light List*, what modern technology replaces most of these?

2-29. What distinguishes BELL, GONG, WHISTLE, and HORN sounds?

2-30. What is printed on the reverse side of 1210 Tr?

2-31. Today's active (ie, not a training chart) navigation chart for the waters covered in the 1210 Tr is NOAA chart 13218, Martha's Vineyard to Block Island 1:80,000). Find a recent copy of this chart or view the one online and identify at least two MAJOR changes that have taken place... (A) regarding soundings datum, and (B) regarding traffic control.

2-32. Considering that a hand span is about 7 inches, and on a 1:10,000 scale chart that covers about 1 miles distance, what distance is covered by a hand span on a 1:40,000 scale chart?

2-33. One handspan on a 1:80,000 scale chart is about how many miles?

2-34. Is a 1:10,000 harbor chart a LARGER scale or a SMALLER scale chart than 1:1,000,000 oceanic chart?

2-35. For close inshore navigation, which chart scale, large or small, would better allow presentation of rocks, kelp beds, and other items of localized concern?

2-36. What is the echart type called that when displayed on an electronic chart plotter allows the user to see an exact copy of a paper chart?

2-37. List at least 4 major differences between ENC and RNC echarts.

2-38. What is the document that a navigator consults to amend and update a paper chart to the latest information, allowing him/her to pencil in buoy, hazard, and other corrections?

  (A) Coast Pilot.
  (B) Local cruising guides.
  (C) Local Notice to Mariners.
  (D) Tides and Current tables.

2-39. East of Nomans Land and south of Squibnocket Point is bell Buoy 1. What is the nature of the seabed in the area of that buoy?

2-40. What is the indicated depth as depicted just NE and adjacent to the Buzzards light, Fl 2.5sec 101ft 22M HORN R BN 314?

2-41. What is the nature of the seabed in the area of that light?

2-42. Approximately 1 mile N of Pasque Island there is a wreck reported at 65 feet. What is the nature of the seabed in the area of the wreck?

2-43. What is the nature of the seabed as depicted about 1/3 mile south of the Butler Flats Buoy (Fl 4sec 4M)?

2-44. What is the prominent fixture charted in the approximate center of Gay Head?

2-45. What is the depth of the sounding contour where the sea color changes from blue to white?

2-46. On Block Island there is charted AERO Rot W & G. What is this?

2-47. South of Point Judith is the lighted whistle Buoy 2. Adjacent to it is the number 35 with an odd underline beneath the number. What does this indicate?

2-48. Southwest of Sow and Pigs Reef is a RB lighted whistle Buoy VS. The RB indicates the color of the buoy as red over black. In the years since publication of the 1210 Tr training chart the black colors of buoys have mostly been replaced by the color green. Nevertheless, what is the light characteristic of this buoy shown on 1210 Tr?

2-49. Keeping vessels off the reef is only part of the purpose of this buoy as charted. What is its other important job?

2-50. Adjacent to Squibnocket Point is an area shaded in light green. What does this color indicate?

2-51. Within this light green area are the following symbols. What do they indicate? (A) * (B) +

2-52. Just off Jacobs Neck, near the entrance to the Cape Cod Canal, is a symbol that looks like a plus sign with four dots. What does this indicate?

2-53. How would the terrain along the west shore of West Passage, in the area of The Bonnet, appear to a small vessel transiting the area?

2-54. As practice with Lat-Lon, please find the Lat and Lon of the following points to the nearest tenth of an arc minute. (A) The WNBH radio tower south of New Bedford, (B) The water tower at Woods Hole, (C) The abandoned light house near the West Passage bridge, (D) The WADK radio tower on Aquidneck Island, (E) The abandoned light house off Sakonnet Point, (F) The monument on Nashawena Island, (G) The unexploded depth charge about 4 miles south of Newport Neck, (H) The wreck about 4 miles WSW of Gay Head.

2-55. As practice measuring distance with dividers, please draw lines as stated in the points below and find the distance between the points. Round to the nearest tenth nmi. Obviously these are not Course lines as some of them traverse charted land masses, (A) From the charted house to the charted monument on Nashawena Island, (B) From the spire on Gay Head to the monument on Nashawena Island, (C) From the south torpedo range W Or "A" Fl 4sec BELL to the north torpedo range W Or "H" Fl 2sec BELL, You may need to draw a fine pencil line to make this an accurate measurement, (D) From the light on Block Island's Sandy Point to the Point Judith light, (E) From the BW "BB" Mo (A) BELL in Buzzards Bay to the BUZZARDS Fl 2,5sec 101ft 22M HORN R Bn 314 light, (F) From the Fl G 4sec BELL east of Nomans Land to the BW "SR" Mo (A) WHISTLE at the entrance to the Sakonnet River, You may need a longer straightedge to draw this line.

2-56. For practice using the parallel ruler and compass rose, please determine the magnetic course of the above defined lines. Your answers should be accurate to within 2 degrees except for problem (A), the very short Nashawena Island course. Use the compass rose that is most convenient for you.

2-57. Explain what the following light and buoy labels mean. (A) RW "NA" Mo (A) WHISTLE, (B) Fl G 4sec BELL, (C) G "31" FL G 4s GONG, (D) F R 25 ft "8", (E) FL 4sec 30ft 8M "2", and (F) Checking a modern Light List, what are the modern abbreviations used for "WHISTLE" and for "sec" (as opposed to those used on 1210 Tr)?

2-58. Departing the Sakonnet River you see the R bell Buoy 2A off Sakonnet Point. Visibility is very limited and no land is in sight. Would you leave that buoy to starboard or to port?

2-59. Which of the following statements concerning buoy location and number sequence is correct?

(A) Can be counted on as accurate and sequential, with no missing numbers.
(B) Is usually sequential, but may occasionally be missing numbers of the sequence.
(C) Can always be relied on for accurate location even though numbering may be off.
(D) Can always be relied on for sequential numbering even though position may be off.

2-60. When tracking a range indicated by painted boards and lights, which board and light set is the set closest to your vessel, the upper or the lower set?

2-61. Ranges can be very accurate aids to navigation but they are not always ahead of us where we need them. What must we do to follow a charted range if the range signals are astern of us?

2-62. Approaching the entrance to a harbor from offshore in restricted visibility you sight a buoy with vertical red and white colors, possibly with a white light atop. On which side must/may you leave this buoy as you pass it?

2-63. Regulatory markers are used for important communications, such as speed limits, no wake zones, etc. What does it indicate when you see a regulatory buoy with a crossed diamond on it?

2-64. What is the 1210 Tr training chart's datum for heights and elevations?

2-65. What do the following navigation abbreviations mean? (A) C, (B) H, (C) R & B, (D) COG, (E) CMG, (F) Trk.

2-66. What are the definitions of the following terms: (A) Course, (B) Heading, (C) Bearing, (D) Course Over Ground, (E) Course Made Good, (F) Track.

2-67. A mark with two black spheres atop, typically black with red horizontal bands indicates what?

2-68. Cardinal marks and buoys indicate which?

(A) Navigable water to their named side.
(B) Hazardous water to their named side.

2-69. A cardinal mark showing two triangles (cones) in a vertical line, point-to-point, indicates safe or hazardous water to which side?

(A) Navigable water to the south
(B) Hazardous water to the west.
(C) Navigable water to the west.
(D) Navigable water to the east.

2-70. A cardinal mark at night showing a very quick sequence of 6 flashes on the top light and a quick series of flashes on the low light indicates what?

(A) Navigable water to the south.
(B) Navigable water to the west.
(C) Navigable water to the north.
(D) Hazardous water to the south.

2-71. What does 'nominal range' mean as applied to a light?

CHAPTER 3 – OTHER NAVIGATION AIDS

The following questions relate to the abridged and modified Coast Pilot and Light List that appear in the Resources section. Both of these publications are available in full format as a download online. See also these corresponding notes to Chapter 2.

3-1. Throughout the Vineyard Sound and Buzzards Bay chapter of Coast Pilot 2 are advisories to strangers. What advice is given to strangers?

(A) Strangers should never attempt certain passages.
(B) Strangers should not enter certain harbors except in daytime and clear weather.
(C) Strangers should attempt certain passages only at slack water.
(D) All of the above.

3-2. The Elizabeth Islands include which of the following?

(A) Gay Head, Nashawena, and Nomans Land.
(B) Martha's Vineyard and Nomans Land.
(C) The islands stretching from Nonamesset to Cuttyhunk.
(D) West Island and other small islets in Nasketucket Bay.

3-3. The Coast Pilot has weather data in two sections of Appendix B. One called Climatological Data, the other called Meteorological Tables. Using the former: In waters near Newport, RI: (A) Which month of the year has the statistically highest number of fog days? (B) What is the mean pressure in Jan? (C) What quadrant do most winds come from in July, and what is the percentage of all observations are from that quadrant? (A quadrant is a direction ±45°). (D) What month has the highest number of calm wind observations? (E) The Coast Pilot Climate data called "Newport, RI" is given with a Lat-Lon? Where is this reference point on the chart? Is there any message here?

3-4. With 12 days of fog as typical in that month, which single electronic tool, other than a VHF radio, would be most appropriate to have onboard? Assume you already have paper charts onboard.

(A) AIS.
(B) Radar, together with an operator who has been trained to use it properly.
(C) Chartplotter.
(D) HF radio.

3-5. Using Coast Pilot Meteorological Table, in the coastal area south of Martha's Vineyard: (A) How many days in a typical February can be expected with waves greater than 9 feet? (B) Are the predictions for this coastal region to have more or less fog days in July than more inland near Newport? (C) Are the severe weather predictions of this table expected to be underestimates or overestimates? (D) What is the mean sea level pressure in Jan according to this table? Does this agree with the Climatological data, and if not what does that tell us? (E) Carrying on with the unusual naming of these weather data tables in the Coast Pilot, what stands out as puzzling in the title of this table?

3-6. Westward of Woods Hole there are several buoyed passages through the Elizabeth Islands, but only one of them is recommended for strangers. Which one?

3-7. Prominent features of Woods Hole are the dome and buildings of an important research center. What agencies do these buildings serve?

3-8. Why is the northern entrance into Woods Hole preferred over the southern entrance?

3-9. The passage through Woods Hole can be dangerous in some conditions without local knowledge. Although a buoyed passage exists, what is the cited risk to safe passage through the channel in some conditions?

3-10. Is the buoyage system in Woods Hole established for vessels proceeding from north to south, or from south to north?

3-11. Canapitsit Channel separating Nashawena and Cuttyhunk Islands, with a controlling depth of 4 ft, should never be used in what conditions? Why not?

3-12. Vessels up to what draft may anchor in New Bedford's Inner Harbor?

3-13. What color(s) and visible arc(s) are characteristics of the Directional Light at Woods Hole Great Harbor?

3-14. How might the Nobska Point lighted bell Buoy 26 be affected by seasonal problems? What is done about it? Why do you think this action is taken?

3-15. What color(s) is displayed by the Nobska Point Light? What is the nominal range of the color(s)?

3-16. What horn characteristic is sounded by the Nobska Point Light?

3-17. What is the nominal visibility of Gay Head Light?

3-18. What is the light characteristic of Gay Head Light?

3-19. What color(s) is the Woods Hole Station Mooring Buoy?

3-20. What is the light characteristic of the Buzzards Bay Entrance Light?

3-21. What is the height of the Buzzards Bay Entrance Light?

3-22. What is the nominal visibility of the Buzzards Bay Entrance Light?

3-23. What is the horn characteristic of the Buzzards Bay Entrance Light?

3-24. The 1210 Tr training chart shows Buzzards Bay Entrance Light to have a radio beacon on the frequency of 314 kHz. Is this radio beacon still operating? If not, what technology might have replaced it?

3-25. Buzzards Bay lighted gong Buoy 8, approximately 2 miles NE of Penikese Island, is replaced when endangered by ice. What is the replacement for this buoy when endangered by ice? An acronym does not count as an answer in this case. (Hint: This question is to motivate external research. Please download a current Light List 1 and do a search for this term.)

3-26. The Cleveland Ledge Channel Range Front and Rear Lights on the southern end of Abiels Ledge are remarked in the Light List to be a structure "KRW on white tower". What kind of structure is this? (Hint: This question is to motivate external research. Please download a current Light List 1 and do a search for this term.)

3-27. What is the height of the Butler Flats light?

3-28. Phinney Rock Buoy, near the entrance to the channel leading to New Bedford Harbor, has changed since the 1210 Tr training chart was issued, such changes being a great reason to refer to the Light List whenever safety of the vessel and crew is on the line. Describe the replacement that is presently serving at Phinney Rock.

3-29. The Hadley Harbor Entrance Daybeacon has a structure on a spindle. A spindle is a piling or pole on which a sign can be mounted. What kind of sign is mounted on the Hadley Harbor Entrance's spindle? (Hint: This question is to motivate external research. Please download a current Light List 1 and do a search for this term.)

3-30. According to the Light List the Hadley Harbor Entrance Daybeacon has a "Ra ref". What is this?

3-31. What color is the Menemsha Bight CG Mooring Buoy?

3-32. You can see Buzzards (Bay) Entrance Light (Fl 2.5s, 41° 24'N, 71° 02'W) while standing on the cabin top (height of eye 15 feet), but not from the cockpit (eye height about 6 feet). The water is calm and it is a clear night. Roughly how far off the light are you? (Use the charted light specifications.)

3-33. According to the Luminous Range Diagram, what is the luminous range of a 26-mile light (nominal range = 26 miles) when the prevailing atmospheric visibility is (A) 5.5 miles, (B) 1 mile, and (C) 500 yards? Use the diagram on page 6 of the Light List. Then figure same values with the approximation: Luminous range = 1 nmi + [(visibility)/10] × nominal range.

3-34. From the cabin top at an eye height of 10 ft above the water, how far could you see Pt. Judith Light if the atmospheric visibility was 5.5 miles? Use charted light specifications.

3-35. From how far off can you see the Dumpling Rocks Light (Fl G 6s, 41° 32'N, 70° 55'W) from an height of eye of 9 feet (A) in clear weather, and (B) with 3 miles visibility? Use the charted light specifications.

3-36. From an eye height of 9 ft, how far off could you see Nomans Land: (A) in clear weather? (B) In atmospheric visibility of 4 miles?

3-37. How far can you see a 5-mile light in 5 miles of visibility?

3-38 (A) If the nominal range of a buoy light is not given on the chart or Light List, what should you assume it is? And (B) more generally, how far off should you assume you can see a typical buoy light with no other information available?

3-39. A light is charted as Fl 4sec, 27 ft, 19M. You can see the light from the cabin top at an eye height of 12 feet, but not from the cockpit at an eye height of 7 feet. How far off the light are you?

3-40. According to the Chart Catalog, what is the largest-scale chart number for Woods Hole?

3-41. (A) What is the Lat, Lon of the Buzzards Bay Midchannel lighted bell Buoy BB as read from the 1210 Tr training chart? (B) What does the Light List give for its location? (C) Approximately how much has the position of the buoy been changed over the years?

3-42. With regard to Rules of the Road, do the Inland or International Navigation rules apply in Vineyard Sound?

3-43. What buoyage scheme if any is in use by the Buzzards Bay Traffic Separation Scheme?

3-44. An aggregation of 7 right whales sighted south of Nantucket has caused NOAA Fisheries to establish a Dynamic Management Area. What action from mariners is requested in this regard?

3-45. Private boats arriving from a foreign port or place must report to the Bureau of Customs and Border Protection...

   (A) As soon as the CBP office opens the following day.
   (B) Immediately upon arrival into the United States.
   (C) If not carrying commercial cargo then within 24 hours.
   (D) All of the above.

3-46. What sound signal is being emitted by the Cleveland Ledge Channel lighted gong Buoy 7?

3-47. The Butler Flats Light is showing what characteristic?

3-48. What clearance should your vessel give to the tugs NAVIGATOR and PATRICK HUNT and their associated working barges?

3-49. What is the present location and status of the Narragansett-Buzzards Bay Approach lighted whistle Buoy A? (Note: this location is not on the 1210 Tr training chart.)

3-50. The Local Notice to Mariners has an excellent check list for safe offshore sailing. (A) To encourage a review of this, how many check points do they list? (B) List another 4 points (of many) we should check that are directly related to good preparation in the navigation department.

3-51. According to the Coast Pilot, what is the maximum draft that can be carried into Broad Cove by way of the East River?

3-52. Besides the nautical charts, what are the five minimum special publications we should have onboard for any extended voyage?

3-53. Are bright lighthouse lights on all the time, or are they controlled by light sensors and just come on at night and during the fog?

CHAPTER 4 – COMPASS USE

Use variation of 15.0° W for all questions. We just override the values listed on 1210 Tr, which vary by 0.5°. Magnetic variation in the charted region in modern times has changed notably.

4-1. (A) What does the rule "Correcting add east" mean? (B) Give at least two jingles that help us remember the meaning and order of compass corrections. (C) What is the correcting direction?

4-2. The local variation is 15.0° W. The true course to our destination is 330 T. (A) What is the compass course assuming no deviation? (B) Same question with Dev = 4° E

4-3. A typical compass rose on a chart has 3 circular scales around it. The outer is true in degrees, the middle is magnetic in degrees; what does the innermost scale represent?

4-4. On course 125 C, you are sailing toward the No. 2 light off of Gunning Pt (1.5 mi N of Woods Hole), and you see its structure aligned precisely with the Standpipe tower on shore. What is your deviation if any on course 125 C? (PS. Both the light and the tower are no longer there!)

4-5. On course 296 C, you are sailing W-NW directly beside and parallel to the Plum Beach Bridge to Conanicut Island and your compass reads 296 C. (A) What is your deviation on course 296 C? (B) From that observation, what can you say about your deviation when you turn south to sail roughly perpendicular to that course?

4-6. If you reason through these various exercises on conversions you will have as much practice as you will likely ever need... except for Exercise 4-16! Solve for the unknowns in each case (blanks in the table). In top one, for example, the true heading is known from the chart, and the compass is known from reading the compass, and the variation in the area is known from a chart. The problem, then, is to figure the proper magnetic heading, and the difference of this from the compass heading is the deviation. This type of problem is best solved using a vertical TVMDC diagram and then filling in the blanks. These are random examples; not related to 1210 Tr. They are 9 separate exercises.

#	Comp	Dev	Mag	Var	True
1	296			16° W	280
2		5°E	014	21° E	
3	354	8° W			007
4	276		276	10° W	
5		5° W	093		114
6	138			4° E	138
7		0°	006	21° W	
8	028	0°			049
9	351		355	17° E	

4-7. The gong Buoy 4 at the west end of Nomans Land bears 339 M and Buoy 2 south of Nomans Land bears 249 M. (A) Are you in the area marked as Prohibited? (B) What is the charted depth at your location? (C) What is your Lat-Lon? (D) What is the course and distance from there to the Buoy 1 ENE of Nomans Land?

4-8. Sailing somewhat NW of Buzzards Light, the Schuyler Ledge Buoy bears 309 M, the tower at Gooseberry neck bears 044 M, and the Cuttyhunk Island lookout tower bears 099 M. (A) What is your Lat-Lon? (B) What is the charted depth? (C) From there, what is the range and bearing to Buzzards Light?

4-9. You are headed straight toward the Midchannel Buoy BB on magnetic heading 100 M and the westernmost edge of Penikese Island bears 197 M. What is your Lat-Lon?

4-10. On a rhumb-line course from the Brenton Reef (horn) Buoy to Buzzards Light, what will be the magnetic bearing to the abandoned light house off Sakonnet Point when you are half way there?

4-11. You are in Rhode Island Sound where the magnetic variation is 15° W. Your compass course is 260, and it has no deviation on this heading. The sun is setting dead ahead. (A) What is true bearing of the setting sun relative to due west? (B) Now a strange question: What time of year must this be?

4-12. Steering course 155 M from Buzzards Light, you measure a radar range of 5.9 nmi at relative bearing 314 R to the westernmost bluff of Gay Head. (A) What is your Lat-Lon? (B) What is the charted depth? (C) What are the main contributions to the uncertainty in this position?

4-13. From a DR position west of Gay Head, you are proceeding on course 290 M. With the compass in your binoculars you get a bearing to the west edge of Cuttyhunk Island of 346 M. Another look gets a 042 M bearing to the east edge of Nashawena Island. (A) What is your Lat-Lon? (B) What is the relative bearing to the Sow and Pigs Reef Buoy from your position?

4-14. Proceeding westward on the course established in the preceding question, you notice a large compass change; yet the sunset you've been watching has not appreciably changed its relative direction. What might be a likely explanation of this change?

4-15. Near Nomans Island there is a compass rose showing variation of 15° 15' W in 1985 with an annual increase of 3' per year. (A) What does this imply the variation at this point should be in 2014? (B) Go online to NOAA to view the latest chart 13218 (modern equivalent) to learn what the variation is now at this location—or use the National Geophysical Data Center online computer (www.ngdc.noaa.gov/geomag-web/#declination). Does this agree, and if not, how much different is it? (C) Is there a message here?

4-16. (A) *For extra practice, here are examples of the worst kind of compass correction problems you would ever run across on any vessel.* For these questions use Deviation Table 1. This one is from Bowditch, and shows rather large deviations, and almost certainly from a steel vessel. We have inserted extra spaces in the table to facilitate practice with interpolation.

In most vessels we cannot hope to steer a course to a tenth of a degree. We are good to *average* within 2° of our goal, but professional compass adjusters will measure and report the deviations precise to the tenth of a degree and some advanced navigation tests will require plotting to at least ±0.25°, and will often give compass questions to this precision. Thus it benefits us to have some practice at interpolation, as it comes up often in navigation whenever tables of any kind are used.

Also, real deviation curves are not always linear over the semi-quadrants shown here, so we are making an approximation with a simple linear interpolation, but this detail is not crucial for the purpose of this exercise. Underway, you may indeed only get two measurements over the region of interest and interpolation will be needed. You need only interpolate the deviations; the magnetic headings follow from these. You can skip to Parts B and C to learn the specific ones that are needed.

Refer to Appendix A2 Interpolation, or use any method of choice, to answer these questions assuming a local variation of 15.0° W.

(B) What compass course would you steer to make a true course of (a) 340 T, (b) 032 T, (c) 152 T?

(C) What is the true course you are steering if the compass reads (d) 335 C, (e) 032 C, (f) 317 C, and (g) 285 C?

(D) Why can we reasonably guess that this table is from a steel vessel?

Deviation Table 1

Compass	Deviation	Magnetic
000°	10.5° E	
015°		
030°		
045°	20.0° E	
060°		
075°		
090°	11.5° E	
105°		
120°		
135°	1.2° W	
150°		
165°		
180°	5.5° W	
195°		
210°		
225°	8.0° W	
240°		
255°		
270°	12.5° W	
285°		
300°		
315°	6.8° W	
330°		
345°		

CHAPTER 5 – DEAD RECKONING

Recall our conventions that times are all 24-hour, ie 1402 means 2:02 PM; time intervals use h for hours, m for minutes, and s for seconds, as 1h 32m 32s. All miles are nautical miles. It does not matter how we solve the speed-time-distance problems, but we all need some consistent quick way so we are never reluctant to figure it out.

5-1 Convert the following to decimal hours (i.e. 1h 30m = 1.50h): (A) 3h 20m, (B) 12h 54m, (C) 2h 18m, (D) 0h 38m, and (E) 1h 5m. Convert the following to hours, minutes, and seconds (i.e. 1.57h = 1h+0.57 × 60m): (F) 2.45h, (G) 12.79h, (H) 2.09h, (I) 0.38h, and (J) 1.73h. Figure the new times of day that result from these additions or subtractions using "today," "tomorrow," or "yesterday" as needed to describe the final time you get. (K) 1934 - 0722, (L) 2312 - 0432, (M) 2312 + 0355, (N) 1425 - 0043, (O) 1232 - 2139, (P) 2209 + 0658.

5-2. (A) To average 200 miles per day what must your average speed be? (B) If your speed is 5.0 kts, how far do you travel in one day and 10.4 hours (34.4h)?

5-3. A Pilot Chart says the current drift is 15 miles per day. What is its speed in knots?

5-4. If Newport is 37 miles away, how long will it take to get there at 4.0 kts?

5-5. (A) If New Bedford is 110 miles away how long will it take to get there at 5.0 kts? (B) How long will it take if the first 50 miles is at 7.0 kts, you stop for 2h and the last leg is at 4.0 kts?

5-6. You have traveled 55 miles in 9h, what was your average speed?

5-7. You travel 12 miles in 3h 40m, what was your average speed?

5-8. On a measured mile course you time the run from beginning to end, it takes 14m 30 sec for the mile, what was your average speed?

5-9. You hold a steady 7 kts according to your knotmeter for a measured mile. (A) How long should it take to travel the course? (B) If the actual time was 2 minutes longer, how many knots or fraction of a knot was your knotmeter off? (C) What was its per cent error? (D) If this knotmeter reads 4 knots, what is your actual speed?

5-10. You want to check your speed. In calm water you approach a floating object and start a stop watch when it passes the bow and stop it when it passes the stern. The time was 4 sec. Your boat is 35 ft. long. Hint: use the rule that boat speed in knots equals boat speed in feet per second times 0.6. (A) What was your speed? (B) If your time was in error by 1 sec, how much in error would your speed be?

5-11 You are traveling at 6.3 kts and have 22.9 miles to go. How long will this take you?

5-12. If you must sail a rhumb-line distance of 18 miles to weather by tacking back and forth across the rhumb line, how long will take at 6.0 knots?

5-13. You must tack to weather for a distance of 4 miles at 5 knots, then reach on course for another distance of 8 miles at 6 knots. How long will it take to get there?

5-14. Consider this route: Leave West Falmouth Harbor Entrance at 11:44 AM, sailing southwest at 6.5 kts SOG to a point 0.25 nmi north of Lone Rock near the entrance to Quicks Hole; thence at an SOG of 5.0 kts to Buoy 2 SE of Gooseberry Neck; thence direct the Fl G 4sec BELL due west of West Falmouth Harbor at SOG 7.2 kts; then a return at SOG 4.8 kts to the West Falmouth Harbor Entrance. Parts (A) to (D) What are the distances, magnetic courses, and time run for each of these 4 legs (each part has 3 answers)? And (E), when do you get back?

5-15. From Buoy 2 south of Nomans Land (departure point) plot a course to the Brenton Reef Light (destination). (A) What is the rhumb line true course and distance? (B) At 7.0 kts under power on the rhumb-line route, how long will this passage take?

The following are a few sailors' questions. Think on these, and if you do not know how to work them, then just read through the answers and plot out the results to learn how to do these. These are fundamental matters for setting optimum sailing courses to weather.

(C) Sailor's question: assume the wind is steady northwesterlies (ie from 315 T) throughout the waterway for the time underway, and choose and plot a tacking route that will get you from departure to destination. Assume you are tacking through 90°, which is equivalent to assuming you are sailing a true wind angle of 45°. Starting on starboard tack, how far would you sail to get there in just one tack and how long would it take? How does this compare to our shortcut estimate of taking distance = 1.5 × rhumb-line distance.

(D) Suppose you chose to not go farther than 5 miles from the rhumb line. What is then the minimum number of tacks to get there and what would be the total distance sailed? What is the message here?

(E) A bit harder sailor's question: Do the same as in part (C), but assume now that we know ahead of time that the wind is veering (shifting to the right) as we proceed and will be pure northerly by about 71° 10'W. Knowing this, choose the optimum route. Again compute distance and time to get there. Speed is again 7 kts in all wind conditions. Discuss the guidelines you used for meeting the new wind in the optimum manner (i.e. shortest time to get there)?

(F) Show how much you saved using the right tactics by also solving the time it takes when doing it as wrong as possible—

ie, sail off to the wrong side of the course and compute the time, taking into account the wind shift.

5-16. Your digital compass manual states that to calibrate your compass you must swing ship (ie turn through 360° at steady rate and speed), taking at least 10 minutes to complete the circuit. Describe a way to do this by listing vessel speed, turning rate or step size, and then compute or plot the diameter of the entire path that you would be following according to your plan—or give any other method you can think of that will accomplish this and tell how to execute it.

5-17. You are 1.5 nmi south of the tower on the south end of West Island and your log reads 5123.4. Lay out the course to pass directly south of the Buoy BB as charted. (A) What is the magnetic course of this leg? (B) What should your log read when you're passing the buoy? (C) You turn to starboard and proceed on C 251 M. What should your log read when Buzzards Light bears 195 M? (D) From this point what is the bearing to the lookout tower on Cuttyhunk Island? (E) From present position sail on toward the Brenton Reef light. What is the magnetic course for this leg? (F) What will the log read passing the Brenton Reef light?

5-18. Starting point is the Buoy 29 off Gay Head. Depart at 1004 at 7 kts on course 203 M. At 1030 change course to 249 M and reduce speed to 4 kts. At 1115 change course again, returning to the Buoy 29 directly at a speed of 10 kts. (A) What will be the bearing back to the buoy at 1115? (B) What is the estimated time of arrival back at the buoy?

5-19. Plot the DR track on your chart that corresponds to the following section of the logbook entries. Subtract successive log readings to find distance run on each leg; it is more accurate than speed × time. C = course, S = knotmeter.

Time	Log	C	S	Comments
1200	651.0	254 M	6.2	Fix at 41° 19.2' N, 70° 40.6' W
1238	654.8	289 M	6.8	Turn to clear Nomans Is.
1312	658.5	327 M	7.3	Head towards Cuttyhunk
1439	668.6	292 M	7.8	Head towards Narragansett
1535	675.6	305 M	7.8	Position Fix here

(A) What is the Lat-Lon of your DR position at log 675.6? (B) You do a position fix at 1535 and find that your true position at that time is 41° 23.6' N, 71° 06.9' W. What is the distance between your fix and your DR position at 1535? (C) What is the direction from the 1535 DR position to the 1535 fix position? (D) Assume that your DR was wrong because you were in a constant current that set you off your DR track. Your first fix was at 1200, the second at 1535. What was the set and drift of the current? The procedure is to assume that during the time you sailed your DR track, the water moved from your final DR position to your final fix position, thus accounting for the discrepancy. (E) In practice, could you conclude from this work that the current you found this way was the true water current over the course you sailed? Explain your answer. (F) Do the logged knotmeter speeds agree with the SMGs that you can figure from the times and log readings given? Can you learn anything from that comparison?

CHAPTER 6 – PILOTING

These exercises can be worked in the traditional manner plotting on a paper chart, or they can be solved digitally using echart and electronic tools. Standard plotting tools are discussed in the Introduction. There is a review of the electronic approach in Appendix A1. Recall we use var = 15.0° W for all locations.

6-1. On a nighttime passage headed for the Cape Cod Canal, you are somewhere on the line created by the range of lights from the Cleveland East Ledge 16-mile light to Buoy BB. With a hand-held compass you measure a 003 M bearing to the WNBH radio tower south of New Bedford. Locate your position along this range. (A) What is your Lat-Lon? (B) Suppose now that this measurement was in error by 5° and the correct bearing should have been 358 M. Find your position from this bearing. What is your real Lat-Lon? (C) How much was your first position fix in error?

6-2. Sailing south (per the ship's compass) you note that the west edges of Gay Head and Nomans Land form a natural range dead on your bow. This information plus a quick hand bearing compass check on the monument on Cuttyhunk Island of 303 M when plotted on your chart gives you… (A) A DR, EP or fix? (B) What is your lat-lon?

6-3. A few days later, you recall the situation as described in the above problem. It occurs to you that you have enough information to check your vessel's deviation on a south heading. What is the deviation on a southerly heading?

6-4. On a voyage near Block Island on magnetic course 305, you note a 052 R radar bearing to Point Judith. Using a hand bearing compass you find that a prominent house near Block Island's Clay Head bears 263. (A) What is your Lat-Lon? (B) What might be a few potential inaccuracies in this fix?

6-5. With a hand bearing compass you measure a bearing of 107 M to Gay Head Light, and 084 M to the monument on Cuttyhunk Island. (A) What is your Lat-Lon? (B) Some hand bearing compasses have card indices that make fine readings of their scales impossible. Assume a conservative error of 4 degrees in your bearings. Redraw the bearing lines 4 degrees one side and then 4 degrees the other. (B) What is the Lat-Lon of your most westerly 'fix'? (C) What is the Lat-Lon of your most easterly 'fix'? (D) How much potential error in distance has your hand bearing compass created? (E) What lesson might one take away from this example?

6-6. You've been proceeding via DR from The Harbor, Block Island, on a heading of 090 M intending to transit Vineyard Sound, as you have done numerous times in the past. Your chartplotter is not functioning but you do have a usable depth sounder, paper charts and VHF. The bad news is that current has set you farther off course than you realize, and you're in restricted visibility in fog. Unknown to skipper or crew, if you continue holding your present course you will go on the rocks of Gay Head at about 41° 20.4' N. You're presently in presumed safe water at a little less than 100 ft depth, if you continue motoring at 8 knots in the fog without realizing your peril, how long do you have before your vessel could be wrecked?

6-7. Proceeding approximately NE abeam the Red "2" Fl 10sec WHISTLE off Point Judith in poor visibility, you wish to follow a sounding to lead you to the entrance to Narragansett Bay. (A) What sounding contour would you choose to lead you to West Passage and why? (B) Would the Fl G 4sec GONG provide sufficient notice for you to resume piloting into the passage? (C) What particular concerns might there be with following this sounding?

6-8. If the tide tables tell us that low water is 2.0 ft, and the charted depth is 2 fathoms, what is the depth of water in feet at low water?

6-9. It is pea soup fog and your estimated position is 3 to 5 miles south of Point Judith. Your course is 226 M. You just noticed that your depth sounder went from about 50 to 90 feet in about 5 minutes or so. Thinking ahead to the land mass somewhere in front of you, you decide to do some depth sounding navigation to home in on your position. You hold a steady speed of 6.0 kts and a steady course of 226 M. You confirm from the current table that the current is about slack at this time. Here is a list of charted depth contours (line of soundings) you crossed, after correcting for draft and tide:

Time	trip log	Depth
1315	0.0	90 ft
1320	0.5	120 ft
1335	2.0	150 ft
1344	2.9	120 ft
1350	3.5	90 ft
1356	4.1	90 ft
1357	4.2	120 ft
1359	4.4	120 ft
1403	4.8	90 ft
1406	5.1	60 ft

(A) Where are you (Lat-Lon plus description) at 1406? *Hint. Using the miles scale from your chart, mark these distances along the edge of a card or paper labeled with the contours, then slide it around on the chart keeping the edge oriented at 226 M till you find the place they match. Or use a Weems Plotter, which has a scale of 1:80,000 on the edge and a dry erase marker.* (B) If you continue on this course, what will be the minimum depth ahead of you? (C) When will you reach that minimum depth? (D) How accurate is this line of soundings fix and how can we prove it?

6-10. You are proceeding in an approximately southeasterly direction with Buzzards Light on your starboard beam, intending to transit Vineyard Sound. The buoy that ordinarily marks the danger of Sow and Pigs Reef has been reported in the LNM as being 'OFF STA'. To avoid the reef, you set up a danger bearing. Giving the deck watch a hand-bearing compass, you tell them that the Gay Head light should bear (A) "No more than" or "No less than" (B) this bearing _____. Choose the proper bearing restriction and give the bearing. Assume you want to pass the reef no closer than 0.25 nmi from the charted position of the missing buoy.

6-11. If your compass had an error of 12° that you did not know about, how far off course would you be after traveling 45 miles? Use 6° rule, or plot it out to scale.

Note that problems 6-12 through 6-24 do not give an initial position, only an approximate location. To work these, estimate a position in the area based on what you know, lay off your course, and go on from there.

6-12. From a DR position south of Martha's Vineyard you are sailing westbound on magnetic course 284 at 5 knots. You note rapidly lowering visibility and need a fix before the fog sets in. A 1745 bearing to the spire at Chilmark (the only landmark in sight by now) reads 330°. One hour later the spire bears 018°. (A) What is your Lat-Lon? (B) What is this charted location called?

6-13. Bow angles. You are sailing course 062 M a few miles east of Point Judith. You do not have a chart of the area (big mistake). The Brenton Reef Light bears 020 M when the log reads 1672.5. (A) What is the angle on the bow of the light? (B) What will the bearing of the light be when you have doubled the angle on the bow staying on your original course? (C) Watching the light and your log, you note that the log reads 1674.2 when the light bears 338 M. What is your distance off the light?

6-14. Running fix. Referring to problem 6-13 above, now using the chart, verify your results by plotting and advancing the first LOP to form a running fix with the second. (A) What is your Lat-Lon at log 1674.2? (B) Is there more than one way to establish this fix?

6-15. Running fix. You are proceeding at night on course 295 M northeast of Gay Head at speed 7 knots. You note that Gay Head light is exactly on your beam at 18:55. (A) What must its magnetic bearing be at 18:55 if it's on your beam and you know your course heading? (B) You continue west on the same course at the same speed. At 19:19 you can just see the Gay Head light well off your port quarter, and it bears 149 M. How far have you traveled? (C) Advance the first LOP to the second to find your position at 19:19 by running fix. What is your Lat-Lon? (D) What hazard lies dead ahead?

6-16. Vertical angle. You are approaching Buzzards Light. With a sextant you measure its height above the water to be 1° 15'. How far off the light are you? (Use the latest information as updated by the Light List and LNM if applicable.)

6-17. Vertical angle. You are west of Gay Head light. Again, you use your sextant and measure its height above the water to be 2° 45'. What is your distance from the light?

6-18. You are running southwest down Vineyard Sound on course 259 M. The monument on Nashawena Island bears 303 M when the log reads 6366.5. (A) What bearing to the monument should you look for in order to double this angle on the bow? Continuing on a steady course, the log reads 6368.5 when the bow angle to the island has been doubled. (B) How far off the island are you now? (C) What is your Lat-Lon at the time of the second bearing?

6-19. Your estimated position is 5 miles southeast of Nomans Land, and your course is 240 M. The Buoy 2 south of Nomans Land bears 280 M when your log reads 6672.3. After sailing for 1.5 miles on course, the buoy bears 312 M. What is your Lat-Lon at the time of the second bearing?

6-20. You are sailing on course 100 M at speed 6.0 kts. At 18:40, when your log reads 16256.5, the monument on Cuttyhunk Island bears 015 M. Later, at log 16259.0, the monument bears 323 M. What is your Lat-Lon at the time of the last bearing?

6-21. You are sailing SE at 7 kts on magnetic course 135. At 1515 a bearing to the Brenton Reef light was 056 M. At 1532, the bearing to the light is 352. What is your Lat-Lon?

6-22. More practice with the RFix. You are SW of Buzzards Light sailing course 085 M at 6.0 kts. The light bears 043 M at 1235, and then 335 M at 1305. (A) What is your Lat-Lon assuming no current? (B) What is your Lat-Lon if the current is 0.6 kts in direction 295 T?

6-23. A follow-on to 6-22, but now assume there is in addition a strong northerly wind which gives you a leeway of 7°. What is your Lat-Lon taking both current and leeway into consideration?

6-24. You appear to be directly north of the Buzzards Light and you estimate your distance off the light as 2.5 miles. You then sail on course 048 M for 3 miles, then change course to 088 M and sail for 4.5 miles. Change again to course 022 M and sail for another 3.2 miles. Now you see Buoy BB, which bears 130 M. (A) Advance your first LOP to the second one to find your running fix. What is your Lat-Lon? (B) From this position work backwards to find out what your actual distance off the light was when you estimated it to be 2.5 miles.

6-25. You are proceeding north northeast on a course of 022 M, when you note the radar range and bearing to Point Judith is 1.8 nmi at 281 Relative. What is your Lat-Lon?

6-26. For a radar fix you plot circles of position from the most westerly bluff of Gay Head at 4.9 nmi, from Buzzards Light at 5.2 nmi, and from the western end of the radar reflective bluff on Cuttyhunk Island at 4.2 nmi. What is your Lat-Lon?

CHAPTER 7 – ELECTRONIC NAVIGATION

The basic electronic instruments we use for navigation are radar, GPS, and depth sounder, along with our knotmeter and log and wind instruments—which are just as valuable for power boats as they are for sail boats. Instrument manuals are often the main reference; they are usually online these days. It often helps to read manuals from other instrument makers, not just those of the brands you use.

7-1. You are westbound on leg 1 of a passage from Buzzards Bay to Vineyard Sound via the following waypoints entered into your GPS:

WPT 1 41° 30.0' N, 70° 54.0' W

WPT 2 41° 25.1' N, 70° 59.5' W

WPT 3 41° 23.3' N, 70° 59.2' W

WPT 4 41° 22.9' N. 70° 56.2 W

WPT 5 41° 26.4' N, 70° 45.8' W

Your GPS is set to automatically switch to the next waypoint when you get within 0.25 nmi of the target. Suppose that somehow after WPT 2 your GPS skipped WPT 3, setting your next course to WPT 4. It is midnight and your speed is 8 kts. (A) What are some consequences of such a goof-up? (B) Name two ways that this type of event could be avoided.

7-2. Suppose you want to tack a rhumb-line route from Buoy A to Buoy B which is upwind, but you do not want to go more than 2 miles off the rhumb line on either tack as you proceed. Explain how you can very easily achieve this with standard echart functions.

7-3. What is the typical accuracy we might expect from a GPS fix without any differential enhancement?

(A) ± 2 ft
(B) ± 20 ft
(C) ± 40 ft
(D) ± 80 ft

7-4. A currently operational differential GPS system that considerably improves resultant fix accuracy is called...

(A) GLONASS
(B) Enhanced LORAN
(C) Wide Area Augmentation System
(D) Radio Direction Beacon

7-5. What is the most likely reason that a fix from a handheld GPS unit is not as good as it was just some time in the recent past?

(A) Batteries are low.
(B) A satellite is temporarily not transmitting.
(C) The relative bearings of the satellites you have been using are no longer as favorable as before.
(D) You have sailed into a region or moved the instrument in such a way that part of the sky is now blocked from view of its antenna.

7-6. Your vessel has a small portable chartplotter and GPS navigation system that is quite accurate when used. However, like most electronics, it has some weaknesses. What is the most likely weakest link in your navigation system?

(A) The cigarette lighter socket and wiring.
(B) The navigation chart memory chip.
(C) The VHF microphone exposed to sea water.
(D) The GPS satellite constellation.

7-7. Your very well-equipped vessel has a chartplotter with a WAAS-enabled GPS input; however the chartplotter gets its directional references from the GPS, not from a flux-gate compass. Your accurately swung helm compass often indicates a significantly different direction from the vessel icon on the chartplotter. Why?

7-8. From a DR position E of Point Judith, you are proceeding on course 072M at a speed of 5.7 knots. From the radar you take a range and bearing to the Brenton Reef light at 1300 and get 4.0 nmi at a bearing of 316R. (A) What is your Lat-Lon? (B) At 1400 you do it again and get 4.5 nmi at 303M. What is your new Lat-Lon? (C) What was the set and drift of the current you were sailing in?

7-9. Sailing S of Cuttyhunk Island at 12 kts, you measure a radar range to the NW corner of Nomans Land as 4.6 nmi. At the same time (within a few seconds) you measure a radar range to the west edge of Gay Head as 3.4 nmi. What is your Lat-Lon?

7-10. From a DR position NE of Block Island you are proceeding on Course 263M at a speed of 12 knots. At 1410 you measure the radar range to the bluff at Clay Head, Block Island and get 7.3 nmi. At 1413 you measure the range to Point Judith, and you get 5.3 nmi. What is your Lat-Lon if you DO NOT take into account the times of the measurements? (B) What is your Lat-Lon if you plot this correctly as a running fix? (C) How much error was in method A?

7-11. Which type of radar fix is the fastest to achieve for comparison with the GPS?

(A) Two bearings
(B) One range and one bearing
(C) Two ranges
(D) All are the same.

7-12. Which type of radar fix is the most accurate for comparison with the GPS?

(A) Two bearings
(B) One range and one bearing
(C) Two ranges
(D) All are the same.

7-13. Explain how an electronic charting system (ECS) can be extremely valuable to you even if you do not plan to use any underway, or in fact do not even have any on the boat?

7-14. When sailing with both radar and ECS, what is the fastest way to identify your approximate location (situation awareness)?

CHAPTER 8 – TIDES AND CURRENTS

This workbook uses tide and current data from 2011. These source books have the same format as the latest editions, whereas the corresponding books from the time of the chart had notably different layouts. In most of these problems you can test yourself with several resources online or in ECS computer or tablet apps that compute tides and currents for any US location on any date. Note the times asked for, standard or daylight; official source books are not always as clear as they might be on this important detail. Data needed are in the Resources.

8-1. What is the time (EST) and height of the highest tide at Newport, Rhode Island, on May 7, 2011?

8-2. What is the time (EST) of the lowest tide at Newport, Rhode Island, on April 17, 2011?

8-3. What is the time (EDT) and height of the highest tide at Newport, Rhode Island, on May 17, 2011?

8-4. What is the time (EDT) and height of the lowest tide at Newport, Rhode Island, on April 22, 2011?

8-5. What is the height of the highest tide at Newport, Rhode Island, on June 7, 2011? Use local time.

8-6. You anchor your 40 ft sailboat (6 ft draft) solidly, in a good seabed north of Sachuest Point around 8 PM local time on May 17 in about 10 feet depth. If you fail to check your tide tables and take appropriate action, what is likely to happen?

8-7. What is the tide range between afternoon low and evening high tides at Newport, Rhode Island, on May 17, 2011? What is the phase of the moon that day?

8-8. What is the Lat-Lon of the tide station at Newport, Rhode Island?

8-9. What is the time (EDT) of the highest tide at Penikese Island on May 18, 2011?

8-10. What is the time (EDT) of the lowest tide at Cuttyhunk on June 16, 2011?

8-11. What is the time (EDT) of the highest tide at The Glen, Sakonnet River on April 20, 2011?

8-12. What is the time (EDT) of the lowest tide at Nannaquaket Neck, Sakonnet River on May 2, 2011?

8-13. Plot the Lat-Lon of Penikese Island and Cuttyhunk subordinate stations. What is the distance between both stations? What do you think explains the significant time differences between the stations even though their locations are so close?

8-14. What is the time (EST) and height of the highest tide at Saint John, New Brunswick on April 6, 2011?

8-15. What is the time (EST) and height of the lowest tide at Saint John, New Brunswick on April 19, 2011?

8-16. What is the tide range between morning low and afternoon high tides at Saint John, New Brunswick on May 21, 2011?

8-17. What is the time (EDT) of the highest tide at Tiverton, St Mary Bay, Nova Scotia on June 4, 2011?

8-18. What is the time (EDT) of the afternoon low tide at Lower East Pubnico, Nova Scotia on May 18, 2011? Q3SJ

8-19. What is the time (EDT) of the highest tide at Burntcoat Head, Minas Basin, Nova Scotia on May 18, 2011?

8-20. What is the time (EDT) of the lowest tide at Joggins, Nova Scotia on June 16, 2011?

8-21. What is the height of the highest tide at North End, Bay Oil Pier, Sakonnet River on June 5, 2011?

8-22. What is the height of the lowest tide at Penikese Island on May 16, 2011?

8-23. What is the height of the highest tide at Weymouth, St Mary Bay, Nova Scotia on April 20, 2011?

8-24. What is the height of the lowest tide at Tiverton, St Mary Bay, Nova Scotia on May 17, 2011?

8-25. What is the height of the highest tide at Burntcoat Head, Minas Basin, Nova Scotia on May 19, 2011?

8-26. What is the height of the lowest tide at Yarmouth Harbor, Nova Scotia on April 4, 2011?

8-27. According to the 1210 Tr training chart the swing bridge at Tiverton, Rhode Island opens completely to a width of 99 ft. Why is there a vertical clearance concern at that location?

8-28. You are the navigator on a sloop intending to transit the Tiverton, Rhode Island bridge and your skipper is relying on your advice for determining whether it is safe to transit this area. Your mast height is 61 ft, including the VHF antenna at the masthead. Would you be able to maintain at least a 2 ft safety margin at 2100 local time of passage on April 18, 2011? Use Anthony Point, Sakonnet River subordinate station data.

8-29. What time (EDT) and velocity is max flood at Pollock Rip Channel on May 18, 2011?

8-30. What time (EDT) and velocity is max ebb at Pollock Rip Channel on April 6, 2011?

8-31. What time (EDT) is the evening slack before ebb at Pollock Rip Channel on June 2, 2011?

8-32. What time (EDT) is morning slack before flood at Pollock Rip Channel on May 4, 2011?

8-33. What is the direction of flood at Pollock Rip Channel? What is the direction of ebb?

8-34. What time (EST) is max flood west of Rose Island on June 17, 2011?

8-35. What time (EDT) is max flood west of Common Fence Point on April 20, 2011?

8-36. What time (EDT) is max ebb at Mount Hope Bridge on June 18, 2011?

8-37. What time (EDT) is max flood at Kickamuit River (Narrows), Mt. Hope Bay on April 6, 2011?

8-38. What time (EDT) is max ebb northeast of Mount Hope Point on April 6, 2011?

8-39. Find the velocity and direction of max flood northeast of Rose Island on April 20, 2011.

8-40. Find the velocity and direction of max ebb 1.4 nmi southwest of Brenton Point on June 19, 2011.

8-41. Find the velocity and direction of max flood east of Bull Point on June 5, 2011.

8-42. Find the velocity and direction of max ebb northeast of Mount Hope point on June 22, 2011.

8-43. What time (EST) is slack before morning flood at Pollock Rip Channel on June 6, 2011?

8-44. What time (EDT) is slack before afternoon ebb at Pollock Rip Channel on June 20, 2011?

8-45. What time (EDT) is slack before afternoon ebb at Pollock Rip Channel on May 6, 2011?

8-46. What time (EDT) is slack before morning flood at Pollock Rip Channel on June 7, 2011?

8-47. What time (EST) is afternoon minimum before flood SW of Black Point, Sakonnet River on April 18, 2011?

8-48. What time (EDT) is afternoon minimum before ebb ENE of Conanicut Point on June 20, 2011?

8-49. What time (EDT) is the earliest minimum before flood of the day west of Common Fence Point on April 17, 2011?

8-50. What time (EDT) is latest minimum before ebb of the day east of Bull Point on June 18, 2011?

8-51. (A) What is the value of Mean High Water at Newport if you compute this from the data in Table 2 of the tide Tables? (B) What does chart 1210 Tr say this value is? (C) What accounts for the difference in these two values? (D) Make the same comparison for Woods Hole.

8-52. You wish to enter Broad Cove during daylight on Monday, May 16, 2011, which calls for passing under the fixed bridge between Onset and Long Neck on the East River. Your air draft is 12 ft. Is this possible, and if so what times of day (EDT) can you do so with a 2 ft clearance? Hint: use the Coast Pilot or chart 13236 (free online viewer) to learn the fixed vertical clearance, which is not listed on 1210 Tr chart.

8-53. (A) On May 20 at Newport station the current is slack at 0443 with peak flood of 2.3 at 0817. Find the current speed at 0543, 0630, and 0717. These times are an hour from the turning points as well as the midpoint. Use Table 3 of the Current Tables and then compare the results you get with the Starpath 50-90 Rule for making these estimates. [*This rule is the counterpart for currents of the Rule of Twelfths for tides.*] (B) Then do the same in the next cycle which goes back to slack at 1131 (i.e. 0917, 0954, and 1031). (C) And for more practice, repeat for the next cycle which peaks at 1.7 ebb at 1412. (i.e. 1231, 1251, and 1312)

8-54. In the vicinity of Buoy VS to the SE of Cuttyhunk Island tidal currents rotate rather than reverse. Reversing currents have just two basic directions, the flood direction and the ebb direction, whereas at some inland locations and most coastal stations the current rotates direction with time as well as chaining speeds. (A) Read about these currents in Table 5 of the Current section of the Resources, and then make a table of the currents you might expect at this location on May 16, from about 8 am to noon EDT. The four table columns would be: Time (EDT), Set, Average Drift, Corrected Drift. (B) Can you think of a way to plot these results that give a better picture of the current flow? (*Nautical charts in other parts of the world use a plot to present rotary current data. An echart program is one convenient way to make such a plot.*)

CHAPTER 9 – NAVIGATION IN CURRENTS

Current sailings are usually vector problems that can be solved by basic plotting or by dedicated calculators programmed for the job. Alternatively, they can be quickly solved with ECS displays as outlined in Appendix A1. There are also approximations for quick estimates adequate for most practical work, keeping in mind we do not often know the currents very precisely. Chapters 5 and 6 have related exercises.

9-1. Current is on your port beam at about 2 kts. Your compass reads 200 and your knotmeter reads 6.0 knots. (A) What is a quick estimate of your CMG? (B) Will your SMG be larger or smaller than your knotmeter speed? (C) What is your exact CMG and SMG from plotting?

9-2. Current is on your starboard quarter at about 2 kts. Your compass reads 200 and your knotmeter reads 6.0 knots. What is your approximate CMG?

9-3. Your knotmeter speed is 5.0 knots. You want to cross a current that you estimate is about 1.5 knots on your beam. How many degrees should you point into the current to track straight across the current?

9-4. Sailor's question: You are beating to weather in strong southerly winds on a port tack. You estimate that your leeway is 10°. There is a current flowing to the north at about 2.0 knots. Your compass reads 205 and your knotmeter reads 6.0 knots. (A) What is your CMG? (B) If you know you tack through 90° in such conditions, what should the compass bearing to a windward buoy be if you intend to pass to weather of it when you tack?

9-5. On a mountain hike you wish to cross a large open meadow to a tree in the far corner. Explain how you might navigate this walk across the field in the least number of steps without being distracted by the beautiful hills and mountains on the other side.

9-6. You want to go across a large open area to your destination, which you can see on the horizon. You know there are currents present but have no idea what they are. You pass by a lighthouse just as you start your crossing. That is, just as you enter the currents the lighthouse is dead astern. Your destination is dead ahead and your compass reads 340. The back bearing to the lighthouse is 160°. After traveling some time you notice that the lighthouse is no longer dead astern, though your destination still lies dead ahead because it is so far away, and your compass course hasn't changed. Using a hand-held bearing compass you find the bearing to the lighthouse is now 135°. What compass course should you steer to get back on track toward your destination? (A long problem with a quick and easy solution.)

9-7. During a passage in tidal waters you notice a prominent tide rip some distance ahead. What can you expect the current to do upon crossing that rip line?

9-8. On Wednesday, May 4, 2011, you depart the Brenton Reef Light at a speed of 4.5 knots. (A) Determine the set and drift of the maximum ebb that afternoon at the nearest substation, and (B) using those figures, determine a magnetic course to the Buzzards Light. You are motoring and there is no leeway to be applied. (C) For extra credit, what will be your CMG? (D) What will be your SMG? (E) and your time to go (TTG) to Buzzards Light?

9-9. At 0915, you depart the Brenton Reef Light on a steady course of 105° M toward Buzzards Bay. You are sailing on a broad reach in calm seas making 6.0 knots through the water. At 1045 you find yourself close aboard the Elisha Ledge Buoy (41° 26.6' N, 71° 09.5' W). What has been the set and drift of the current during the trip?

9-10. Consider the following deck log records, starting from when you passed Buoy 1B1 north of Block Is. Wind is steady at W 15.

Time	Log	Course	Remarks
1330	10.5	050 M	Port jibe at Buoy 1B1
1430	16.0	110 M	Starboard jibe
1518	20.4	050 M	Port jibe
1552	23.5	050 M	

(A) Plot the DR track from these records assuming no current present. What is your DR Lat-Lon at 1552 and the range and bearing to Pt. Judith Light from that position? (B) What was your CMG and SMG between 1330 and 1552? (C) Assume now there had been a steady current with set of 270 and a drift of 1.1 kts over this full time period. In that case what would be your EP at 1552 and the range and bearing to the same light at that time? (D) What was your CMG and SMG between 1330 and 1552 taking into account this estimate of the current?

9-11. The following are standard current sailing problems. H= boat heading, S=knotmeter speed. All directions true.

(A) Fill in the missing data. For example in #1 you are steering 200 T at a knotmeter speed of 6.0 and the tables tell you to expect a current of 2.0 kts in direction 150. What do you anticipate will be your CMG and SMG in these conditions. In #4, you want to cross a current of 2.0 kts in direction 150 making good a course of 200, running at a knotmeter speed of 6.0. What course should you steer and what will be your SMG on this course? In #7, you are steering a steady course of 180 with a steady knotmeter speed of 7.4, but your trail of past positions shows you are making good a steady 205 and your SOG on the GPS shows that you have had a steady SOG of 6.8. If this difference is due to current alone, what would be the set and drift of this current?

#	S	H	Set	Drift	CMG	SMG
1	6.0	200	150	2.0		
2	5.0	100	315	1.5		
3	7.5	350	260	1.8		
4	6.0		150	2.0	200	
5	5.0		315	1.5	100	
6	7.5		260	1.8	350	
7	7.4	180			205	6.8
8	6.2	130			110	5.6
9	6.2	130			110	7.0

(B) Compare the headings you get from 4, 5, and 6 with those of 1, 2, and 3 to evaluate how accurate it is to just assume the correction to make good a course is just the opposite of what happens if you do not correct the course. That is, if I am being set 15° to the right, I can correct by steering 15° to the left. (C) Compare the answers you get to 1 through 7 with the simple Starpath 40-60 Rule for current sailing.

9-12. You are sailing in a region with only one current station covering the full area you will be transiting. The current report for this reversing current pattern is as follows:

2103	slack
0035	1.7 F
0326	slack
0613	1.4 E

Practice using the 50-90 Rule given in the Resources to answer these questions: (A) If you were sailing in this current from slack to slack (about 2100 to 0330) what would be an equivalent average current that could be used for figuring an average SMG during this period? (B) Same question, but now entering the current at 0130 (about an hour after the peak) and leaving it at 0330 (about slack)?, and (C) Entering at 0230 (about an hour before slack) and leaving at 0530 about an hour before next peak?

CHAPTER 10 – NAVIGATION RULES

Refer to the Navigation Rules to answer these questions. An electronic copy (any format) would be convenient for finding answers. These questions are selected from the USCG database of license exam questions. Each question applies to both the International Rules and to the US Inland Rules, thus if the Rules differ you must choose the answer with the common rules. The Answers list the specific Rules that apply.

**Nav Rules Parts A and B.
Definitions and Right of Way**

10-1. If you are the stand-on vessel in a crossing situation, you may take action to avoid collision by your maneuver alone. When may this action be taken?

(A) At any time you feel it is appropriate.
(B) Only when you have reached extremis.
(C) When you determine that your present course will cross ahead of the other vessel.
(D) When it becomes apparent to you that the give-way vessel is not taking appropriate action.

10-2. Which statement is true concerning a vessel equipped with operational radar?

(A) She must use this equipment to obtain early warning of risk of collision.
(B) The radar equipment is only required to be used in restricted visibility.
(C) The use of a radar excuses a vessel from the need of a lookout.
(D) The safe speed of such a vessel will likely be greater than that of vessels without radar.

10-3. A vessel must proceed at a safe speed...

(A) in restricted visibility. (B) in congested waters.
(C) during darkness. (D) at all times.

10-4. A sailing vessel is overtaking a tug and tow as shown in DIAGRAM 43. Which statement is correct?

(A) The sailing vessel is the stand-on vessel because it is overtaking.
(B) The sailing vessel is the stand-on vessel because it is under sail.
(C) The tug is the stand-on vessel because it is being overtaken.
(D) The tug is the stand-on vessel because it is towing.

10-5. The word "vessel", in the Rules, includes...

(A) sailing ships. (B) nondisplacement craft.
(C) seaplanes. (D) All of the above.

10-6. If two sailing vessels are running free with the wind on the same side, which one must keep clear of the other?

(A) The one with the wind closest abeam.
(B) The one with the wind closest astern.
(C) The one to leeward.
(D) The one to windward.

10-7. The *NAVIGATION RULES* define a "vessel not under command" as a vessel which...

(A) from the nature of her work is unable to keep out of the way of another vessel.
(B) through some exceptional circumstance is unable to maneuver as required by the rules.
(C) by taking action contrary to the rules has created a special circumstance situation.
(D) is moored, aground or anchored in a fairway.

10-8. A vessel "restricted in her ability to maneuver" is one which...

(A) from the nature of her work is unable to maneuver as required by the rules.
(B) through some exceptional circumstance is unable to maneuver as required by the rules.
(C) due to adverse weather conditions is unable to maneuver as required by the rules.
(D) has lost steering and is unable to maneuver.

10-9. You are seeing another vessel and its compass bearing does not significantly change. This would indicate that...

(A) you are the stand-on vessel.
(B) risk of collision exists.
(C) a special circumstances situation exists.
(D) the other vessel is dead in the water.

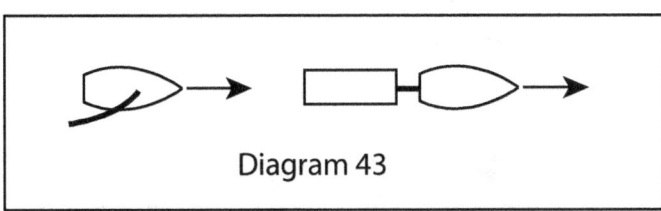

Diagram 43

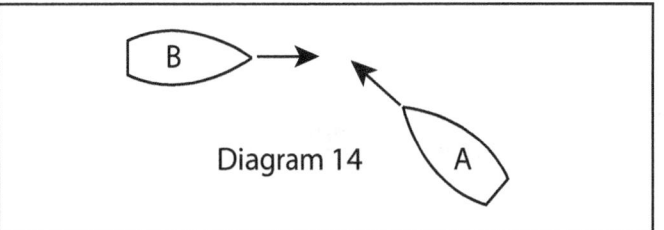

Diagram 14

10-10. You are the watch officer on a power-driven vessel and notice a large sail vessel approaching from astern. You should...

(A) slow down.
(B) sound one short blast and change course to starboard.
(C) sound two short blasts and change course to port.
(D) hold course and speed.

10-11. You are underway on vessel "A" and sight vessel "B" which is a vessel underway and fishing. Which statement is true? (see DIAGRAM 14)

(A) Vessel "A" must keep out of the way of vessel "B" because "B" is to port.
(B) Vessel "A" must keep out of the way of vessel "B" because " B" is fishing.
(C) Vessel "B" must keep out of the way of vessel "A" because "A" is to starboard.
(D) In this case, both vessels are required by the Rules to keep clear of each other.

10-12. If it becomes necessary for a stand-on vessel to take action to avoid collision, she shall, if possible...

(A) not decrease speed.
(B) not increase speed.
(C) not turn to port for a vessel on her own port side.
(D) not turn to starboard for a vessel on her own port side.

10-13. Your vessel is NOT making way, but is not in any way disabled, another vessel is approaching you on your starboard beam. Which statement is true?

(A) The other vessel must give way since your vessel is stopped.
(B) Your vessel is the give-way vessel in a crossing situation.
C . You should be showing the lights or shapes for a vessel not under command.
(D) You should be showing the lights or shapes for a vessel restricted in her ability to maneuver.

10-14. Two vessels meeting in a "head on" situation are directed by the Rules to...

(A) alter course to starboard and pass port to port.
(B) alter course to port and pass starboard to starboard.
(C) decide on which side the passage will occur by matching whistle signals.
(D) slow to bare steerageway.

10-15. A vessel is "engaged in fishing" when...

(A) her gear extends more than 100-meters from the vessel.
(B) she is using any type of gear, other than lines.
(C) she is using fishing apparatus which restricts her maneuverability.
(D) she has any fishing gear on board.

10-16. When shall the stand-on vessel change course and speed?

(A) The stand-on vessel may change course and speed at any time as it has the right-of-way.
(B) After the give-way vessel sounds one blast in a crossing situation.
(C) When action by the give-way vessel alone cannot prevent collision.
(D) When the two vessels become less than one-half mile apart.

10-17. Which factor is listed in the Rules as one which must be taken into account when determining safe speed?

(A) The construction of the vessel.
(B) The maneuverability of the vessel.
(C) The experience of vessel personnel.
(D) All of the above.

10-18. Which statement is true concerning seaplanes on the water?

(A) A seaplane must show appropriate lights but need not exhibit shapes.
(B) A seaplane should exhibit the lights for a vessel constrained by her draft.
(C) In situations where a risk of collision exists, a seaplane should always give way.
(D) A seaplane on the water shall, in general, keep well clear of all vessels.

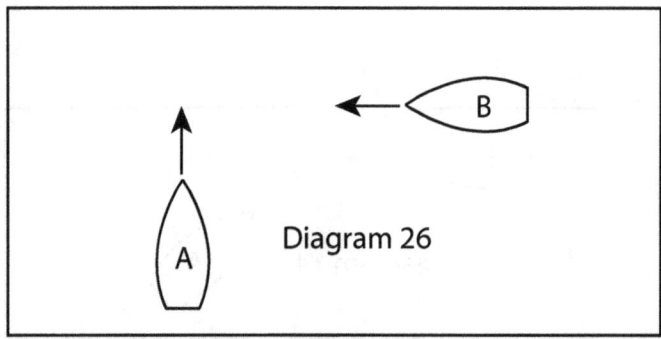

Diagram 26

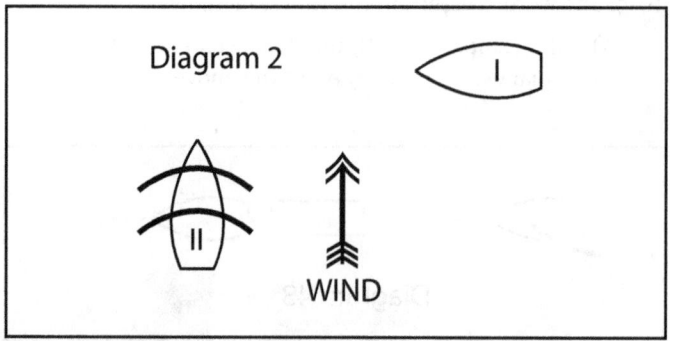

Diagram 2

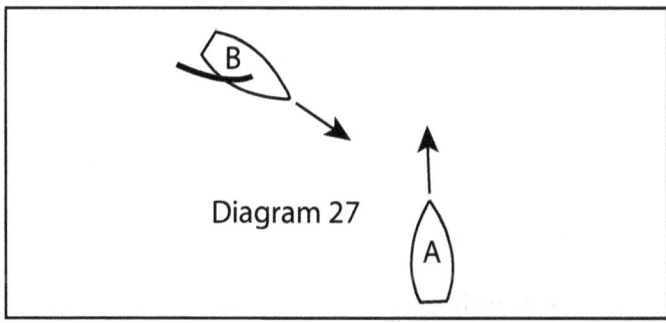

Diagram 27

10-19. A vessel approaching your vessel from 235 degrees relative is in what type of situation?

(A) Meeting. (B) Overtaking.
(C) Crossing. (D) Passing.

10-20. Vessels "A" and "B" are crossing as shown in DIAGRAM 26. Which statement is true?

(A) The vessels should pass starboard to starboard.
(B) Vessel "B" should pass under the stern of vessel "A".
(C) Vessel "B" should alter course to the right.
(D) Vessel "A" must keep clear of vessel "B".

10-21. In the situation illustrated in DIAGRAM 2, Vessel I is a power-driven vessel. Vessel II is a sail vessel with the wind dead aft. Which of the following statements about this situation is correct?

(A) Vessel I should keep out of the way of Vessel II.
(B) Vessel II should keep out of the way of Vessel I.
(C) Vessel II would normally be the stand-on vessel, but should stay out of the way in this particular situation.
(D) The Rules of Special Circumstances applies, and neither vessel is the stand-on vessel.

10-22. You are aboard vessel "A" on open waters and vessel "B", a sailing vessel, is sighted off your port bow as shown in DIAGRAM 27. Which vessel is the stand on vessel?

(A) Vessel "A" because it is towing.
(B) Vessel "A" because it is to starboard of vessel "B".
(C) Vessel "B" because it is sailing.
(D) Vessel "B" because it is to port of vessel "A".

10-23. You are on vessel "A" and approaching vessel "B" as shown in DIAGRAM 15. You are not sure whether your vessel is crossing or overtaking vessel "B". You should...

(A) change course to make the situation definitely either crossing or overtaking.
(B) consider it to be a crossing situation.
(C) consider it to be an overtaking situation.
(D) consider it a crossing situation if you can cross ahead safely.

10-24. The term "restricted visibility" as used in the Rules refers...

(A) only to fog.
(B) only to visibility of less than one-half of a mile.
(C) to visibility where you cannot see shore.
(D) to any condition where visibility is restricted.

10-25. Which statement(s) is (are) true concerning the Rules of the Road?

(A) Distress signals are in the Annexes of the Rules.
(B) Spacing and positioning requirements for lights are in the Annexes to the Rules.
(C) Radar information is in the main body of the Rules.
(D) All of the above.

10-26. According to the Navigation Rules, you may depart from the Rules when...

(A) no vessels are in sight visually.
(B) no vessels are visible on radar.
(C) you are in immediate danger.
(D) out of sight of land.

10-27. Which statement is true concerning two sailing vessels?

(A) A sailing vessel with the wind forward of the beam on her port side shall keep out of the way of a sailing vessel with the wind forward of the beam on the starboard side.
(B) When both vessels have the wind on the same side, the vessel to leeward shall keep out of the way.
(C) A sail vessel with the wind aft of the beam must keep out of the way of a vessel sailing into the wind.
(D) None of the above.

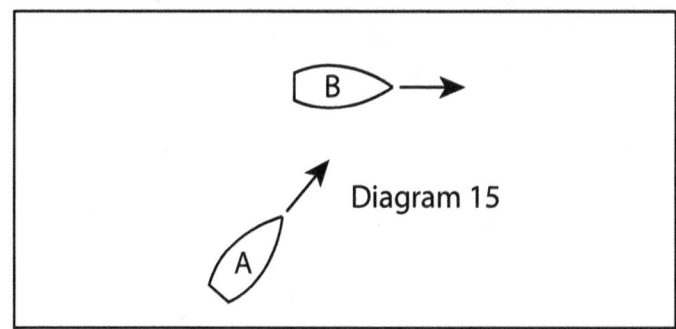

Diagram 15

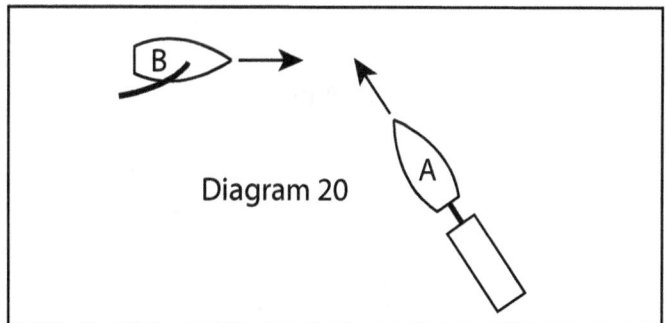

Diagram 20

10-28. You are aboard vessel "A" which is towing on open waters when vessel "B", a sailing vessel, is sighted off your port bow, as shown in DIAGRAM 20. Which vessel has the right of way?

(A) Vessel "A" is the stand-on vessel because it is towing.
(B) Vessel "A" is the stand-on vessel because it is to starboard of vessel "B".
(C) Vessel "B" is the stand-on vessel because it is sailing.
(D) Vessel "B" is the stand-on vessel because it is to port of vessel "A".

10-29. When underway in a channel, you should keep....

(A) in the middle of the channel.
(B) to the starboard side of the channel.
(C) to the port side of the channel.
(D) to the side of the channel that has the widest turns.

10-30. When navigating in restricted visibility, a power-driven vessel shall...

(A) if risk of collision does not exist, still stop her engines when hearing a fog signal forward of her beam.
(B) have her engines ready for immediate maneuver.
(C) when making way, sound one prolonged blast at intervals of not more than one minute.
(D) operate at a speed to be able to stop in the distance of her visibility.

10-31. A vessel is "in sight" of another vessel when...

(A) she can be observed visually or by radar.
(B) she can be observed visually from the other vessel.
(C) she can be seen well enough to determine her heading.
(D) her fog signal can be heard.

10-32. Which statement is true concerning two sailing vessels approaching each other?

(A) A sailing vessel overtaking another is the give-way vessel.
(B) When each is on a different tack, the vessel on the starboard tack shall keep out of the way.
(C) A sailing vessel seeing another to leeward on an undetermined tack shall hold her course.
(D) All of the above.

10-33. A power-driven vessel has on her port side a sailing vessel which is on a collision course. The power-driven vessel is to...

(A) maintain course and speed.
(B) keep clear.
(C) sound one blast and turn to starboard.
(D) stop her engines.

10-34. A sailing vessel is NOT required to keep out of the way of a...

(A) power-driven vessel.
(B) vessel not under command.
(C) vessel restricted in her ability to maneuver.
(D) vessel engaged in fishing.

10-35. In DIAGRAM 28, vessel "A" is underway and towing, when vessel "B" is sighted off the starboard bow. Which vessel is the stand-on vessel?

(A) Vessel "A" is the stand-on vessel because it is to port.
(B) Vessel "A" is the stand-on vessel because it is towing.
(C) Vessel "B" is the stand-on vessel because it is to starboard of vessel "A".
(D) Neither vessel is the stand-on vessel.

10-36. A sailing vessel is meeting a vessel engaged in fishing in a narrow channel. Which statement is true?

(A) The fishing vessel shall not hinder the passage of the sail vessel.
(B) The fishing vessel has the right of way.
(C) Each vessel should move to the edge of the channel on her port side.
(D) Each vessel should be displaying signals for a vessel constrained by her draft.

10-37. Vessel "A" is overtaking vessel "B" as shown in DIAGRAM 9. Which vessel is the stand-on vessel?

(A) Vessel "A".
(B) Vessel "B".
(C) Neither vessel.
(D) Both vessels must keep clear of the other.

10-38. A vessel is being propelled both by sail and by engines. Under the Rules, the vessel is...

(A) considered a "special circumstance" vessel.
(B) not covered under any category.
(C) considered a sail vessel.
(D) considered a power-driven vessel.

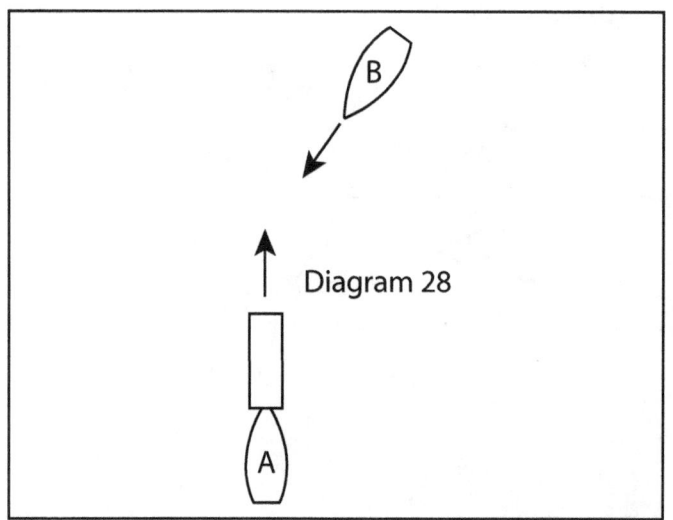

Diagram 28

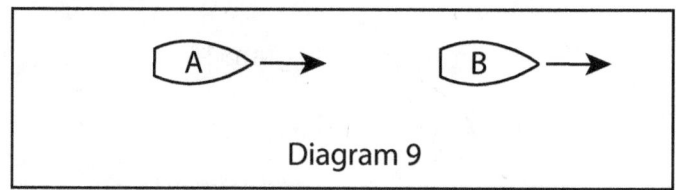

Diagram 9

10-39. The rule regarding lookouts applies...

(A) in restricted visibility.
(B) between dusk and dawn.
(C) in heavy traffic.
(D) All of the above.

10-40. When taking action to avoid collision, you should...

(A) make sure the action is taken in enough time.
(B) not make any large course changes.
(C) not make any large speed changes.
(D) All of the above.

10-41. A vessel transferring cargo while underway is classified by the Rules as a vessel...

(A) not under command.
(B) in special circumstances.
(C) restricted in her ability to maneuver.
(D) constrained by her draft.

10-42. Which vessel is "underway" under the Rules of the Road?

(A) A vessel at anchor with the engine running.
(B) A vessel with a line led to a tree onshore.
(C) vessel drifting with the engine off.
(D) A vessel aground.

10-43. You are on watch in the fog. The vessel is proceeding at a safe speed when you hear a fog signal ahead of you. The Rules require you to navigate with caution until the danger of collision is over and to...

(A) slow to less than 2 knots.
(B) reduce to bare steerageway.
(C) stop your engines.
(D) begin a radar plot.

10-44. In order for a stand-on vessel to take action in a situation, she must determine that the other vessel...

(A) is restricted in her ability to maneuver.
(B) has sounded the danger signal.
(C) is not taking appropriate action.
(D) has not changed course since risk of collision was determined.

Nav Rules Part C. Lights and Dayshapes

10-45. At night, a barge being towed astern must display...

(A) red and green sidelights only.
(B) a white sternlight only.
(C) sidelights and a sternlight.
(D) one all-round white light.

10-46. Which of the following may be used as a distress signal?

(A) Directing the beam of a searchlight at another vessel.
(B) A smoke signal giving off orange colored smoke.
(C) A whistle signal of one prolonged and three short blasts.
(D) International Code Signal PAN.

10-47. A pilot vessel on pilotage duty at night will show sidelights and a sternlight...

(A) when at anchor.
(B) only when making way.
(C) at any time when underway.
(D) only when the identifying lights are not being shown.

10-48. A vessel which displays the day signal as shown in DIAGRAM 6 is engaged in...

(A) submarine cable laying.   (B) pilotage duty.
(C) fishing.   (D) mine sweeping.

10-49. A vessel displaying the dayshapes illustrated in DIAGRAM 11, is...

(A) towing.   (B) conducting underwater operations.
(C) drifting.   (D) aground.

10-50. Which vessel must show forward and after masthead lights when making way?

(A) A 75-meter vessel restricted in her ability to maneuver.
(B) A 100-meter sailing vessel.
(C) A 150-meter vessel engaged in fishing.
(D) A 45-meter vessel engaged in towing.

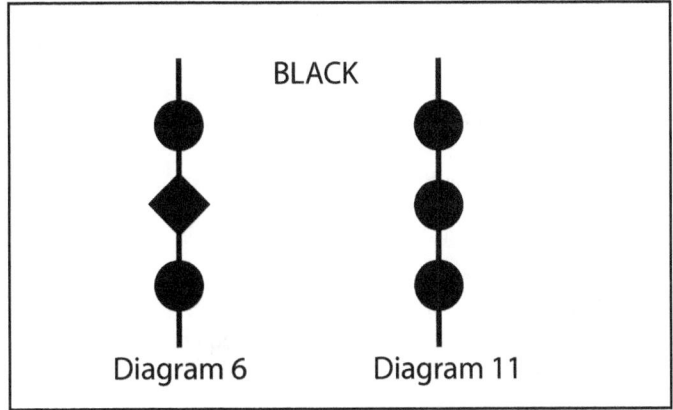

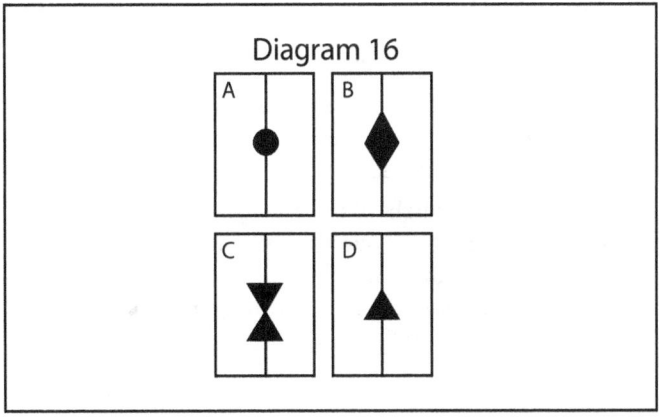

10-51. A light signal of three flashes means...

(A) "I am in doubt as to your actions".
(B) "My engines are full speed astern".
(C) "I desire to overtake you".
(D) "I am operating astern propulsion".

10-52. If a towing vessel and her tow are severely restricted in their ability to change course, they may show lights in addition to their towing identification light. These additional lights may be shown if the tow is...

(A) pushed ahead.
(B) towed alongside.
(C) towed astern.
(D) Any of the above.

10-53. Additional light signals are provided in the Annexes to the Rules for vessels...

(A) engaged in fishing.
(B) not under command.
(C) engaged in towing.
(D) under sail.

10-54. Which vessel may combine her sidelights in one lantern on the fore and aft centerline of the vessel?

(A) A 16-meter sail vessel.
(B) A 25-meter power-driven vessel.
(C) A 28-meter sail vessel.
(D) Any non-self propelled vessel.

10-55. Which of the following dayshapes, in DIAGRAM 16, indicates a vessel with a tow exceeding 200-meters in length?

(A) A.
(B) B.
(C) C.
(D) D.

10-56. What lights are required for a barge being towed alongside?

(A) Sidelights and a stern light.
(B) Sidelights, a special flashing light, and a sternlight.
(C) Sidelights and a special flashing light.
(D) Sidelights, a towing light, and a sternlight.

10-57. A towing vessel pushing a barge ahead which is rigidly connected in composite unit shall show the lights of...

(A) a vessel towing by pushing ahead.
(B) a power-driven vessel, not towing.
(C) a barge being pushed ahead.
(D) either answer A or answer B.

10-58. You see a vessel's green sidelight bearing due east from you. The vessel might be heading...

(A) east.
(B) northeast.
(C) northwest.
(D) southwest.

10-59. A vessel shall be deemed to be overtaking when she is in such a position with reference to the vessel she is approaching that she can see, at night...

(A) only the sternlight of the vessel.
(B) the sternlight and one sidelight of the vessel.
(C) only a sidelight of the vessel.
(D) any lights except the masthead lights of the vessel.

10-60. A vessel trawling will display a...

(A) red light over a white light.
(B) green light over a white light.
(C) white light over a red light.
(D) white light over a green light.

10-61. The rules concerning lights shall be complied with in all weathers from sunset to sunrise. The lights...

(A) shall be displayed in restricted visibility during daylight hours.
(B) need not be displayed when no other vessels are in the area.
(C) shall be set at low power when used during daylight hours.
(D) need not be displayed by unmanned vessels.

10-62. You are in charge of a power-driven vessel navigating at night. You sight the red sidelight of another vessel on your port bow. Its after masthead light is to the right of the forward masthead light. You should...

(A) hold course and speed.
(B) alter course to port.
(C) stop engines.
(D) sound the danger signal.

10-63. A 30-meter tug is underway and not towing. At night, this vessel must show sidelights and...

(A) one masthead light and a sternlight.
(B) two masthead lights and a sternlight.
(C) three masthead lights and a sternlight.
(D) a sternlight.

10-64. A vessel at anchor shall display between sunrise and sunset on the forward part of the vessel where it can best be seen...

(A) one black ball.
(B) two black balls.
(C) one red ball.
(D) two orange and white balls.

10-65. Which vessel must exhibit three white masthead lights in a vertical line?

(A) Any vessel towing astern.
(B) A vessel whose tow exceeds 200-meters astern.
(C) A vessel not under command, at anchor.
(D) A vessel being towed.

10-66. Which vessel must show an after masthead light, if over 50-meters in length?

(A) A vessel engaged in fishing.
(B) A vessel at anchor.
(C) A vessel not under command.
(D) A vessel trawling.

10-67. A "flashing light" is a light that...

(A) is red in color.
(B) is visible over an arc of the horizon of 360 degrees.
(C) flashes at regular intervals at a frequency of 120. flashes or more per minute.
(D) All of the above.

10-68. An authorized light to assist in the identification of submarines operating on the surface is a/an...

(A) blue rotating light.
(B) intermittent flashing amber/yellow light.
(C) flashing white light.
(D) flashing sidelight.

10-69. During the day, a dredge will indicate the side on which it is safe to pass by displaying...

(A) two balls in a vertical line.
(B) two diamonds in a vertical line.
(C) a single black ball.
(D) no shape is shown during the day.

10-70. What type of vessel or operation is indicated by a vessel showing two cones with the apexes together?

(A) Sailing vessel.   (B) Vessel trawling.
(C) Mineclearing.   (D) Dredge.

10-71. A vessel, which is unable to maneuver due to some exceptional circumstance, shall exhibit...

(A) during the day, three balls in a vertical line.
(B) during the day, three shapes, the highest and lowest being balls and the middle being a diamond.
(C) when making way at night, two all-round red lights, sidelights, and a sternlight.
(D) when making way at night, masthead lights, sidelights, and a sternlight.

10-72. One of the signals, other than a distress signal, that can be used by a vessel to attract attention is a/an...

(A) searchlight.
(B) continuous sounding of a fog-signal apparatus.
(C) burning barrel.
(D) orange smoke signal.

10-73. A lantern combining the two sidelights of a vessel's running lights may be shown on a...

(A) 15-meter sailing vessel.
(B) 20-meter vessel engaged in fishing and making way.
(C) 25-meter power-driven vessel trolling.
(D) 25-meter pilot vessel.

10-74. A vessel engaged in fishing during the day would show...

(A) one black ball.
(B) two cones with bases together.
(C) a cone, point downward.
(D) two cones, points together.

10-75. By day, when it is impracticable for a small vessel engaged in diving operations to display the shapes for a vessel engaged in underwater operations, it shall display...

(A) three black balls in a vertical line.
(B) two red balls in a vertical line.
(C) a black cylinder.
(D) a rigid replica of the International Code flag "A".

10-76. A vessel will NOT show sidelights when...

(A) underway but not making way.
(B) making way, not under command.
(C) not under command, not making way.
(D) trolling underway.

10-77. Which vessel may show two masthead lights in a vertical line?

(A) A vessel less than 5.0-meters in length with a 20-meter tow.
(B) A sail vessel towing a small vessel astern.
(C) A vessel restricted in her ability to maneuver.
(D) A vessel engaged in dredging.

10-78. What dayshape should a vessel being towed exhibit if the tow EXCEEDS 200-meters?

(A) Two balls.   (B) Two diamonds.
(C) One ball.   (D) One diamond.

10-79. Which statement is true when you are towing more than one barge astern at night?

(A) Only the last barge in the tow must be lighted.
(B) Only the first and last barges in the tow must be lighted.
(C) Each barge in the tow must be lighted.
(D) Only manned barges must be lighted.

10-80. The white masthead light required for a power-driven vessel under the Rules is visible over how many degrees of the horizon?

(A) 22.5 degrees.   (B) 112.5 degrees.
(C) 225.0 degrees.   (D) 360.0 degrees.

10-81. Which statement is true concerning lights and shapes for towing vessels?

(A) If a tow exceeds 200-meters in length, the towing vessel will display a black ball during daylight.
(B) When towing astern, a vessel will carry her identification lights at the masthead in addition to her regular masthead light.
(C) When towing astern, the towing vessel may show either a sternlight or a towing light, but not both.
(D) If the towing vessel is over 50-meters in length, she must carry forward and after masthead lights.

10-82. A vessel may use any sound or light signals to attract the attention of another vessel as long as...

(A) white lights are not used.
(B) red and green lights are not used.
(C) the vessel signals such intentions over the radiotelephone.
(D) the signal cannot be mistaken for a signal authorized by the Rules.

10-83. Which vessel may exhibit identifying lights when not actually engaged in her occupation?

(A) a trawler.   (B) a fishing vessel.
(C) a tug.   (D) none of the above.

10-84. What lights, if any, would you exhibit at night if your vessel was broken down and being towed by another vessel?
(A) none.
(B) same lights as for a power driven vessel underway.
(C) a white light forward and a white light aft.
(D) side lights and a stern light.

Nav Rules Part D. Sound Signals

10-85. While underway in fog, you hear a prolonged blast from another vessel. This signal indicates a...
(A) sailboat underway.
(B) vessel underway, towing.
(C) vessel underway, making way.
(D) vessel being towed.

10-86. Which of the following may be used as a distress signal?
(A) Directing the beam of a searchlight at another vessel.
(B) A smoke signal giving off orange colored smoke.
(C) A whistle signal of one prolonged and three short blasts.
(D) International Code Signal PAN.

10-87. If your vessel is approaching a bend and you hear a prolonged blast from around the bend, you should...
(A) back your engines.
(B) stop your engines and drift.
(C) answer with one prolonged blast.
(D) sound the danger signal.

10-88. Failure to understand the course or intention of an approaching vessel should be indicated by...
(A) one short blast.
(B) one prolonged blast.
(C) no less that five short blasts.
(D) not less that five prolonged blasts.

10-89. If your vessel is underway in fog and you hear one prolonged and three short blasts, this is a...
(A) vessel not under command.
(B) sailing vessel.
(C) vessel in distress.
(D) vessel being towed.

10-90. A power-driven vessel underway in fog making NO way must sound what blast(s) on the whistle?
(A) One long.
(B) Two prolonged.
(C) One prolonged.
(D) One prolonged and two short.

10-91. Which of the following is a distress signal?
(A) A triangular flag above or below a ball.
(B) The International Code Signal of distress indicated by JV.
(C) A green smoke signal.
(D) Flames on the vessel as from a burning tar barrel.

10-92. A sailing vessel with the wind abaft the beam is navigating in fog. She should sound...
(A) three short blasts.
(B) one prolonged blast.
(C) one prolonged and two short blasts.
(D) two prolonged blasts.

10-93. Which of the following actions would indicate a distress signal?
(A) Firing of green star shells.
(B) Deploying dye marker in the water.
(C) Answering a one blast signal with two blasts.
(D) Sounding 5 short blasts on the whistle.

10-94. The duration of a prolonged blast of the whistle is...
(A) 2 to 4 seconds. (B) 4 to 6 seconds.
(C) 6 to 8 seconds. (D) 8 to 10 seconds.

10-95. When underway in restricted visibility, you might hear, at intervals of two minutes, any of the following fog signals EXCEPT...
(A) one prolonged blast.
(B) two prolonged blasts.
(C) one prolonged and two short blasts.
(D) ringing of a bell for five seconds.

10-96. What is the identity fog signal which may be sounded by a vessel engaged on pilotage duty?
(A) 2 short blasts. (B) 3 short blasts.
(C) 4 short blasts. (D) 5 short blasts.

10-97. A bell is used to sound a fog signal for a...
(A) power-driven vessel underway.
(B) sailing vessel at anchor.
(C) vessel engaged in fishing.
(D) vessel not under command.

10-98. You are on lookout watch, when you sight a vessel displaying the code flag "LIMA" below which is a red ball, this indicates...
(A) a vessel with trolling lines out.
(B) a vessel getting ready to receive aircraft.
(C) a vessel aground.
(D) a vessel in distress.

10-99. You are underway in fog when you hear the rapid ringing of a bell for five seconds followed by the sounding of a gong for five seconds. This signal indicates a vessel...
(A) aground.
(B) more than 100-meters in length, at anchor.
(C) fishing while making no way through the water.
(D) fishing in company with another vessel.

10-100. The wind is ESE, and a sailing vessel is steering NW. What tack is she on, and what fog signal should she sound?

(A) Port tack - one blast at one-minute intervals.
(B) Starboard tack - one blast at one-minute intervals.
(C) Starboard tack - two blasts at one-minute intervals.
(D) Starboard tack - one prolonged and two short blasts at two-minute intervals.

10-101. You are underway and sight a vessel which is continuously sounding its fog whistle. This indicates...

(A) the other vessel desires to communicate by radio.
(B) the other vessel desires a pilot.
(C) a distress signal.
(D) the vessel is aground.

10-102. A tug is towing three barges in line in restricted visibility. The second vessel of the tow should sound...

(A) one prolonged and two short blasts.
(B) one prolonged and three short blasts.
(C) one short blast.
(D) no fog signal.

10-103. You are approaching another vessel on crossing courses. She is about one mile distant and is on your starboard bow. You believe she will cross ahead of you. She then sounds a whistle signal of five short blasts. You should...

(A) answer the signal and hold course and speed.
(B) reduce speed slightly to make sure she will have room to pass.
(C) make a large course change, and slow down if necessary.
(D) wait for another whistle signal from the other vessel.

10-104. You are underway in fog and hear a fog signal of two prolonged blasts on your starboard quarter. You should...

(A) stop your vessel.
(B) change your course to the left.
(C) change course to the right.
(D) hold your course and speed.

10-105. You are underway, in fog, when you hear a whistle signal of one prolonged blast followed by two short blasts. This signal could indicate a vessel...

(A) not under command.   (B) being towed.
(C) aground.   (D) All of the above.

10-106. A 35-ft power-driven vessel must carry for sound signaling...

(A) Whistle.
(B) Bell.
(C) Bell and Whistle.
(D) Any device that makes an efficient sound.

10-107. A 35-ft sailing vessel must carry for sound signaling...

(A) Whistle.
(B) Bell.
(C) Bell and Whistle.
(D) Any device that makes an efficient sound.

10-108. Which of the following statements is true concerning the danger signal?

(A) Vessels must be in sight of each other in order to use the danger signal.
(B) Only the stand-on vessel can sound the danger signal.
(C) Distress signals may be used in place of the danger signal.
(D) The danger signal consists of 4 or more short blasts of the whistle.

10-109. A distress signal...

(A) consists of 5 or more short blasts of the fog signal apparatus.
(B) may be used separately or with other distress signals.
(C) consists of the raising and lowering of a large white flag.
(D) is used to indicate doubt about another vessel's intentions.

10-110. What is the danger signal?

(A) A continuous sounding of the fog signal.
(B) Firing a gun every minute.
(C) Five or more short rapid blasts on the whistle.
(D) One long blast on the whistle.

10-111. At specified intervals, a 40-ft vessel anchored in fog shall sound...

(A) no sound signal needed .
(B) bell.
(C) any efficient sound.
(D) bell and gong.

10-112. Continuous sounding of a fog whistle by a vessel is a signal...

(A) that the vessel is anchored.
(B) for a request that the draw span of a bridge be opened.
(C) of distress.
(D) that the vessel is broken down and drifting.

10-113. Which statement is true concerning the light used with whistle signals?

(A) Use of such a light is required.
(B) The light shall have the same characteristics as a masthead light.
(C) It is only used to supplement short blasts of the whistle.
(D) All of the above.

10-114. What is the minimum sound signaling equipment required aboard a vessel 14-meters in length?

[ed. note: sailing both Inland and International waters]

(A) A bell only.
(B) A whistle only.
(C) A bell and a whistle.
(D) Any means of making an efficient sound signal.

10-115. When should the fog signal of a vessel being towed be sounded?

(A) After the towing vessel's fog signal.
(B) Before the towing vessel's fog signal.
(C) Approximately one minute after the towing vessel's fog signal.
(D) If the towing vessel is sounding a fog signal, the vessel towed is not required to sound any fog signal.

10-116. Which vessel may sound the danger signal?

(A) The stand-on vessel in a crossing situation.
(B) The give-way vessel in a crossing situation.
(C) A vessel at anchor.
(D) All of the above

10-117. The duration of each blast of whistle signals used in meeting, and crossing, situations is...

(A) about 1 second.   (B) 2 or 4 seconds.
(C) 4 to 6 seconds.   (D) 8 to 10 seconds.

10-118. A fog signal of one short, one prolonged, and one short blast can be sounded by...

(A) a vessel at anchor.   (B) a vessel aground.
(C) a trawler shooting its nets.   (D) All of the above.

10-119. While underway in fog you hear a whistle signal consisting of one prolonged blast followed immediately by two short blasts. Such a signal is sounded in fog by...

(A) vessels at anchor, not engaged in fishing.
(B) vessels underway and towing.
(C) vessels in danger.
(D) pilot vessels.

10-120. When a vessel signals her distress by means of a gun or other explosive signal, the firing should be at intervals of approximately...

(A) 10 minutes.   (B) 1 minute.
(C) 1 hour.   (D) 3 minutes.

10-121. Your vessel is underway in reduced visibility. You hear, about 30 degrees on the starboard bow, a fog signal of another vessel. Which of the following actions should you take?

(A) Alter course to starboard to pass around the other vessel's stern.
(B) Slow your engines and let him pass ahead of you.
(C) Reduce your speed to bare steerageway.
(D) Alter course to port and pass him on his port side.

10-122. A power-driven vessel making way through the water sounds a fog signal of ...

(A) one prolonged blast at intervals of not more than two minutes.
(B) two prolonged blasts at intervals of not more than two minutes.
(C) one prolonged blast at intervals of not more than one minute.
(D) two prolonged blasts at intervals of not more than one minute.

10-123. In restricted visibility, a vessel fishing with nets shall sound at intervals of two minutes...

(A) one prolonged blast.
(B) one prolonged followed by two short blasts.
(C) one prolonged followed by three short blasts.
(D) two prolonged blasts in succession.

10-124. You are underway and approaching a bend in the channel where vessels approaching from the opposite direction cannot be seen. You should sound...

(A) one blast, 4 to 6 seconds in duration.
(B) three blasts, 4 to 6 seconds in duration.
(C) one continuous blast until you are able to see around the bend.
(D) one blast, 8 to 10 seconds in duration.

10-125. Fog signals, required under the Rules for vessels underway, shall be sounded...

(A) only on the approach of another vessel.
(B) only when vessels are in sight of each other.
(C) at intervals of not more than one minute.
(D) at intervals of not more than two minutes.

10-126. Five or more short blasts on a vessel's whistle indicates that she is...

(A) in doubt that another vessel is taking sufficient action to avoid a collision.
(B) altering course to starboard.
(C) altering course to port.
(D) the stand-on vessel and will maintain course and speed.

10-127. A person aboard a vessel, signaling by raising and lowering his outstretched arms to each side, is indicating...

(A) danger, stay away.
(B) all is clear, it is safe to pass.
(C) the vessel is anchored.
(D) a distress signal.

CHAPTER 11 – NAVIGATION PLANNING AND PRACTICE

This chapter includes exercises that review topics covered in earlier chapters, presented sequentially along two boat trips. Use information from the Resources section of this workbook as needed. With sequential problems that rely to some extent on previous answers, it might be best to check the solutions as you proceed, rather than working through all of them before looking at the solutions. There is no specific order to the three trips. You might look over each to decide which would be the best to start with.

Trip 1.

The following are examples of questions asked on USCG deck license exams. There is no order to the presentation. Variation is 15.0 W.

11-1. Your eye height is 25 feet (7.6 meters). The visibility is 5.5 nmi. (A) What is the luminous range of Buzzards Bay Entrance Light (*use the charted light description*). (B) As an aside, compare the charted height and nominal range of this light with the modern values given in the Light List.

11-2. (A) What chart gives the most detail for Point Judith Harbor? (B) What is its scale? (C) Is this considered a LARGE scale or a SMALL scale chart?

11-3. Near Buzzards Bay Buoy BB you see two dashed lines emanating from the lighted Buoy VS. What do these lines indicate?

(A) Fish trap area.
(B) Prohibited anchoring.
(C) Underwater cable area.
(D) Light obscured boundaries.

11-4. You are on course 090 M. Your speed is 7.0 kts. You passed close abeam of Pt Judith Buoy 2 at 2010. It is now 2053. You see a bright white light on your port beam. (A) What is the name of this light? (B) Approximately how far off is it?

11-5. What kind of bottom is found in the center of Sippican Harbor? (A) Hard, (B) Muddy, (C) Rocky, (D) Sandy.

11-6. You are on course 270 M and Buoy 2 south of Nomans Land is dead ahead. Gay Head Light bears 340 M. What is your Lat-Lon? (B) Proceeding on toward the buoy on the same course sometime later you notice that Gay Head Light disappears. What is your approximate Lon when that happens?

11-7. At 0725 your position is 41°20.3'N, 71°18.7'W. What is the range and true bearing to Pt. Judith Light?

11-8. At 1425 you are heading 054 T and Pt Judith Light is abeam to port at 3.1 nmi. The current is 135 T at 1.8 kts. (A) At a knotmeter speed of 8.0 which true course must you steer to make good 048 T? (B) What is the corresponding compass course?

11-9. At 1130 you are located between Buoy 3 and Buoy 4 headed south along the Cleveland Ledge Channel. Your course is 195 T. You take a bearing to Nyes Neck of 127 T. What is the relative bearing to that point?

(A) 292 R.   (B) 142 R.
(C) 068 R.   (D) 277 R.

11-10. At 0825 your position is 41° 24.5'N, 71° 10.0'W and your heading is 350 T. You see a buoy at a relative bearing of 340 R. What does this buoy mark?

11-11. At 1215 you are headed toward Robinson's Hole on course 288 M in 80 ft of water about to cross Lucas Shoal. Your depth sounder draft is 2 ft and the tide is 4.0 ft. What is the minimum depth you expect to see on the sounder?

11-12. You are sailing SW along the Buzzard's Bay Channel, just passing the midchannel Buoy BB, proceeding to the ocean. When will you enter waters governed by the International Rules.

(A) You are already in International Rules waters.
(B) When Gooseberry Neck Lt bears 317 T.
(C) When Gay Head Light bears 090 T.
(D) When you cross the line between Block Is. and Nomans Land Is.

11-13. At 0845 you are headed east passing close abeam the Brenton Reef Light. You plan to rendezvous with a boat at 1200 at a meeting point 1.0 nmi due south of Buoy 1, charted as having a 6s isophase green light (North of Buzzards Light). (A) What is the true course to the meeting point? (B) What is the distance to the meeting point? (C) Assuming still water, what knotmeter speed should you hold to arrive at the meeting point at 1200?

11-14. You want to make good a course of 172 T. An east wind is causing 3° of leeway and the current is 1.2 kt setting toward 320 T. What true course should you steer to make good 172 at a knotmeter speed of 9.0 kts?

11-15 to 11-19 are Reserved.

Trip 2.

This is passage from Buoy 12 at the exit of the Cape Cod Canal to the breakwater Light 1A at The Harbor on the east side of Block Island. We use true bearings throughout, although compass bearings might be more common underway.

Also, even though it is crucial to check the Light List for all aids you rely on when underway, in this exercise we use only the 1210 Tr charted information for all aids. Many of these have changed over the years. Use EDT for all of this exercise.

11-20. Plan the route in two legs, Buoy 12 to Buzzards Bay midchannel Buoy BB, and from there to the Fl G 8M breakwater Light 1A at The Harbor, Block Island. What is the true course and distance of (A) leg 1 and (B) leg 2?

11-21. What is (A) the range and (B) true bearing from the breakwater Light 1A to the unlighted bell Buoy 1 on the approach to The Harbor?

11-22. We depart at 0600 EDT on May 16, 2011. Assuming an SMG on course of 5.0 kts, which is what we see on the knotmeter: (A) What is the ETA Buoy BB and then (B) ETA at Light 1A?

11-23. Since departure, you have been steering a steady compass course of 221 T and your knotmeter has been steady at 5.0 kts. At about 0650 you note you have Buoy 10 dead ahead. Assuming Buoy 10 is indeed on station at the charted location: (A) Is this consistent with the plotted route? and if not, (B) How far off what side had you planned to pass this buoy?

11-24. At 0702 you are passing the Buoy 10 very close abeam. What is your estimate of the average current you have been sailing in since departure?

11-25. You decide you want to get back in control of your navigation and pass close abeam of Buoy BB. What true heading would you choose to reach Buoy BB taking into account the record of your navigation so far? Your knotmeter speed is staying at 5.0.

11-26. You pass close abeam Buoy BB at 0742. What has been your SMG since departure at 0600?

11-27. Tracking directly toward your destination of Light 1A, (A) what times do you expect to pass abeam the Buoys 8, 6, 4, and 2 as you proceed, assuming you make good 5.0 kts? (B) At what time should you cross the Colregs demarcation lines, and how would you note this by piloting?

11-28. At 0937 you are on heading 238 T and knotmeter speed 5.0, and take a bearing to the large light structure of Buzzards Light and find it to be 203 T. Then later at 0949 on the same course and speed the bearing to the Buzzards Light structure is now 168 T. (A) What is your Lat-Lon? (B) Describe two different ways to come to this result.

11-29. We suspect we are being set to the SE, so we need to look ahead and figure anticipated currents. The next leg is long open water run. Luckily, the visibility has begun to deteriorate slightly and the Buzzards Light is now on and very prominent. (A) What are the primary two current stations that might help us with predictions as we proceed to the SW? (B) Make a table of the forecasted currents; times, sets and drifts. *Note: We want EDT and there are astronomical corrections needed.* (C) How do the predictions from these two stations compare. *We can consider ± 20% in speed and ± 20° in direction as in agreement . This is the approximate (optimistic) uncertainty of this type of data. Review Exercise 8-54 for background on the process.*

11-30. (A) What is the range and bearing to the destination (Light 1A) from your 0949 position? (B) What is the time to go (TTG) at 5.0 kts? Starting from your 0949 position, make an estimate of the net tidal current vector affecting your navigation over then next 5 hours. That is, what average set and drift would account for the changing currents you expect over this period.

11-31. Using your estimate of the average set and drift, (A) what true course would you steer to make good the direct course to the Light 1A from your 0949 position at a knotmeter speed of 5.0 kts. (B) What do you expect for an average SMG?

11-32. You proceed on your chosen heading and doing DR with your estimated SMG. To make a quick check of your progress, you take a bearing to Buzzards light at 1003 and get 104 T, then at 1015 the bearing has changed to 082. (A) Find a running fix from these bearings. (B) Plot your DR position at 1015. What is the range and bearing from your expected DR position at 1015 and what you got from the running fix. Note this is a rough check only as the running fix assumes our CMG and SMG are correct, which we do not know for certain till we get a better fix.

11-33. At 1108 you notice that you can see Brenton Reef Light from the cabin top (Height of eye = 10 ft) at a bearing of 295 T and you can see the Buzzards Light at 064 T, so you now have a good fix. (A) What is your fix Lat-Lon? (B) Suppose each of these bearings had an uncertainty of ± 2°, what would that imply your position uncertainty is? Hint: you can plot the new lines, or measure the range to the lights and use the small-angle rule. (C) How does your 1108 DR compare to this fix at 1108? (D) What is your new course and distance to your destination?

11-34. We can see Buzzards Light, but we can no longer see the huge structure it is mounted on. Checking the log, we lost visual sight of the tower with good binoculars at about 1053, which we noted because this tells us something about the atmospheric visibility. Looking back over our DR plot, what would be a rough estimate of the visibility based on that observation?

11-35. We are counting on the bright lights (now turned on in this light fog) for our navigation over an open water run to

Block Island. Make a table of the bright lights we might see or care about, along with their anticipated visual ranges (i.e. smaller of geographic range and luminous range). The table should have columns: Light name, Height, Nominal range, and Geo range at HE = 10 ft and Luminous Range at visibility = x. Often it is useful to draw range rings at these distances about the lights so we can anticipate when we see which ones. Check the answer to 11-34 to see what we are calling the visibility in this exercise.

11-36. Our navigation has been pretty good, but seems we are still being set slightly to the SE. So now that we have a reasonable fix at 1108, we will do another test of the current. That is we will steer a steady heading direct to the mark (answer to 11-33 D), and hold our knotmeter speed of 5.0 and then do another fix in 60m to check our set. We have several lights to use for bearing fix. At 1208 we take these bearings: Buzzards Light 059T and Brenton Reef Light 323 T. (A) What is your DR position at 1208? (B) What is the Lat-Lon of your 1208 fix? (C) What is the range and bearing DR to fix at 1208? (D) What tidal current (set and drift) would account for this difference? (E) Checking your list of predicted currents at Brown's Ledge, is this consistent with those predictions for this time frame? (F) What is the new course and distance to the Light 1A?

11-37. We have about 3h to go. Checking your current table, we will make the assumption that the average current over this period will be 0.4 kts to the SW (225T). (A) Is this consistent with your current tables? (B) What is the course to steer and anticipated SMG to account for that current and track to the Light 1A on the rhumb line course (Answer 11-36 F) at knotmeter speed of 5.0?

11-38. Using your anticipated SMG (Answer 11-37B) tracking along the rhumbline course (Answer 11-33B), noting your depth sounder draft is 2 ft, (A) what time would you expect to read the deepest water during the next hour and (B) what would the depth sounder read?

11-39. Carrying on from 1208 position, you take these bearings at 1354: Block Is SE Light 226 T, Pt Judith Light 346 T, and Brenton Reef Light 011 T. (A) What is your Lat-Lon from the bearing fix? (B) What is the new course and distance to Light 1A? (C) What is your DR at this time—use the SMG you computed from 11-21B and the track you assumed you were making good. (D) Was the course you chose to steer at 1208 (Answer 11-37B) the right one to keep you on track? What is the range and bearing of 1354 DR to 1354 fix? (E) What does this tell us about our assumptions of what the current was going to be? (F) Thinking over this result more generally, what does this tell us about our navigation procedures so far?

11-40. Considering what you steered from 1208 to 1354 and what you made good during this time, (A) what is now the best course to steer to make good the new course to the Light 1A and the associated SMG, assuming still a knotmeter speed of 5.0? There are several ways to approach this: you are either correcting a correction or reevaluating the last leg from scratch. In other words, you know what you steered (Answer 11-37B) and you know what the knotmeter read (5.0) and now you know what you made good—quite independent of any reasoning that went into deciding what to steer. (B) Assuming Answer A is the best you can compute, what is an alternative way to make a quick estimate of the new course to steer and new SMG?

11-41. You proceed from the 1354 position with your new heading (Answer 11-40A) hoping to make good direct to the Light 1A. You believe the visibility is still about 5 to 6 mi. (A) At what time would you expect to see the Light 1A? (B) What will be the bearing to Block Island Southeast Light at that time?

11-42. What do you expect the tide height to be at Old Harbor (the current name of The Harbor) when you arrive there?

11-43. (A) At what time do you expect to first see 90 ft on your depth sounder and (B) and what should be the bearing to the eastern most tangent to Block Island. (C) How far are you from the Light 1A at that time?

11-44. As you approach Old Harbor the fog has thickened, but the wind is calm and the seas are flat. You passed the bell Buoy 1, but you did not hear any bell as you passed although you could see the buoy clearly about 100 yards off. List several factors that could account for that, and note the most likely one.

11-45. Recall that we had large corrections to the rotary currents of up to 40% (factor 1.4) due to astronomical effects (relative location of sun and moon). Why do we not have to make these corrections for the other current predictions in the current book?

11-46 to 11-49 are Reserved.

Trip 3.

This short trip departs mid channel abeam the entrance to The Cove, across the river from Tiverton, and proceeds down the Sakonnet River to anchor in Sakonnet Harbor. There are optional right answers on some questions, so self grading will be called for. We will use buoys for navigation in the exercise, but as a rule, we should always have back-ups when using buoys as they could be off station or missing.

11-50. We will work this exercise on 1210 Tr, but this is clearly not the best chart for the trip. The NOAA chart viewer online is one way to see options. (A) What are the best paper charts for this trip? (B) What other mapping resources might be useful for this trip? (C) What are the RNC electronic chart numbers that correspond to the paper charts you chose? (D) What are the ENC electronic chart numbers corresponding to the charts you chose?

11-51. Using the 1210 Tr chart and assuming all charted navigation aids are on station and functioning as intended, select a set of waypoints for this trip along with a brief note of why you selected them.

11-52. Trip planning: (A) What is the total distance of this trip? (B) What is the total time to go (TTG) at an SMG of 5.0 kts?

11-53. What is the main factor that determines a best time to depart?

11-54. What are the two current stations that provide information appropriate to this trip?

11-55. There is a very good reason why the Gould Island current subordinate station should NOT be used for this trip. What is it?

11-56. You would like to depart on your trip at the time of morning minimum before ebb on April 20, 2011. What time (local) will your trip begin?

11-57. You are beginning the trip at minimum before ebb, so the current at Stone Bridge should be insignificant. But for future information, possibly affecting our return planning, what would be the time and velocity of the first maximum ebb on that same day?

11-58. Using your proposed waypoints, and assuming a departure at the min before ebb calculated in 11-7 above, what is (A) the course and distance for each leg of the trip, and (B) the ETA at each waypoint assuming 5.0 kts SMG?

11-59. Monitoring a USCG radio Broadcast Notices to Mariners, you have learned that the Old Bull Rock Buoy is off station and can no longer be used to maintain a safe clearance from the Rock. (A) What danger bearing based on a look ahead to Sakonnet Point (that anchors the Sakonnet Harbor breakwater) would you choose that would ensure a minimum 0.2 nmi clearance from the Rock? (B) Then state whether that danger bearing should be NO GREATER or NO LESS than your bearing to stay in safe water. (C) Using bearings to the Little Compton church spire, at what bearing should you begin monitoring your danger bearing? (D) And passing what bearing can you leave the Rock to history and be concerned with the approaching Sakonnet Harbor?

11-60. After anchoring in the Harbor in 9 feet of water, you pause to consider the expected tide range over the next 24 hours that you plan to remain here. Your boat draws 6 feet. The question is, Are you anchored safely?

CHAPTER 12 – IN DEPTH...

This section is a review of basics and some new material on special topics.

12-1. What is the most important book in navigation?

12-2. (A) What are the three primary electronic navigation instruments?

12-3. (A) Which of the following is the most accurate LOP?

(a) compass bearing to a lighthouse,
(b) natural range between an exposed rock and the lighthouse,
(c) depth contour at known tide height,
(d) radar bearing to an islet.

(B) Which is the least accurate?

12-4 (A) What would be a fair estimate of your DR uncertainty when traveling at 5 kts for 24h in coastal waters? (B) Same question when traveling at 12 kts for 24 hr?

12-5. Of all the many options for plotting tools, which would most navigators consider the two basic tools?

12-6. What is the navigator's trick play for notes and labels?

12-7. (A) What is the sailor's formula for a quick estimate of an ETA to weather when tacking, for example? (B) The buoy upwind of you that you must go around is 2 miles away; your speed is 6 kts; how long will it take to get to the buoy?

12-8. What is the approximate speed of a wind-created current after it has blown in the same direction for about a day?

12-9. Your compass deviation is 5° E headed south. Without further information, what would you guess your deviation is headed north?

12-10. What is the name of the free software program from National Geodetic Center that calculates accurate magnetic variation for any time and place?

12-11. You just motored along a measured mile in still water and calm wind at a constant rpm with your knotmeter reading 6.0 ± 0.05 kts. This took you 9m and 23 sec. (A) is your knotmeter correct, high, or low? (B) If incorrect, what is the percentage correction you must apply?

12-12. (A) At 6 kts, what is your speed in miles in minutes per mile? (B) At 10 kts, what is your speed in minutes per mile? (C) At 1 kt, what is your speed in feet per min?

12-13. What is the difference between ECDIS and ECS?

12-14. Which statements are True and which are False? (Hint: Read all carefully before answering any.)

(A) Current affects both our CMG and our SMG.
(B) Leeway affects both our CMG and our SMG.
(C) To find our distance made good during a given time accounting for current, we must correct our compass course steered and the logged distance run.
(D) To find our distance made good during a given time accounting for leeway, we must correct our compass course steered and the logged distance run.
(E) To find our best estimated position, the correction for current depends on our heading.
(F) To find our best estimated position, the correction for current depends on our heading.
(G) Sailing to weather with a 6° leeway, a 6° current set into the wind direction cancels out the leeway leaving our DR accurate.
(H) I can change my heading to minimize the effect of current.
(I) I can change my heading to minimize the effect of leeway.
(J) I can measure a usable value of the current underway using the GPS.
(K) I can measure a usable value of the leeway underway using GPS.
(L) Leeway is only important in strong winds.
(M) A specific current correction on inland waters is rarely the same for more than an hour or so.

12-15. VMG is commonly used in two different ways in modern instruments. What is the distinction between them.

12-16. Assuming all else is equal and assumed to remain constant, what is the derived parameter that we want to optimize when choosing the favored tack?

12-17. What are the two VHF channels that you can use to communicate with both recreational and commercial vessels after contact is made on Channel 16?

12-18. (A) What are three advantages of the new POD nautical charts? (B) What are two disadvantages of the new POD nautical charts?

12-19. (A) A NOAA current prediction at a specific midchannel station reports a max ebb of 2.7 kts at 1220 EST. What is the range of variance from this prediction in speed and time that we can fairly expect right at the location of the current station? (B) What are the same variances in max speed and time (and direction) we might expect along the shoreline nearest to this station, which is about 1 mile away?

12-20. List at least three advantages AIS offers to supplement a radar.

12-21. It is generally a good approximation to assume the correction for a set detected on the GPS will be the same as the set itself. That is, you are under power steering 045 T at knotmeter speed 6.0, but your COG is 055 T and your SOG is 6.5. You are getting set 10°, so a first guess would be to turn 10°

into the current (steer 035) and you will hope to then track at the desired course of 045. (A) Solve for the current (set and drift) and (B) then with that information figure what your heading should be to make good 045 at knotmeter speed 6.0. (C) Then compare the proper correction with the approximation to see how close it was.

12-22. You are in pea soup fog navigating only by radar. (A) You see a target approaching from 045R. Who has the right of way. (B) Once you see that risk of collision might develop with this target, what should you do? (C) Later you see a similar target approaching from 315R on the radar. What should you do? (D) Later another target approaches from 200R, clearly overtaking you, what should you do, and (E) Later a target is seen you approaching from 165 R, overtaking you on a parallel course, estimated to pass within just under half a mile on your starboard side. What should you do?

12-23. As a stand on vessel in a close encounter, you have a right to maneuver to avoid collision when...

(A) you decide the other vessel is not going to obey the Rules.
(B) you decide that the only way to avoid a collision is your own maneuver.
(C) the vessel has approached into what you have defined as your "close quarters" range for this encounter.
(D) Any of the above reasons can be used to justify your maneuver.

12-24. Which of the following are true about the 5-short blast danger signal.

(A) It can be used by both sail and power vessels.
(B) It can be used in both fog and clear weather.
(C) A long steady blast is more effective in most situations.
(D) We should be stopping by the time we sound it a second time.

12-25. What is the advantage of showing both a tricolor sidelights at the masthead and deck sidelights when sailing?

(A) Better visibility.
(B) Indicates you are under sail.
(C) Confuses your racing competitors.
(D) None. It is illegal and you will be fined.

12-26. What is the closest distance off you can pass a cruise ship in a harbor, even traveling dead slow?

12-27. What can be said about folding charts?

(A) There is a specific optimum way to fold them.
(B) We should not fold charts, only roll them.
(C) Usually we must fold them, but it really doesn't matter how.
(D) We should fold them so the large chart name and number printed on the chart shows in the corner.

12-28. It is now 1525, sunset is 1907, your steady speed is 7.4 kts, how far can you travel before sunset?

12-29. Use your best estimate of a range of values for each. (A) What is typical best accuracy of a GPS fix in feet? (B) What is a typical poor accuracy of a GPS fix in feet?

12-30. Give two conditions necessary for your GPS to use the WAAS system for enhanced accuracy?

12-31. What are various factors that might account for your VMG into the wind to be different on one tack compared to the other?

RESOURCES

The following are excerpts from standard resources used in navigation. The Light List and Coast Pilot also have custom made indices, which just cover the sections excerpted. Page numbers from the original Tide and Current Table pages are included on the samples as they are cross referenced. Book page numbers are in the headers of each page.

Resources Contents

Tide Tables	44
Current Tables	48
Light List	55
Light List Luminous Range Diagram	60
Light List Characteristics of Lights	61
Local Notice to Mariners	62
Excerpts from NOAA Chart Catalog No. 1	68
US Coast Pilot Vol. 2, Chapter 5	70
Coast Pilot Chapter 5 Index	78
Coast Pilot Climate Data (Appendix B)	79
Coast Pilot Marine Weather Statistics (Appendix B)	80

Tide Tables

Newport, Rhode Island, 2011
Times and Heights of High and Low Waters

	April							May							June					
	Time	Height		Time	Height			Time	Height		Time	Height			Time	Height		Time	Height	
	h m	ft	cm	h m	ft	cm		h m	ft	cm	h m	ft	cm		h m	ft	cm	h m	ft	cm
1 F	0623 1143 1835	3.3 0.1 3.7	101 3 113	**16** Sa	0551 1130 1817	4.0 -0.5 4.8	122 -15 146	**1** Su	0626 1139 1837	3.2 0.1 3.9	98 3 119	**16** M	0001 0622 1146 1849	-0.4 4.0 -0.5 5.0	-12 122 -15 152	**1** W ●	0055 0710 1226 1920	0.2 3.3 0.1 4.0	6 101 3 122	**16** Th	0132 0747 1304 2012	-0.2 3.9 -0.1 4.6	-6 119 -3 140
2 Sa	0024 0659 1217 1909	0.0 3.3 0.0 3.8	0 101 0 116	**17** Su O	0015 0642 1216 1907	-0.7 4.2 -0.7 5.1	-21 128 -21 155	**2** M	0036 0701 1217 1911	0.1 3.3 0.0 3.9	3 101 0 119	**17** Tu O	0054 0713 1235 1939	-0.5 4.0 -0.5 5.0	-15 122 -15 152	**2** Th	0137 0751 1308 2000	0.1 3.4 0.1 4.1	3 104 3 125	**17** F	0216 0836 1354 2101	-0.1 3.9 0.0 4.4	-3 119 0 134
3 Su ●	0059 0733 1252 1942	-0.1 3.4 -0.1 3.8	-3 104 -3 116	**18** M	0107 0732 1302 1957	-0.8 4.2 -0.7 5.1	-24 128 -21 155	**3** Tu ●	0115 0737 1255 1945	0.1 3.3 0.0 3.9	3 101 0 119	**18** W	0144 0804 1324 2030	-0.4 4.0 -0.4 4.8	-12 122 -12 146	**3** F	0216 0834 1350 2043	0.1 3.4 0.1 4.1	3 104 3 125	**18** Sa	0254 0925 1441 2149	0.0 3.8 0.1 4.1	0 116 3 125
4 M	0135 0806 1327 2014	-0.1 3.3 -0.1 3.8	-3 101 -3 116	**19** Tu	0158 0823 1349 2048	-0.7 4.2 -0.6 4.9	-21 128 -18 149	**4** W	0152 0815 1333 2021	0.0 3.3 0.0 3.9	0 101 0 119	**19** Th	0232 0855 1413 2121	-0.3 3.9 -0.2 4.6	-9 119 -6 140	**4** Sa	0254 0919 1433 2129	0.1 3.5 0.1 4.0	3 107 3 122	**19** Su	0330 1015 1527 2236	0.1 3.7 0.3 3.8	3 113 9 116
5 Tu	0210 0841 1402 2047	-0.1 3.3 -0.1 3.7	-3 101 -3 113	**20** W	0247 0914 1435 2140	-0.6 4.0 -0.5 4.7	-18 122 -15 143	**5** Th	0229 0855 1411 2100	0.1 3.3 0.1 3.9	3 101 3 119	**20** F	0317 0947 1500 2213	-0.2 3.8 0.0 4.2	-6 116 0 128	**5** Su	0330 1008 1519 2218	0.1 3.5 0.2 4.0	3 107 6 122	**20** M	0406 1103 1614 2323	0.2 3.6 0.5 3.5	6 110 15 107
6 W	0245 0917 1436 2123	0.0 3.2 0.0 3.6	0 98 0 110	**21** Th	0334 1007 1520 2234	-0.3 3.8 -0.2 4.3	-9 116 -6 131	**6** F	0304 0938 1449 2144	0.2 3.2 0.2 3.8	6 98 6 116	**21** Sa	0400 1036 1548 2305	0.0 3.6 0.3 3.9	0 110 9 119	**6** M	0409 1058 1608 2311	0.1 3.6 0.2 3.8	3 110 6 116	**21** Tu	0443 1150 1704	0.3 3.5 0.7	9 107 21
7 Th	0318 0958 1511 2203	0.1 3.1 0.1 3.5	3 94 3 107	**22** F	0422 1102 1608 2330	0.0 3.6 0.1 3.9	0 110 3 119	**7** Sa	0341 1025 1530 2233	0.2 3.2 0.2 3.7	6 98 6 113	**22** Su	0443 1133 1639 2357	0.3 3.5 0.5 3.5	9 107 15 107	**7** Tu	0452 1151 1704	0.2 3.7 0.3	6 113 9	**22** W	0008 0525 1236 1803	3.2 0.4 3.4 0.9	98 12 104 27
8 F	0354 1042 1549 2249	0.3 2.9 0.2 3.4	9 88 6 104	**23** Sa	0515 1158 1701	0.3 3.4 0.5	9 104 15	**8** Su	0421 1115 1617 2325	0.3 3.2 0.3 3.6	9 98 9 110	**23** M	0528 1225 1738	0.5 3.4 0.8	15 104 24	**8** W O	0005 0542 1245 1813	3.7 0.2 3.8 0.4	113 6 116 12	**23** Th O	0053 0612 1321 1917	3.0 0.5 3.3 1.0	91 15 101 30
9 Sa	0434 1132 1633 2341	0.4 2.9 0.3 3.3	12 88 9 101	**24** Su O	0026 0626 1255 1810	3.5 0.5 3.2 0.7	107 15 98 21	**9** M	0508 1208 1714	0.4 3.3 0.4	12 101 12	**24** Tu O	0049 0620 1317 1902	3.2 0.6 3.3 0.9	98 18 101 27	**9** Th	0101 0642 1341 1936	3.6 0.2 4.0 0.4	110 6 122 12	**24** F	0139 0705 1408 2032	2.8 0.6 3.3 0.9	85 18 101 27
10 Su	0524 1225 1728	0.5 2.9 0.4	15 88 12	**25** M	0124 0754 1353 2027	3.2 0.6 3.2 0.8	98 18 98 24	**10** Tu O	0021 0608 1304 1824	3.5 0.4 3.4 0.5	107 12 104 15	**25** W	0140 0716 1410 2034	3.0 0.6 3.3 0.9	91 18 101 27	**10** F	0200 0746 1441 2057	3.5 0.1 4.2 0.3	107 3 128 9	**25** Sa	0229 0801 1459 2129	2.7 0.6 3.3 0.8	82 18 101 24
11 M O	0038 0634 1323 1840	3.3 0.6 3.0 0.5	101 18 91 15	**26** Tu	0224 0847 1452 2133	3.0 0.7 3.2 0.8	91 21 98 24	**11** W	0120 0718 1402 1949	3.5 0.3 3.7 0.4	107 9 113 12	**26** Th	0234 0809 1502 2128	2.8 0.6 3.3 0.8	85 18 101 24	**11** Sa	0303 0846 1542 2202	3.4 0.0 4.4 0.2	104 0 134 6	**26** Su	0323 0854 1552 2218	2.7 0.5 3.4 0.7	82 15 104 21
12 Tu	0141 0801 1424 2005	3.3 0.5 3.2 0.3	101 15 98 9	**27** W	0324 0922 1549 2214	2.9 0.6 3.3 0.6	88 18 101 18	**12** Th	0223 0824 1503 2107	3.5 0.2 4.0 0.2	107 6 122 6	**27** F	0328 0856 1554 2210	2.8 0.5 3.4 0.7	85 15 104 21	**12** Su	0407 0941 1643 2259	3.5 -0.1 4.6 0.0	107 -3 140 0	**27** M	0419 0943 1643 2304	2.8 0.4 3.6 0.5	85 12 110 15
13 W	0247 0907 1528 2121	3.4 0.2 3.6 0.1	104 6 110 3	**28** Th	0420 0953 1640 2248	2.9 0.5 3.5 0.5	88 15 107 15	**13** F	0327 0920 1604 2211	3.6 0.0 4.3 -0.1	110 0 131 -3	**28** Sa	0419 0939 1642 2250	2.8 0.4 3.5 0.5	85 12 107 15	**13** M	0508 1033 1740 2352	3.6 -0.2 4.7 -0.1	110 -6 143 -3	**28** Tu	0511 1029 1730 2349	3.0 0.3 3.8 0.4	91 9 116 12
14 Th	0354 0958 1628 2224	3.6 0.0 4.0 -0.2	110 0 122 -6	**29** F	0507 1026 1724 2322	3.0 0.4 3.6 0.3	91 12 110 9	**14** Sa	0430 1009 1702 2307	3.7 -0.2 4.6 -0.3	113 -6 140 -9	**29** Su	0506 1021 1725 2331	2.9 0.3 3.7 0.4	88 9 113 12	**14** Tu	0604 1123 1833	3.7 -0.2 4.8	113 -6 146	**29** W	0558 1115 1814	3.1 0.2 4.0	94 6 122
15 F	0455 1044 1724 2321	3.8 -0.3 4.5 -0.5	116 -9 137 -15	**30** Sa	0548 1101 1802 2359	3.1 0.2 3.8 0.2	94 6 116 6	**15** Su	0528 1058 1757	3.8 -0.4 4.9	116 -12 149	**30** M	0549 1103 1804	3.1 0.2 3.8	94 6 116	**15** W O	0044 0656 1214 1924	-0.1 3.9 -0.2 4.8	-3 119 -6 146	**30** Th	0035 0643 1201 1857	0.2 3.3 0.1 4.1	6 101 3 125
											31 Tu	0013 0630 1144 1842	0.3 3.2 0.1 3.9	9 98 3 119							

Time meridian 75° W. 0000 is midnight. 1200 is noon. Times are not adjusted for Daylight Saving Time.
Heights are referred to mean lower low water which is the chart datum of soundings.

TABLE 2 – TIDAL DIFFERENCES AND OTHER CONSTANTS

No.	PLACE	POSITION		DIFFERENCES				RANGES		Mean Tide Level
		Latitude	Longitude	Time		Height		Mean	Spring	
				High Water	Low Water	High Water	Low Water			
		North	West	h m	h m	ft	ft	ft	ft	ft
	MASSACHUSETTS Martha's Vineyard Time meridian, 75° W			on Newport, p. 53						
933	Wasque Point, Chappaquiddick Island	41° 21.8'	70° 27.0'	+2 02	+3 20	*0.31	*0.31	1.1	1.4	0.6
935	Squibnocket Point	41° 18.7'	70° 46.1'	−0 45	−0 02	*0.82	*0.82	2.9	3.7	1.6
937	Nomans Land	41° 15.7'	70° 49.0'	−0 19	+0 18	*0.85	*0.85	3.0	3.6	1.6
939	Gay Head	41° 21.2'	70° 49.8'	−0 06	+0 45	*0.82	*0.82	2.9	3.5	1.5
941	Cedar Tree Neck	41° 26.1'	70° 41.8'	+0 10	+1 32	*0.62	*0.62	2.2	2.8	1.2
				on Boston, p.40						
943	Oak Bluffs	41° 27.5'	70° 33.3'	+0 32	−0 12	*0.18	*0.18	1.7	2.0	0.9
945	Edgartown	41° 23.3'	70° 30.7'	+0 57	+0 18	*0.20	*0.20	1.9	2.3	1.0
	Vineyard Sound			on Newport, p. 53						
	Woods Hole									
947	Little Harbor	41° 31.2'	70° 39.9'	+0 32	+2 21	*0.40	*0.40	1.4	1.8	0.8
949	OCEANOGRAPHIC INSTITUTION	41° 31.4'	70° 40.3'	Daily predictions, p.48				1.8	2.33	1.0
951	Uncatena Island (south side)	41° 30.9'	70° 42.2'	+0 12	+0 22	*1.02	*1.02	3.6	4.5	1.9
953	Quicks Hole, North side	41° 26.9'	70° 51.4'	−0 08	−0 08	*0.99	*0.99	3.5	4.4	1.8
955	Cuttyhunk	41° 25.5'	70° 55.0'	+1 20	+1 15	*0.97	*0.93	3.37	4.25	1.81
	Buzzards Bay									
957	Penikese Island	41° 27.0'	70° 55.3'	−0 17	−0 16	*0.97	*0.97	3.4	4.2	1.8
959	Chappaquoit Point, West Falmouth Harbor	41° 36.3'	70° 39.1'	+0 06	+0 08	*1.11	*1.14	3.82	4.70	2.07
961	Monument Beach	41° 42.9'	70° 37.0'	+0 16	+0 30	*1.15	*1.15	3.97	5.00	2.17
963	Gray Gables	41° 44.1'	70° 37.4'	+0 37	+1 16	*1.05	*1.21	3.62	4.45	1.98
965	Cape Cod Canal, RR. bridge <6>	41° 44.5'	70° 37.0'	+1 17	+2 50	*1.01	*1.01	3.43	4.22	1.93
967	Onset Beach, Onset Bay	41° 44.5'	70° 39.5'	+0 41	+1 25	*1.03	*1.03	3.50	4.41	1.97
969	Great Hill	41° 42.7'	70° 42.9'	+0 12	+0 12	*1.14	*1.21	3.96	4.99	2.15
971	Marion, Sippican Harbor	41° 43.2'	70° 45.6'	+0 10	+0 12	*1.13	*1.29	4.0	4.9	2.2
973	Piney Point	41° 41.7'	70° 43.2'	+0 10	+0 10	*1.13	*1.21	3.91	4.81	2.13
975	Mattapoisett, Mattapoisett Harbor	41° 39'	70° 49'	+0 11	+0 20	*1.09	*1.00	3.9	4.8	2.1
977	Clarks Point	41° 35.6'	70° 54.0'	+0 14	+0 23	*1.03	*1.07	3.56	4.49	1.93
979	New Bedford	41° 38.4'	70° 55.1'	+0 07	+0 07	*1.05	*1.05	3.7	4.6	1.9
981	Round Hill Point	41° 32.3'	70° 55.7'	+0 14	+0 22	*0.99	*1.00	3.43	4.32	1.85
	Westport River									
983	Westport Harbor	41° 31'	71° 05'	+0 09	+0 33	*0.85	*0.85	3.0	3.7	1.6
985	Hix Bridge, East Branch	41° 34.2'	71° 04.4'	+1 40	+2 30	*0.77	*0.77	2.7	3.4	1.4
	RHODE ISLAND, and MASSACHUSETTS Narragansett Bay									
	Sakonnet River									
987	Sakonnet	41° 27.9'	71° 11.6'	−0 09	+0 13	*0.91	*0.86	3.17	3.99	1.70
989	Sachuest, Flint Point	41° 29.2'	71° 14.3'	−0 05	+0 15	*0.90	*0.93	3.13	3.94	1.69
991	The Glen	41° 33.5'	71° 14.2'	−0 13	−0 03	*0.98	*1.00	3.40	4.28	1.84
993	Nannaquaket Neck	41° 37.1'	71° 12.2'	−0 12	−0 13	*1.01	*1.01	3.50	4.41	1.91
995	Anthony Point	41° 38.3'	71° 12.7'	+0 00	−0 01	*1.09	*1.09	3.75	4.73	2.05
997	North End, Bay Oil pier	41° 39.1'	71° 12.6'	+0 20	+0 01	*1.20	*1.07	4.17	5.25	2.24
999	Castle Hill	41° 27.8'	71° 21.7'	−0 05	+0 13	*0.94	*1.00	3.25	4.10	1.77
1001	NEWPORT	41° 30.3'	71° 19.6'	Daily predictions				3.47	4.38	1.87
	Conanicut Island									
1003	Beavertail Point	41° 27.1'	71° 24.1'	−0 05	+0 04	*0.98	*0.98	3.34	4.21	1.86
1005	West Jamestown, Dutch Island Harbor	41° 29.8'	71° 23.2'	+0 05	+0 04	*1.00	*1.00	3.46	4.36	1.87
1007	Conanicut Point	41° 34.4'	71° 22.3'	+0 07	−0 06	*1.07	*1.07	3.8	4.7	2.0
1009	Prudence Island, (south end)	41° 34.8'	71° 19.3'	+0 08	−0 03	*1.08	*1.14	3.74	4.71	2.03
1011	Bristol Ferry	41° 38.2'	71° 15.3'	+0 15	+0 00	*1.17	*1.14	4.08	5.14	2.20
1013	Bristol, Bristol Harbor	41° 40.1'	71° 16.7'	+0 13	+0 00	*1.16	*1.14	4.1	5.1	2.2
1015	Bristol Highlands	41° 41.8'	71° 17.6'	+0 13	−0 07	*1.18	*1.21	4.2	5.2	2.2
1017	Fall River, Massachusetts	41° 42.3'	71° 09.8'	+0 18	+0 03	*1.25	*1.21	4.36	5.41	2.35
1019	Steep Brook, Taunton River	41° 44.4'	71° 07.9'	+0 26	+0 05	*1.30	*1.29	4.51	5.68	2.44
1021	Bay Spring, Bullock Cove	41° 45.1'	71° 21.1'	+0 12	+0 01	*1.22	*1.21	4.25	5.23	2.30
1023	Pawtuxet, Pawtuxet Cove	41° 45.7'	71° 23.3'	+0 06	−0 11	*1.25	*1.29	4.35	5.35	2.35
1025	Providence, State Pier no.1	41° 48.4'	71° 24.1'	+0 13	+0 00	*1.27	*1.29	4.41	5.63	2.40
1027	Rumford, Seekonk River	41° 50.4'	71° 22.4'	+0 12	+0 06	*1.34	*1.29	4.66	5.73	2.51
1029	Pawtucket, Seekonk River	41° 52.1'	71° 22.8'	+0 18	+0 09	*1.31	*1.29	4.6	5.8	2.5
1031	East Greenwich	41° 39.9'	71° 26.7'	+0 13	+0 03	*1.14	*1.14	4.0	5.0	2.1
1033	Wickford	41° 34.3'	71° 26.7'	+0 03	−0 06	*1.07	*1.07	3.71	4.56	2.01
1035	Watson Pier, Boston Neck	41° 27.6'	71° 25.7'	−0 03	+0 16	*0.96	*0.93	3.32	4.18	1.79
1037	Narragansett Pier	41° 25.3'	71° 27.3'	−0 11	+0 11	*0.91	*0.93	3.2	4.0	1.7
	RHODE ISLAND, Outer Coast									
1039	Point Judith, Harbor of Refuge	41° 21.8'	71° 29.4'	+0 00	+0 33	*0.87	*0.93	3.00	3.13	1.63
1041	Block Island (Old Harbor)	41° 10.4'	71° 33.4'	−0 13	+0 15	*0.82	*0.86	2.85	3.51	1.54
1043	Southwest Point, Block Island	41° 09.8'	71° 36.6'	+0 05	+0 42	*0.75	*0.79	2.60	3.20	1.41
1045	Weekapaug Point, Block Island Sound	41° 19.7'	71° 45.7'	+0 41	+1 06	*0.74	*0.93	2.53	3.11	1.39
1047	Watch Hill Point	41° 18.3'	71° 51.6'	+0 41	+1 16	*0.74	*0.71	2.6	3.2	1.4
				on New London, p.60						
1049	Westerly, Pawcatuck River	41° 22.9'	71° 49.9'	−0 21	+0 03	*1.02	*1.00	2.6	3.1	1.5

Endnotes can be found at the end of table 2.

Saint John, New Brunswick, 2011
Times and Heights of High and Low Waters

	April							May							June					
	Time	Height		Time	Height			Time	Height		Time	Height			Time	Height		Time	Height	
	h m	ft	cm	h m	ft	cm		h m	ft	cm	h m	ft	cm		h m	ft	cm	h m	ft	cm
1 F	0425 1034 1646 2252	4.6 24.3 4.3 24.3	140 740 130 740	**16 Sa** 0337 0946 1602 2211	1.3 26.9 1.0 27.9	40 820 30 850	**1 Su**	0435 1045 1651 2256	4.3 23.6 4.9 24.6	130 720 150 750	**16 M** 0411 1021 1633 2242	0.7 26.2 1.6 28.2	20 800 50 860	**1 W** ●	0519 1129 1732 2338	3.9 23.6 5.2 25.3	120 720 160 770	**16 Th** 0541 1150 1800	1.6 25.3 3.3	50 770 100
2 Sa	0505 1114 1723 2328	4.3 24.6 4.3 24.6	130 750 130 750	**17 Su** ○ 0430 1039 1653 2302	0.3 27.2 0.7 28.5	10 830 20 870	**2 M**	0512 1122 1727 2331	3.9 23.6 4.9 24.6	120 720 150 750	**17 Tu** ○ 0504 1114 1725 2334	0.3 26.6 2.0 28.2	10 810 60 860	**2 Th**	0556 1205 1810	3.3 23.6 4.9	100 720 150	**17 F** 0008 0630 1239 1849	26.9 2.0 25.3 3.6	820 60 770 110
3 Su ●	0541 1150 1758	3.9 24.3 4.3	120 740 130	**18 M** 0522 1130 1744 2352	-0.3 27.6 0.7 28.9	-10 840 20 880	**3 Tu** ●	0547 1157 1801	3.6 23.6 4.9	110 720 150	**18 W** 0556 1205 1816	0.7 26.2 2.3	20 800 70	**3 F**	0015 0635 1243 1850	25.6 3.3 24.0 4.6	780 100 730 140	**18 Sa** 0057 0718 1327 1938	26.6 2.3 24.9 3.9	810 70 760 120
4 M	0002 0615 1224 1831	24.6 3.6 24.3 4.6	750 110 740 140	**19 Tu** 0613 1222 1834	-0.3 27.2 1.0	-10 830 30	**4 W**	0005 0622 1231 1836	24.9 3.6 23.6 4.9	760 110 720 150	**19 Th** 0024 0646 1256 1907	27.9 1.0 25.9 3.0	850 30 790 90	**4 Sa**	0055 0715 1322 1931	25.6 3.0 24.3 4.6	780 90 740 140	**19 Su** 0145 0805 1414 2026	26.2 3.0 24.6 4.6	800 90 750 140
5 Tu	0034 0649 1257 1903	24.6 3.9 24.0 4.6	750 120 730 140	**20 W** 0043 0704 1313 1925	28.2 0.3 26.6 2.0	860 10 810 60	**5 Th**	0040 0657 1306 1912	24.9 3.6 23.6 4.9	760 110 720 150	**20 F** 0115 0737 1347 1958	27.2 1.6 25.3 3.6	830 50 770 110	**5 Su**	0136 0757 1405 2016	25.6 3.0 24.6 4.3	780 90 750 130	**20 M** 0233 0852 1502 2115	25.3 3.6 24.3 4.9	770 110 740 150
6 W	0107 0722 1330 1937	24.6 3.9 25.6 4.9	750 120 780 150	**21 Th** 0134 0756 1406 2018	27.6 1.0 25.6 3.0	840 30 780 90	**6 F**	0116 0735 1343 1951	24.9 3.6 23.6 5.2	760 110 720 160	**21 Sa** 0206 0828 1438 2050	26.2 2.6 24.6 4.6	800 80 750 140	**6 M**	0221 0843 1451 2104	25.6 3.0 24.6 4.3	780 90 750 130	**21 Tu** 0322 0940 1551 2205	24.6 4.3 24.0 5.6	750 130 730 170
7 Th	0141 0758 1405 2014	24.6 4.3 23.3 5.6	750 130 710 170	**22 F** 0227 0849 1500 2112	26.6 2.3 24.6 4.3	810 70 750 130	**7 Sa**	0156 0816 1424 2034	24.9 3.9 23.6 5.2	760 120 720 160	**22 Su** 0258 0920 1532 2144	25.3 3.6 24.0 5.2	770 110 730 160	**7 Tu**	0310 0932 1542 2157	25.6 3.3 24.9 4.3	780 100 760 130	**22 W** 0413 1030 1643 2258	23.6 5.2 23.6 6.2	720 160 720 190
8 F	0219 0837 1445 2055	24.3 4.6 23.0 5.9	740 140 700 180	**23 Sa** 0322 0945 1558 2211	25.6 3.6 23.6 5.2	780 110 720 160	**8 Su**	0240 0901 1510 2122	24.6 4.3 23.3 5.6	750 130 710 170	**23 M** 0353 1014 1627 2241	24.6 4.3 23.6 5.9	750 130 720 180	**8 W** ◐	0404 1025 1636 2254	25.3 3.3 24.9 3.9	770 100 760 120	**23 Th** ◐ 0507 1122 1735 2353	23.0 5.9 23.0 6.6	700 180 700 200
9 Sa	0301 0922 1530 2142	24.0 4.9 22.6 6.2	730 150 690 190	**24 Su** ◐ 0421 1045 1659 2313	24.3 4.6 23.0 5.9	740 140 700 180	**9 M**	0329 0952 1601 2216	24.6 4.3 23.6 5.6	750 130 720 170	**24 Tu** ◐ 0451 1111 1725 2341	23.6 5.2 23.3 6.2	720 160 710 190	**9 Th**	0502 1122 1735 2355	24.9 3.3 25.3 3.6	760 100 770 110	**24 F** 0603 1215 1829	22.3 6.6 23.0	680 200 700
10 Su	0349 1012 1622 2236	23.6 5.2 22.3 6.6	720 160 680 200	**25 M** 0524 1147 1802	23.6 5.2 22.6	720 160 690	**10 Tu** ◐	0423 1047 1658 2314	24.3 4.3 23.6 5.2	740 130 720 160	**25 W** 0551 1208 1823	23.0 5.6 23.0	700 170 700	**10 F**	0603 1222 1835	24.9 3.6 25.6	760 110 780	**25 Sa** 0048 0659 1309 1922	6.6 22.0 6.9 23.0	200 670 210 700
11 M ◐	0445 1109 1721 2336	23.6 5.2 22.6 6.2	720 160 690 190	**26 Tu** 0017 0629 1249 1904	6.2 23.3 5.6 22.6	190 710 170 690	**11 W**	0523 1146 1758	24.3 4.3 24.3	740 130 740	**26 Th** 0040 0650 1305 1919	6.6 22.6 5.9 23.0	200 690 180 700	**11 Sa**	0057 0707 1322 1935	3.3 24.6 3.3 26.2	100 750 100 800	**26 Su** 0142 0754 1401 2013	6.6 21.7 6.9 23.0	200 660 210 700
12 Tu	0546 1211 1823	23.6 4.9 23.0	720 150 700	**27 W** 0120 0731 1348 2002	6.2 23.0 5.6 23.0	190 700 170 700	**12 Th**	0016 0626 1246 1859	4.6 24.6 3.6 24.9	140 750 110 760	**27 F** 0137 0747 1359 2011	6.2 22.6 6.2 23.3	190 690 190 710	**12 Su**	0159 0809 1422 2035	2.6 24.9 3.3 26.6	80 760 100 810	**27 M** 0234 0845 1450 2101	5.9 22.0 6.6 23.3	180 670 200 710
13 W	0039 0650 1313 1925	5.6 24.3 4.3 24.0	170 740 130 730	**28 Th** 0218 0828 1442 2053	5.9 23.3 5.2 23.6	180 710 160 720	**13 F**	0119 0728 1346 1958	3.6 24.9 3.0 26.2	110 760 90 800	**28 Sa** 0230 0840 1448 2058	5.9 22.6 5.9 23.6	180 690 180 720	**13 M**	0259 0909 1521 2132	2.3 24.9 3.3 26.9	70 760 100 820	**28 Tu** 0321 0933 1537 2146	5.2 22.3 6.2 24.0	160 680 190 730
14 Th	0142 0752 1413 2024	4.3 24.9 3.3 25.6	130 760 100 780	**29 F** 0309 0919 1530 2139	5.2 23.3 5.2 24.0	160 710 160 730	**14 Sa**	0219 0828 1444 2055	2.6 25.6 2.3 26.9	80 780 70 820	**29 Su** 0317 0928 1534 2142	5.2 22.6 5.9 24.0	160 690 180 730	**14 Tu**	0355 1006 1616 2227	1.6 25.3 3.0 27.2	50 770 90 830	**29 W** 0406 1017 1621 2229	4.6 23.0 5.6 24.6	140 700 170 750
15 F	0241 0851 1509 2119	3.0 25.9 2.0 26.9	90 790 60 820	**30 Sa** 0355 1004 1612 2219	4.9 23.6 4.9 24.3	150 720 150 740	**15 Su**	0317 0926 1539 2150	1.6 26.2 2.0 27.9	50 800 60 850	**30 M** 0400 1011 1615 2222	4.9 23.0 5.6 24.3	150 700 170 740	**15 W** ○	0449 1059 1709 2319	1.6 25.3 3.0 27.2	50 770 90 830	**30 Th** 0448 1058 1703 2310	3.9 23.6 4.9 25.6	120 720 150 780
							31 Tu	0440 1051 1654 2300	4.3 23.3 5.2 24.6	130 710 160 750										

Time meridian 60° W. 0000 is midnight. 1200 is noon. Times are not adjusted for Daylight Saving Time.
Heights are referred to the Canadian chart datum of soundings.

TABLE 2 – TIDAL DIFFERENCES AND OTHER CONSTANTS

No.	PLACE	POSITION Latitude	POSITION Longitude	DIFFERENCES Time High Water	DIFFERENCES Time Low Water	DIFFERENCES Height High Water	DIFFERENCES Height Low Water	RANGES Mean	RANGES Spring	Mean Tide Level
		North	West	h m	h m	ft	ft	ft	ft	ft
	NOVA SCOTIA, Gulf of St. Lawrence Time meridian, 60° W			on Pictou, p.8						
435	Pugwash	45° 51'	63° 40'	+1 00	+1 03	+1.8	0.0	5.0	6.0	4.8
437	PICTOU	45° 41'	62° 42'	Daily predictions				3.2	3.9	3.9
439	Merigomish Harbour	45° 39'	62° 27'	-0 13	-0 01	-0.3	0.0	2.9	3.4	3.8
441	Cape George	45° 53'	61° 53'	-0 54	-0 51	-1.6	-0.8	2.4	3.2	2.7
443	Antigonish Harbour	45° 40'	61° 53'	+0 09	+0 17	-1.7	-0.5	2.0	2.5	2.8
445	Cape Jack	45° 42'	61° 33'	-1 11	-1 18	-1.8	-0.7	2.1	2.6	2.7
447	Auld Cove	45° 39'	61° 26'	-0 27	-0 33	(*0.62+1.3)		2.0	2.6	3.7
	Cape Breton Island									
449	Port Hood	46° 01'	61° 32'	-0 46	-0 45	-1.6	-0.9	2.5	3.2	2.7
451	Mabou River entrance	46° 06'	61° 28'	-0 53	-1 04	*0.66	*0.61	2.2	2.9	2.5
453	Cheticamp	46° 37'	61° 02'	-1 23	-1 20	*0.56	*0.74	1.4	1.8	2.4
	NOVA SCOTIA, Outer Coast									
	Cape Breton Island–cont.									
455	Neil Harbour	46° 48'	60° 20'	-1 44	-1 45	*0.69	*0.65	2.4	3.1	2.7
457	Ingonish Island	46° 40'	60° 23'	-1 40	-1 33	-1.5	-0.9	2.6	3.2	2.7
459	St. Anns Harbour	46° 15'	60° 34'	-1 37	-1 40	-1.4	-1.0	2.8	3.5	2.7
461	North Sydney	46° 13'	60° 15'	-1 54	-1 49	*0.73	*0.61	2.6	3.2	2.7
463	Glace Bay	46° 12'	59° 55'	-1 59	-1 54	-1.6	-0.9	2.5	3.2	2.7
				on Halifax, p.20						
465	Louisburg Harbour	45° 54'	59° 59'	-0 08	-0 14	-1.6	-0.7	3.5	4.2	3.2
467	Gabarus Cove	45° 51'	60° 10'	+0 08	+0 10	-1.4	-0.7	3.7	4.4	3.3
469	St. Peter Bay	45° 38'	60° 52'	-0 12	-0 07	-0.6	-0.4	4.2	5.1	3.8
471	Arichat	45° 31'	61° 02'	-0 25	-0 14	-0.9	-0.5	4.0	4.8	3.6
473	Port Hastings, Strait of Canso	45° 39'	61° 24'	-0 16	-0 12	0.0	+0.2	4.2	5.1	4.4
475	Guysborough	45° 23'	61° 29'	+0 06	+0 18	-1.1	-0.5	3.8	4.6	3.5
477	Canso Harbour	45° 21'	61° 00'	-0 05	-0 04	-1.1	-0.6	3.9	4.7	3.5
479	Whitehaven Harbour	45° 14'	61° 12'	-0 10	-0 02	-1.1	-0.4	3.7	4.7	3.6
481	Isaacs Harbour	45° 11'	61° 40'	-0 03	+0 04	-0.6	-0.1	3.9	4.6	4.0
483	Sonora, St. Mary River	45° 03'	61° 55'	-0 02	+0 09	-0.7	-0.6	4.3	5.2	3.7
485	Liscomb Harbour	45° 00'	62° 02'	-0 11	-0 05	-0.6	-0.4	4.2	5.0	3.8
487	Sheet Harbour	44° 54'	62° 30'	-0 08	-0 04	-1.1	-0.9	4.2	5.0	3.3
489	Ship Harbour	44° 47'	62° 49'	-0 07	-0 04	-0.6	-0.4	4.2	5.1	3.8
491	Jeddore Harbour	44° 45'	63° 01'	-0 06	-0 03	-0.5	-0.4	4.3	5.2	3.9
493	HALIFAX	44° 40'	63° 34'	Daily predictions				4.4	5.3	4.3
495	Sable Island, north side	43° 57'	60° 06'	-0 06	-0 12	-2.7	-0.9	2.6	3.2	2.5
497	Sable Island, south side	43° 56'	59° 54'	-0 02	-0 06	-2.1	-1.6	3.9	4.8	2.5
499	St. Margarets Bay	44° 31'	63° 56'	+0 08	+0 07	-0.5	-0.3	4.2	4.9	3.9
501	Chester, Mahone Bay	44° 34'	64° 18'	+0 01	-0 04	-0.2	-0.2	4.4	5.3	4.1
503	Mahone Harbour, Mahone Bay	44° 27'	64° 22'	+0 03	-0 01	-0.1	-0.2	4.5	5.5	4.2
505	Lunenburg	44° 22'	64° 19'	+0 07	+0 07	-0.1	+0.1	4.2	4.9	4.3
507	Riverport, La Have River	44° 17'	64° 20'	+0 12	+0 05	-0.3	-0.4	4.5	5.3	4.0
509	Bridgewater, La Have River	44° 23'	64° 31'	+0 09	+0 06	-0.2	-0.3	4.5	5.5	4.1
511	Liverpool Bay	44° 02'	64° 41'	+0 14	+0 04	-0.5	-0.4	4.3	5.1	3.9
513	Lockeport	43° 44'	65° 05'	+0 27	+0 02	-0.2	-0.4	4.6	5.4	4.0
515	Shelburne	43° 45'	65° 18'	+0 30	+0 35	+0.1	-0.3	4.8	5.8	4.2
517	Barrington Passage	43° 32'	65° 36'	+0 51	+0 30	+1.6	+0.6	5.4	6.2	5.4
519	Swim Point	43° 26'	65° 38'	+1 41	+1 03	+2.9	+0.1	7.2	8.4	5.8
	NOVA SCOTIA, Bay of Fundy			on Saint John, N.B., p.24						
521	Lower East Pubnico	43° 38'	65° 46'	-1 52	-2 07	*0.43	*0.48	8.7	10.0	6.3
523	Yarmouth Harbour	43° 48'	66° 08'	-1 07	-1 15	*0.53	*0.42	11.5	13.4	7.5
525	Westport, St. Mary Bay	44° 16'	66° 21'	-0 35	-0 30	*0.72	*0.72	15.0	16.7	10.4
527	Tiverton, St. Mary Bay	44° 24'	66° 13'	-0 38	-0 30	-5.6	-0.7	15.9	18.3	11.3
529	Weymouth, St. Mary Bay	44° 27'	66° 01'	-0 26	-0 22	-6.5	-0.7	15.0	17.0	10.8
531	Digby, Annapolis Basin	44° 38'	65° 45'	-0 09	-0 07	+0.7	+0.3	21.2	24.6	14.9
533	Annapolis Royal, Annapolis River	44° 45'	65° 30'	+0 06	+0 10	+2.2	+0.4	22.6	25.7	15.7
535	Port George	45° 01'	65° 10'	-0 06	-0 06	+6.7	+0.8	26.7	30.5	18.2
537	Ile Haute	45° 15'	65° 00'	-0 02	-0 02	+7.4	+0.7	27.5	31.5	18.5
539	Spencer Island	45° 20'	64° 42'	+0 17	+0 21	*1.47	*1.50	30.5	35.0	21.2
	Minas Basin									
541	Parrsboro (Partridge Island) <2>	45° 22'	64° 20'	+0 51	+0 49	+14.7	- - -	34.4	39.0	22.3
543	Horton Bluff, Avon River	45° 06'	64° 13'	+0 58	+1 02	*1.76	*1.38	38.1	43.6	24.6
545	Windsor <2>	45° 00'	64° 08'	+1 03	- - -	+19.5	- - -	- -	- -	- -
547	Burntcoat Head	45° 18'	63° 49'	+1 06	+1 12	*1.90	*2.18	38.4	43.5	27.9
549	Truro <2>	45° 22'	63° 20'	+1 43	- - -	+26.1	- - -	- -	- -	- -
551	Spicer Cove, Chignecto Bay	45° 26'	64° 54'	+0 12	+0 16	+7.0	+0.8	27.0	30.0	18.3
553	Joggins <2>	45° 41'	64° 28'	+0 14	+0 26	+14.2	+1.8	33.2	37.0	22.4
555	Amherst Point, Cumberland Basin	45° 50'	64° 17'	+0 33	+0 45	*1.69	*1.55	35.6	40.5	24.0
	NEW BRUNSWICK, Bay of Fundy									
	Petitcodiac River <3>									
557	Grindstone Island	45° 43'	64° 37'	+0 21	+0 28	*1.49	*1.45	31.1	35.6	21.4
559	Hopewell Cape	45° 52'	64° 35'	+0 14	+0 39	*1.64	*1.85	33.2	38.0	24.0
561	Moncton <2> <3>	46° 05'	64° 46'	+0 46	- - -	+17.2	- - -	- -	- -	- -
563	Salisbury	46° 01'	65° 03'	+1 31	- - -	+18.2	- - -	- -	- -	- -
565	Herring Cove	45° 35'	64° 58'	+0 22	+0 20	+8.4	+0.9	28.3	32.4	19.1
567	Quaco Bay	45° 20'	65° 32'	+0 11	+0 12	+2.0	-0.3	23.1	26.3	15.3

Endnotes can be found at the end of table 2.

Current Tables

Pollock Rip Channel, Massachusetts, 2011

F–Flood, Dir. 035° True   E–Ebb, Dir. 225° True

	April						May						June				
	Slack	Maximum		Slack	Maximum		Slack	Maximum		Slack	Maximum		Slack	Maximum		Slack	Maximum
	h m	h m	knots	h m	h m	knots	h m	h m	knots	h m	h m	knots	h m	h m	knots	h m	h m	knots
1 F	0146 0806 1402 2029	0514 1105 1734 2326	2.0F 1.7E 2.1F 1.7E	**16 Sa**	0056 0727 1320 1953	0418 1011 1643 2237	2.1F 2.0E 2.2F 2.0E	**1 Su**	0149 0818 1408 2030	0521 1108 1737 2321	2.1F 1.7E 2.0F 1.8E	**16 M**	0124 0802 1353 2017	0451 1045 1714 2305	2.3F 1.9E 2.1F 2.0E	**1 W** ●	0230 0911 1456 2115	0602 1150 1815 2358	2.1F 1.6E 1.8F 1.8E	**16 Th**	0252 0936 1527 2142	0628 1222 1849	2.3F 1.7E 1.9F
2 Sa	0225 0847 1440 2106	0554 1141 1811 2358	2.1F 1.7E 2.1F 1.8E	**17 Su**	0146 0818 1411 2040	0508 1102 1731 2325	2.3F 2.1E 2.3F 2.1E	**2 M**	0226 0858 1446 2108	0558 1143 1811 2354	2.1F 1.7E 1.9F 1.8E	**17 Tu** ○	0214 0855 1446 2107	0543 1138 1805 2354	2.3F 1.9E 2.1F 2.0E	**2 Th**	0307 0952 1535 2154	0636 1228 1848	2.1F 1.7E 1.8F	**17 F**	0341 1026 1617 2231	0033 0718 1312 1939	1.9E 2.3F 1.7E 1.8F
3 Su ●	0300 0925 1516 2141	0629 1213 1843	2.1F 1.7E 2.1F	**18 M**	0234 0908 1501 2127	0556 1152 1818	2.4F 2.1E 2.3F	**3 Tu** ●	0301 0937 1523 2144	0631 1217 1843	2.1F 1.7E 1.9F	**18 W**	0304 0947 1538 2156	0634 1229 1856	2.4F 1.9E 2.0F	**3 F**	0345 1032 1615 2234	0036 0710 1307 1923	1.8E 2.1F 1.7E 1.8F	**18 Sa**	0429 1115 1705 2320	0121 0806 1359 2027	1.8E 2.2F 1.7E 1.8F
4 M	0333 1003 1551 2216	0028 0700 1245 1913	1.8E 2.1F 1.8E 2.0F	**19 Tu**	0321 0959 1551 2215	0012 0644 1242 1906	2.2E 2.4F 2.1E 2.2F	**4 W**	0336 1016 1600 2222	0027 0702 1252 1914	1.8E 2.1F 1.8E 1.8F	**19 Th**	0354 1038 1629 2247	0044 0725 1320 1947	2.0E 2.3F 1.8E 1.9F	**4 Sa**	0424 1114 1657 2317	0116 0747 1349 2002	1.9E 2.2F 1.8E 1.8F	**19 Su**	0517 1202 1753	0208 0853 1446 2116	1.8E 2.2F 1.6E 1.8F
5 Tu	0406 1040 1626 2252	0058 0730 1318 1942	1.8E 2.1F 1.8E 1.9F	**20 W**	0409 1050 1642 2304	0100 0733 1332 1956	2.1E 2.4F 2.0F 2.1F	**5 Th**	0411 1055 1638 2300	0102 0734 1330 1947	1.8E 2.1F 1.7E 1.8F	**20 F**	0443 1131 1721 2339	0133 0817 1412 2040	1.9E 2.3F 1.7E 1.8F	**5 Su**	0506 1158 1741	0200 0827 1433 2046	1.9E 2.2F 1.8E 1.8F	**20 M**	0010 0604 1250 1841	0256 0941 1533 2205	1.7E 2.1F 1.6E 1.7F
6 W	0440 1119 1703 2330	0132 0800 1355 2013	1.8E 2.0F 1.7E 1.8F	**21 Th**	0459 1144 1735 2357	0149 0825 1424 2050	2.0E 2.3F 1.9E 1.9F	**6 F**	0448 1137 1719 2342	0141 0809 1411 2024	1.8E 2.1F 1.7E 1.7F	**21 Sa**	0535 1223 1815	0224 0910 1505 2136	1.8E 2.2F 1.6E 1.7F	**6 M**	0003 0552 1244 1829	0246 0912 1520 2134	1.9E 2.2F 1.8E 1.8F	**21 Tu**	0101 0653 1338 1931	0344 1029 1621 2257	1.6E 2.0F 1.6E 1.7F
7 Th	0516 1201 1742	0209 0834 1435 2050	1.8E 2.0F 1.7E 1.8F	**22 F**	0552 1240 1831	0241 0922 1520 2150	1.9E 2.2F 1.7E 1.8F	**7 Sa**	0529 1222 1804	0223 0849 1455 2107	1.8E 2.1F 1.7E 1.7F	**22 Su**	0033 0628 1317 1910	0317 1006 1600 2234	1.7E 2.1F 1.6E 1.7F	**7 Tu**	0053 0642 1334 1921	0336 1002 1611 2227	1.9E 2.2F 1.8E 1.8F	**22 W**	0154 0743 1427 2022	0435 1120 1710 2350	1.5E 1.9F 1.6E 1.7F
8 F	0011 0556 1246 1827	0250 0914 1519 2132	1.8E 2.0F 1.6E 1.7F	**23 Sa**	0053 0648 1339 1931	0337 1024 1620 2256	1.7E 2.1F 1.6E 1.6F	**8 Su**	0028 0615 1310 1853	0309 0934 1544 2157	1.8E 2.0F 1.7E 1.7F	**23 M**	0129 0723 1411 2006	0414 1104 1657 2335	1.6E 2.0F 1.5E 1.6F	**8 W**	0148 0736 1426 2015	0429 1056 1704 2326	1.8E 2.1F 1.8E 1.8F	**23 Th** ◐	0248 0835 1517 2113	0529 1212 1802	1.5E 1.8F 1.5E
9 Sa	0056 0641 1336 1916	0335 1000 1608 2222	1.7E 1.9F 1.6E 1.6F	**24 Su** ○	0153 0749 1440 2035	0438 1131 1726	1.6E 2.0F 1.5E	**9 M**	0118 0705 1401 1946	0359 1026 1636 2252	1.7E 2.0F 1.7E 1.7F	**24 Tu** ○	0227 0820 1506 2103	0513 1202 1755	1.5E 1.9F 1.5E	**9 Th**	0246 0834 1521 2113	0526 1155 1801	1.8E 2.0F 1.8E	**24 F**	0344 0929 1607 2206	0045 0624 1306 1854	1.7F 1.4E 1.8F 1.5E
10 Su	0146 0732 1429 2011	0426 1052 1702 2318	1.6E 1.9F 1.5E 1.5F	**25 M**	0257 0852 1541 2139	0006 0545 1238 1834	1.6F 1.5E 1.9F 1.4E	**10 Tu**	0213 0800 1456 2043	0454 1122 1731 2352	1.7E 2.0F 1.7E 1.7F	**25 W** ◐	0326 0917 1600 2159	0035 0613 1300 1853	1.7F 1.4E 1.9F 1.5E	**10 F**	0347 0935 1618 2213	0029 0626 1257 1859	1.9F 1.7E 2.0F 1.8E	**25 Sa**	0439 1024 1658 2257	0140 0720 1400 1947	1.8F 1.4E 1.7F 1.5E
11 M ◐	0242 0828 1526 2110	0520 1152 1759	1.6E 1.8F 1.5E	**26 Tu**	0400 0956 1640 2240	0112 0654 1341 1939	1.6F 1.4E 1.9F 1.5E	**11 W**	0312 0859 1552 2142	0551 1224 1829	1.7E 2.0F 1.7E	**26 Th**	0424 1014 1652 2253	0132 0713 1355 1947	1.7F 1.4E 1.9F 1.5E	**11 Sa**	0449 1038 1715 2312	0135 0728 1402 1959	1.9F 1.7E 1.9F 1.8E	**26 Su**	0534 1118 1748 2347	0234 0815 1452 2037	1.8F 1.7E 1.7F 1.6E
12 Tu	0341 0928 1624 2211	0021 0619 1256 1859	1.5F 1.6E 1.9F 1.5E	**27 W**	0501 1057 1735 2336	0212 0759 1438 2036	1.7F 1.4E 2.0F 1.5E	**12 Th**	0413 1001 1648 2240	0056 0652 1326 1928	1.7F 1.7E 2.0F 1.7E	**27 F**	0520 1109 1742 2343	0226 0810 1447 2038	1.8F 1.4E 1.9F 1.6E	**12 Su**	0551 1141 1811	0240 0832 1506 2058	2.0F 1.7E 1.9F 1.8E	**27 M**	0626 1210 1836	0324 0908 1542 2125	1.9F 1.4E 1.7F 1.6E
13 W	0441 1030 1720 2309	0127 0720 1359 1958	1.6F 1.6E 1.9F 1.6E	**28 Th**	0558 1152 1825	0307 0856 1529 2126	1.8F 1.5E 2.0F 1.6F	**13 F**	0513 1102 1743 2337	0200 0753 1428 2025	1.9F 1.7E 2.0F 1.8E	**28 Sa**	0612 1201 1829	0317 0902 1535 2124	1.9F 1.5E 1.9F 1.6E	**13 M**	0010 0652 1242 1907	0343 0934 1607 2156	2.1F 1.7E 1.9F 1.8E	**28 Tu**	0034 0715 1300 1921	0412 0957 1627 2209	1.9F 1.5E 1.7F 1.7E
14 Th	0539 1130 1813	0229 0820 1458 2054	1.8F 1.7E 2.0F 1.8E	**29 F**	0025 0649 1242 1910	0356 0946 1616 2209	1.8F 1.6E 2.0F 1.7E	**14 Sa**	0611 1202 1836	0301 0853 1526 2121	2.0F 1.8E 2.1F 1.9E	**29 Su**	0029 0701 1249 1913	0404 0950 1620 2206	2.0F 1.5E 1.9F 1.7E	**14 Tu**	0107 0749 1340 2000	0441 1034 1704 2251	2.2F 1.7E 1.9F 1.9E	**29 W**	0118 0801 1346 2005	0455 1041 1709 2251	2.0F 1.5E 1.7F 1.7E
15 F	0005 0634 1226 1904	0326 0917 1552 2147	1.9F 1.8E 2.1F 1.9E	**30 Sa**	0109 0735 1327 1951	0441 1029 1658 2247	2.0F 1.6E 2.0F 1.7E	**15 Su**	0031 0707 1259 1927	0358 0950 1621 2214	2.1F 1.9E 2.1F 2.0E	**30 M**	0112 0747 1334 1955	0447 1032 1702 2245	2.0F 1.6E 1.8F 1.7E	**15 W** ○	0200 0844 1435 2052	0536 1130 1758 2343	2.3F 1.7E 1.9F 1.9E	**30 Th**	0200 0844 1429 2047	0534 1123 1747 2331	2.1F 1.6E 1.8F 1.8E
								31 Tu	0152 0830 1416 2036	0526 1112 1740 2321	2.1F 1.6E 1.8F 1.7E									

Time meridian 75° W. 0000 is midnight. 1200 is noon. Times are not adjusted for Daylight Saving Time.

TABLE 2 – CURRENT DIFFERENCES AND OTHER CONSTANTS

No.	PLACE	Meter Depth (ft)	POSITION Latitude North	POSITION Longitude West	TIME DIFFERENCES Min. before Flood (h m)	TIME DIFFERENCES Flood (h m)	TIME DIFFERENCES Min. before Ebb (h m)	TIME DIFFERENCES Ebb (h m)	SPEED RATIOS Flood	SPEED RATIOS Ebb	AVERAGE SPEEDS AND DIRECTIONS Minimum before Flood knots	AVERAGE SPEEDS AND DIRECTIONS Minimum before Flood Dir.	AVERAGE SPEEDS AND DIRECTIONS Maximum Flood knots	AVERAGE SPEEDS AND DIRECTIONS Maximum Flood Dir.	AVERAGE SPEEDS AND DIRECTIONS Minimum before Ebb knots	AVERAGE SPEEDS AND DIRECTIONS Minimum before Ebb Dir.	AVERAGE SPEEDS AND DIRECTIONS Maximum Ebb knots	AVERAGE SPEEDS AND DIRECTIONS Maximum Ebb Dir.
	NARRAGANSETT BAY <8> Time meridian, 75° W				on Pollock Rip Channel, p.37													
2031	Sakonnet River (except Narrows)		- -	- -	Current weak and variable													
2036	Black Point, SW of, Sakonnet River	15	41° 30.4'	71° 13.2'	−2 54	−1 55	−2 13	−2 26	0.2	0.2	—	—	0.4	012°	—	—	0.4	194°
2041	Almy Point Bridge, south of, Sakonnet River		41° 37.3'	71° 13.2'	−3 00	−2 10	−2 30	−3 13	0.2	0.8	—	—	0.4	034°	—	—	1.5	180°
2046	Tiverton, Stone bridge, Sakonnet R. <9>	15	41° 37.5'	71° 13.0'	−2 58	−5 02	−2 26	−3 06	1.4	1.6	—	—	2.7	010°	—	—	2.7	190°
						−2 54			0.3				0.6	010°				
						−0 36			1.3				2.5	010°				
2051	Tiverton, RR. bridge, Sakonnet R. <10>		41° 38.3'	71° 12.9'	−3 26	−5 06	−2 48	−3 41	1.2	1.4	—	—	2.3	000°	—	—	2.4	180°
						−3 04			—				1.5	000°				
2056	Common Fence Point, northeast of	10	41° 39.5'	71° 12.5'	−2 38	−4 50	−2 32	−2 41	0.8	0.2	—	—	0.2	026°	—	—	0.3	210°
						−2 25			0.1				0.1	058°				
						−0 58			0.0				0.1	046°				
2061	Brenton Point, 1.4 n.mi. southwest of	7	41° 25.9'	71° 22.6'	−1 03	−0 38	−1 20	−1 04	0.2	0.4	—	—	0.4	347°	—	—	0.6	170°
2066	Castle Hill, west of, East Passage	15	41° 27.4'	71° 22.7'	−0 06	−0 42	−1 07	−0 29	0.4	0.7	—	—	0.7	013°	—	—	1.2	237°
2071	Bull Point, east of	10	41° 28.8'	71° 21.0'	−1 10	−0 47	−1 10	−1 33	0.6	0.8	—	—	1.2	001°	—	—	1.5	206°
2076	Mackerel Cove		41° 28.5'	71° 22.8'	Current weak and variable													
2081	Newport Harbor, S and E of Goat Island		41° 29'	71° 20'	Current weak and variable													
2086	Rose Island, northeast of	15	41° 30.2'	71° 19.9'	−1 57	−0 07	−1 17	−2 08	0.4	0.5	—	—	0.8	310°	—	—	1.0	124°
2091	Rose Island, northwest of	15	41° 30.4'	71° 21.1'	−1 38	−0 26	−1 38	−1 39	0.4	0.5	0.1	105°	0.7	007°	0.1	102°	1.0	190°
2096	Rose Island, west of		41° 29.8'	71° 21.0'	−0 42	−0 34	−1 20	−1 28	0.4	0.6	—	—	0.7	001°	—	—	1.0	172°
2101	Gould Island, southeast of	7	41° 31.5'	71° 20.2'	−1 40	−1 28	−1 14	−1 16	0.3	0.4	—	—	0.5	033°	—	—	0.7	217°
2106	Gould Island, west of	15	41° 31.9'	71° 21.5'	−0 16	−0 32	−1 13	−1 07	0.4	0.4	—	—	0.6	351°	—	—	0.8	193°
2111	Dyer Island–Carrs Point (between)		41° 34.5'	71° 17.8'	−1 56	−1 13	−0 50	−1 37	0.4	0.4	0.1	279°	0.8	040°	0.1	—	0.6	236°
2116	Conanicut Point, ENE of	15	41° 34.5'	71° 20.5'	−2 05	−0 24	−1 18	−1 13	0.4	0.2	—	—	0.4	018°	—	—	0.4	183°
2121	Dyer Island, west of	7	41° 35.2'	71° 18.5'	−1 04	−0 46	−0 53	−1 34	0.4	0.6	0.1	111°	0.8	023°	0.1	106°	1.0	216°
2126	QUONSET POINT	16	41° 35.01'	71° 23.74'	Daily Predictions, p.32								0.3	021°			0.4	200°
2131	Mount Hope Bridge	7	41° 38.4'	71° 15.5'	−1 22	−1 34	−1 08	−0 58	0.6	0.8	—	—	1.1	047°	—	—	1.4	230°
2136	Hog Island, northwest of		41° 38.8'	71° 17.7'	−2 16	−0 04	−0 30	−1 04	0.2	0.2	0.1	282°	0.4	011°	0.1	133°	0.4	199°
2141	Common Fence Point, west of	10	41° 39.0'	71° 14.7'	−1 13	+0 08	−1 00	−0 37	0.2	0.4	—	—	0.5	050°	0.1	121°	0.7	224°
2146	Mount Hope Point, northeast of	10	41° 40.8'	71° 12.7'	−2 01	−0 20	−1 03	−0 57	0.7	0.2	—	—	0.4	038°	—	—	0.4	217°
2151	Kickamuit R. (Narrows), Mt. Hope Bay		41° 41.9'	71° 14.7'	−2 04	−1 40	−1 19	−0 48	0.5	1.0	—	—	0.9	000°	—	—	1.7	191°
	VINEYARD SOUND																	
1791	West Chop, 0.2 mile west of		41° 29.0'	70° 36.6'	+1 19	+1 34	+1 50	+1 16	1.3	0.8	—	—	2.7	059°	—	—	1.4	241°
1796	Nobska Point, 1 mile southeast of		41° 30.1'	70° 38.6'	+2 33	+2 15	+2 25	+2 19	1.3	1.4	—	—	2.6	071°	—	—	2.4	259°
1801	Norton Point, 0.5 mile north of		41° 28.1'	70° 39.9'	+1 55	+1 44	+2 01	+1 12	1.7	1.4	—	—	3.4	050°	—	—	2.4	240°
1806	Tarpaulin Cove, 1.5 miles east of		41° 28.3'	70° 43.5'	+2 49	+2 07	+2 12	+2 33	1.0	1.2	—	—	1.9	055°	—	—	2.1	232°
1811	Robinsons Hole, 1.2 miles southeast of		41° 26.1'	70° 46.8'	+2 30	+1 51	+2 11	+2 02	1.0	1.2	—	—	1.9	060°	—	—	2.1	240°
1816	Gay Head, 3 miles northeast of		41° 23.1'	70° 47.0'	+2 25	+1 50	+1 42	+2 11	0.5	0.8	—	—	0.9	081°	—	—	1.3	238°
1821	Menemsha Bight <6>		41° 21.3'	70° 46.3'														
1826	Gay Head, 3 miles north of		41° 24.1'	70° 51.2'	+2 13	+1 24	+1 55	+1 17	0.6	0.7	—	—	1.1	074°	—	—	1.2	255°
1831	Gay Head, 1.5 miles northwest of		41° 21.8'	70° 51.8'	+1 30	+0 54	+1 42	+1 16	1.0	1.2	—	—	2.0	012°	—	—	2.0	249°
1836	Cuttyhunk Island, 3.2 miles southwest of		41° 23'	71° 00'	See table 5.													
1841	Browns Ledge		41° 19.8'	71° 05.9'	See table 5.													

TABLE 3.—SPEED OF CURRENT AT ANY TIME

TABLE A

	Interval between slack and maximum current													
	h. m. 1 20	h. m. 1 40	h. m. 2 00	h. m. 2 20	h. m. 2 40	h. m. 3 00	h.m. 3 20	h.m. 3 40	h.m. 4 00	h.m. 4 20	h.m. 4 40	h.m. 5 00	h.m. 5 20	h.m. 5 40
h. m.	knots	knots	knots	knots	knots	knots	knots	knots	knots	knots	knots	knots	knots	knots
0 20	0.4	0.3	0.3	0.2	0.2	0.2	0.2	0.1	0.1	0.1	0.1	0.1	0.1	0.1
0 40	0.7	0.6	0.5	0.4	0.4	0.3	0.3	0.3	0.3	0.2	0.2	0.2	0.2	0.2
1 00	0.9	0.8	0.7	0.6	0.6	0.5	0.5	0.4	0.4	0.4	0.3	0.3	0.3	0.3
1 20	1.0	1.0	0.9	0.8	0.7	0.6	0.6	0.5	0.5	0.5	0.4	0.4	0.4	0.4
1 40	----	1.0	1.0	0.9	0.8	0.8	0.7	0.7	0.6	0.6	0.5	0.5	0.5	0.4
2 00	----	----	1.0	1.0	0.9	0.9	0.8	0.8	0.7	0.7	0.6	0.6	0.6	0.5
2 20	----	----	----	1.0	1.0	0.9	0.9	0.8	0.8	0.7	0.7	0.7	0.6	0.6
2 40	----	----	----	----	1.0	1.0	1.0	0.9	0.9	0.8	0.8	0.7	0.7	0.7
3 00	----	----	----	----	----	1.0	1.0	1.0	0.9	0.9	0.8	0.8	0.8	0.7
3 20	----	----	----	----	----	----	1.0	1.0	1.0	0.9	0.9	0.9	0.8	0.8
3 40	----	----	----	----	----	----	----	1.0	1.0	1.0	0.9	0.9	0.9	0.9
4 00	----	----	----	----	----	----	----	----	1.0	1.0	1.0	1.0	0.9	0.9
4 20	----	----	----	----	----	----	----	----	----	1.0	1.0	1.0	1.0	0.9
4 40	----	----	----	----	----	----	----	----	----	----	1.0	1.0	1.0	1.0
5 00	----	----	----	----	----	----	----	----	----	----	----	1.0	1.0	1.0
5 20	----	----	----	----	----	----	----	----	----	----	----	----	1.0	1.0
5 40	----	----	----	----	----	----	----	----	----	----	----	----	----	1.0

(Side label: Interval between slack and desired time)

TABLE B

	Interval between slack and maximum current													
	h. m. 1 20	h. m. 1 40	h. m. 2 00	h. m. 2 20	h. m. 2 40	h. m. 3 00	h. m. 3 20	h. m. 3 40	h. m. 4 00	h. m. 4 20	h. m. 4 40	h. m. 5 00	h. m. 5 20	h. m. 5 40
h. m.	knots	knots	knots	knots	knots	knots	knots	knots	knots	knots	knots	knots	knots	knots
0 20	0.5	0.4	0.4	0.3	0.3	0.3	0.3	0.3	0.2	0.2	0.2	0.2	0.2	0.2
0 40	0.8	0.7	0.6	0.5	0.5	0.5	0.4	0.4	0.4	0.4	0.3	0.3	0.3	0.3
1 00	0.9	0.8	0.8	0.7	0.7	0.6	0.6	0.5	0.5	0.5	0.4	0.4	0.4	0.4
1 20	1.0	1.0	0.9	0.8	0.8	0.7	0.7	0.6	0.6	0.6	0.5	0.5	0.5	0.5
1 40	----	1.0	1.0	0.9	0.9	0.8	0.8	0.7	0.7	0.7	0.6	0.6	0.6	0.6
2 00	----	----	1.0	1.0	0.9	0.9	0.9	0.8	0.8	0.7	0.7	0.7	0.7	0.6
2 20	----	----	----	1.0	1.0	1.0	0.9	0.9	0.8	0.8	0.8	0.7	0.7	0.7
2 40	----	----	----	----	1.0	1.0	1.0	0.9	0.9	0.9	0.8	0.8	0.8	0.7
3 00	----	----	----	----	----	1.0	1.0	1.0	0.9	0.9	0.9	0.9	0.8	0.8
3 20	----	----	----	----	----	----	1.0	1.0	1.0	0.9	0.9	0.9	0.9	0.9
3 40	----	----	----	----	----	----	----	1.0	1.0	1.0	1.0	0.9	0.9	0.9
4 00	----	----	----	----	----	----	----	----	1.0	1.0	1.0	1.0	0.9	0.9
4 20	----	----	----	----	----	----	----	----	----	1.0	1.0	1.0	1.0	0.9
4 40	----	----	----	----	----	----	----	----	----	----	1.0	1.0	1.0	1.0
5 00	----	----	----	----	----	----	----	----	----	----	----	1.0	1.0	1.0
5 20	----	----	----	----	----	----	----	----	----	----	----	----	1.0	1.0
5 40	----	----	----	----	----	----	----	----	----	----	----	----	----	1.0

(Side label: Interval between slack and desired time)

Use Table A for all places except those listed below for Table B.
Use Table B for Cape Code Canal, Hell Gate, Chesapeake and Delaware Canal, and all stations in table 2 which are referred to them.

1. From predictions find the time of slack water and the time and velocity of maximum current (flood or ebb), one of which is immediately before and the other after the time for which the velocity is desired.
2. Find the interval of time between the above slack and maximum current, and enter the top of Table A or B with the interval which most nearly agrees with this value.
3. Find the interval of time between the above slack and the time desired, and enter the side of Table A or B with the interval which most nearly agrees with this value.
4. Find, in the Table, the factor corresponding to the above two intervals, and multiply the maximum velocity by this factor. The result will be the approximate velocity at the time desired.

ASTRONOMICAL DATA, 2011

January

	d	h	m
S	1	02	..
●	4	09	03
E	9	16	..
A	10	05	..
☽	12	11	31
N	16	23	..
○	19	21	21
P	22	00	..
E	23	05	..
☾	26	12	57
S	29	17	..

February

	d	h	m
●	3	02	31
E	6	00	..
A	6	23	..
☽	11	07	18
N	13	09	..
○	18	08	36
P	19	07	..
E	19	15	..
☾	24	23	26
S	25	22	..

March

	d	h	m
●	4	20	46
E	5	06	..
A	6	08	..
N	12	17	..
☽	12	23	45
E	19	02	..
○	19	18	10
P	19	19	..
☉m	20	23	21
S	25	05	..
☾	26	12	07

April

	d	h	m
E	1	12	..
A	2	09	..
●	3	14	32
N	8	23	..
☽	11	12	05
E	15	13	..
P	17	06	..
○	18	02	44
S	21	14	..
☾	25	02	47
E	28	18	..
A	29	18	..

May

	d	h	m
●	3	06	51
N	6	04	..
☽	10	20	33
E	12	20	..
P	15	11	..
○	17	11	09
S	19	00	..
☾	24	18	52
E	26	00	..
A	27	04	..

June

	d	h	m
●	1	21	03
N	2	10	..
☽	9	02	11
E	9	02	..
P	12	01	..
S	15	09	..
○	15	20	14
☉j	21	17	16
E	22	08	..
☾	23	11	48
A	24	04	..
N	29	18	..

July

	d	h	m
●	1	08	54
E	6	08	..
P	7	14	..
☽	8	06	29
S	12	17	..
○	15	06	40
E	19	17	..
A	21	23	..
☾	23	05	02
N	27	03	..
●	30	18	40

August

	d	h	m
E	2	15	..
P	2	21	..
☽	6	11	08
S	9	00	..
○	13	18	57
E	16	01	..
A	18	16	..
☾	21	21	54
N	23	13	..
●	29	03	04
E	30	00	..
P	30	17	..

September

	d	h	m
☽	4	17	39
S	5	05	..
E	12	08	..
○	12	09	27
A	15	06	..
N	19	21	..
☾	20	13	39
☉s	22	09	05
E	26	11	..
●	27	11	09
P	28	01	..

October

	d	h	m
S	2	12	..
☽	4	03	15
E	9	14	..
○	12	02	06
A	12	12	..
N	17	03	..
☾	20	02	30
E	23	21	..
P	26	12	..
●	26	19	56
S	29	20	..

November

	d	h	m
☽	2	16	38
E	5	19	..
A	8	13	..
○	10	20	16
N	13	08	..
☾	18	15	09
E	20	05	..
P	23	23	..
●	25	06	10
S	26	07	..

December

	d	h	m
☽	2	09	52
E	3	02	..
A	6	01	..
N	10	14	..
○	10	14	36
E	17	11	..
☾	18	00	48
P	22	03	..
☉d	22	05	30
S	23	18	..
●	24	18	06
E	30	10	..

LUNAR DATA
- ● -- new Moon
- ☽ -- first quarter
- ○ -- full Moon
- ☾ -- last quarter
- A -- Moon in apogee
- P -- Moon in perigee
- N -- Moon farthest north of Equator
- E -- Moon on Equator
- S -- Moon farthest south of Equator

SOLAR DATA
- ☉m -- March equinox
- ☉j -- June solstice
- ☉s -- September equinox
- ☉d -- December solstice

Greenwich mean time (GMT) or universal time (UT) is the mean solar time on the Greenwich meridian reckoned in days of 24 mean solar hours written as 00^h at midnight and 12^h at noon. To convert the above times to those of other standard time meridians, add 1 hour for each $15°$ of east longitude of the desired meridian and subtract 1 hour for each $15°$ of west longitude. This table was compiled from data supplied by the Nautical Almanac Office, United States Naval Observatory.

TABLE 5.—ROTARY TIDAL CURRENTS
EXPLANATION

Offshore and in some of the wider indentations of the coast, the tidal current is quite different from that found in the more protected bays and rivers. In these inside waters the tidal current is of the reversing type. The current sets in one direction for a period of 6 hours after which is ceases to flow momentarily and then sets in the opposite direction during the following 6 hours. The offshore tidal current, not being confined to a definite channel, changes its direction continually and never slows to a true slack water. Thus in a tidal cycle of 12 ½ hours it will have set in all directions of the compass. This type of current is referred to as a rotary current.

A characteristic feature of the rotary current is the absence of slack water. Although the current generally varies from hour to hour, this variation from greatest current to least current and back again to greatest does not give rise to a period of slack water. When the speed of the rotary tidal current is least, it is known as the minimum current, and when it is greatest it is known as the maximum current. The minimum and maximum speeds of the rotary current are related to each other in the same way as slack and strength of current. A minimum speed of the current follows a maximum speed by an interval of approximately 3 hours and followed in turn by another maximum after a further interval of 3 hours.

The following table provides the direction and speed of the rotary current for each hour at a number of offshore stations. The times and speeds are referred to predictions for a reference station in Table 1. All times are in local standard time for the secondary station.

The speeds given in the table are the average speeds for the station. The Moon when new, full, or at perigee tends to increase the speeds 15 to 20 percent above average. When perigee occurs at or near the time of new or full Moon, the current speeds will be 30 to 40 percent above average. The Moon when at first and third quarter or at apogee tend to decrease the current speeds below average by 15 to 20 percent. When apogee occurs at or near the first or third quarter Moon, the currents will be 30 to 40 percent below average. The speeds will be about average when apogee occurs at or near the time of the new or full Moon and also when perigee occurs at or near the first or third quarter Moon. (See table of astronomical data for dates of Moon phases and other data.)

The direction of the current is given in degrees, true, reading clockwise from 0° at north, and is the direction toward which the water is flowing.

The speeds and directions are for tidal current only and do not include the effect of the wind. When a wind is blowing, a wind-driven current will be set up as is superimposed on the normal tidal current. The actual current encountered will thus be a combination of the wind-driven current and the tidal current. See the chapters on "Wind-Driven Currents" and "The Combination of Currents".

As an example, in the following table the current at Nantucket Shoals is given for each hour after maximum flood at Pollock Rip Channel. Suppose it is desired to find the direction and speed of the current at Nantucket Shoals at 3:15 p.m. (15:15) on a day when the maximum flood at Pollock Rip Channel is predicted in Table 1 to occur at 13:20. The desired time is therefore 2 hours after the maximum flood at Pollock Rip Channel. From the table the tidal current at Nantucket Shoals at 2 hours is setting 015° true with an average speed of 0.8 knots. If this day is near the time of new Moon and about half way between apogee and perigee, then the distance effect of the moon will be nil and the phase effect alone will increase the speed by about 15 percent, to 0.9 knots.

Caution - Speeds from 1 ½ to 3 knots have been observed at most of the stations in this table. Near Diamond Shoal Light a speed of 4 knots has occurred.

At some offshore stations, such as those near the entrance to Chesapeake Bay, the tidal current is directed alternately toward and away from the bay entrance with intervening periods of slack water. At these stations the current is essentially a reversing current. For such places, differences for predicting the current are given in Table 2.

TABLE 5.—ROTARY TIDAL CURRENTS

Station Name	Depth	Hourly time increments												
		0	1	2	3	4	5	6	7	8	9	10	11	
		After Maximum Flood at POLLOCK RIP CHANNEL											
Davis Bank, Nantucket Shoals, 15 miles SE of Nantucket Island		0.9	1.2	1.3	1.1	0.8	0.9	0.8	1.2	1.1	0.9	0.7	0.7	knots
		346	028	047	073	103	132	182	215	240	251	267	302	degrees
Davis Bank, Nantucket Shoals, 17.5 miles SE of Nantucket Island		0.8	1.5	1.9	1.8	1.1	0.4	1.2	1.9	1.7	1.5	0.9	0.2	knots
		023	027	028	029	046	115	191	202	215	225	233	270	degrees
Great South Channel, Georges Bank 40°31'N 68°47'W		0.7	0.9	1.1	1.0	0.8	0.4	0.7	0.9	1.0	1.0	0.8	0.6	knots
		320	331	342	003	023	063	129	140	164	179	190	221	degrees
Davis Bank, Nantucket Shoals, 18.5 miles SE of Nantucket Island		0.6	1.3	1.5	1.4	1.1	0.8	0.6	1.3	1.7	1.4	1.0	0.3	knots
		030	036	038	050	080	105	178	230	235	238	241	265	degrees
Nantucket Island, 28 miles east of		0.9	1.3	1.4	1.1	0.5	0.3	0.8	1.1	1.1	0.9	0.7	0.1	knots
		019	007	359	351	334	221	198	185	184	184	183	060	degrees
Monomoy Point, 23 miles east of		0.7	1.0	0.9	0.7	0.3	0.1	0.5	0.8	0.9	0.8	0.5	0.1	knots
		320	324	326	330	334	144	145	146	147	148	150	230	degrees
Nauset Beach Light, 5 miles NE		0.5	0.6	0.5	0.2	0.1	0.2	0.4	0.6	0.6	0.4	0.2	0.2	knots
		315	327	340	357	016	124	132	135	139	145	269	297	degrees
Great Round Shoal Channel entrance		1.6	1.4	1.3	1.1	0.8	1.2	1.5	1.5	1.2	0.9	0.8	1.2	knots
		032	045	068	095	140	192	210	220	235	264	303	350	degrees
Great Round Shoal Channel, 4 miles NE of Great Point		0.8	1.1	1.3	1.0	0.5	0.5	1.1	1.4	1.2	0.7	0.2	0.4	knots
		080	088	096	104	129	213	267	275	280	284	328	042	degrees
Cuttyhunk Island, 3.25 miles SW		0.4	0.3	0.2	0.3	0.5	0.5	0.4	0.3	0.2	0.3	0.3	0.4	knots
		356	015	080	123	146	158	173	208	267	306	322	335	degrees
Gooseberry Neck, 2 miles SSE of		0.6	0.4	0.2	0.3	0.4	0.5	0.5	0.3	0.2	0.2	0.3	0.5	knots
		052	065	108	168	210	223	232	249	274	321	016	038	degrees
Browns Ledge, Massachusetts		0.3	0.3	0.3	0.4	0.4	0.4	0.3	0.2	0.3	0.3	0.4	0.5	knots
		330	012	028	104	118	123	168	205	201	270	282	318	degrees
		After Maximum Flood at THE RACE											
Point Judith, Harbor of Refuge		0.2	0.2	0.4	0.5	0.5	0.5	0.4	0.2	0.1	0.1	0.1	0.1	knots
		197	160	151	159	146	124	109	104	090	030	336	209	degrees

Current Sailing Resources

The 50-90 Rule for figuring current speeds between slack and peak flow

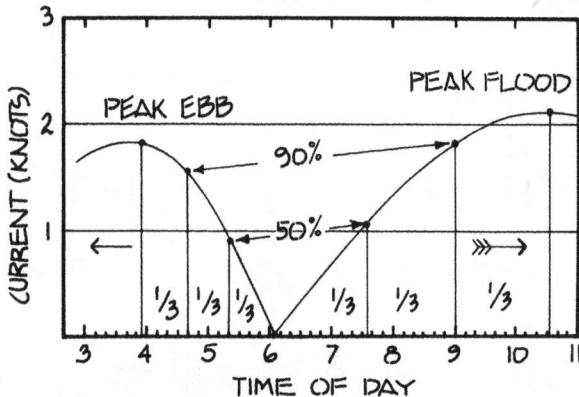

Divide the time between slack water and peak flow into three steps. In many cases, each step will be approximately one hour long. During the first step the current increases to 50 percent of its maximum value, and during the next step it increases to 90 percent of its maximum value. The same procedure will reproduce the fall in current speed after maximum flow.

The 40-60 approximation for estimating current set

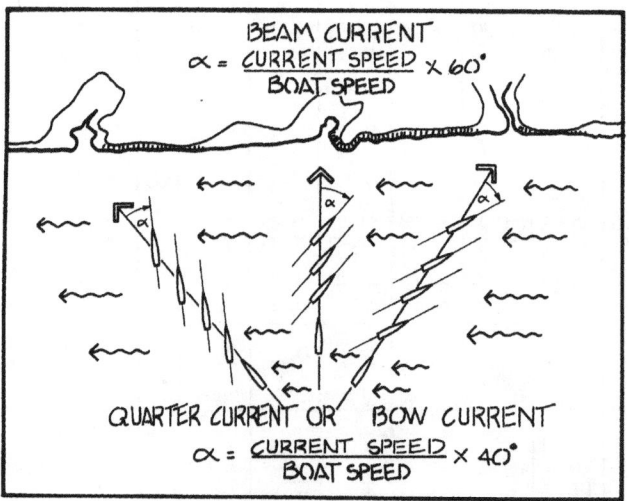

The rule works adequately well for set angles up to 42° or so, which is equivalent to limiting its use to currents that are less than some three quarters of your boat speed. In most cases, knowledge of current speed and direction is not accurate enough to justify precise vector solutions. This formula is useful and easy to remember. Bow and quarter currents take less of a correction, but they are the same in each case. The only difference is the resulting SMG. Bow currents slow you down, quarter currents speed you up. Bow, beam, and quarter current directions are defined for this application with the boat pointed toward the destination, as in the starting position shown on each route.

Use of the 50-90 Rule to estimate the effect of a changing tidal current on net progress

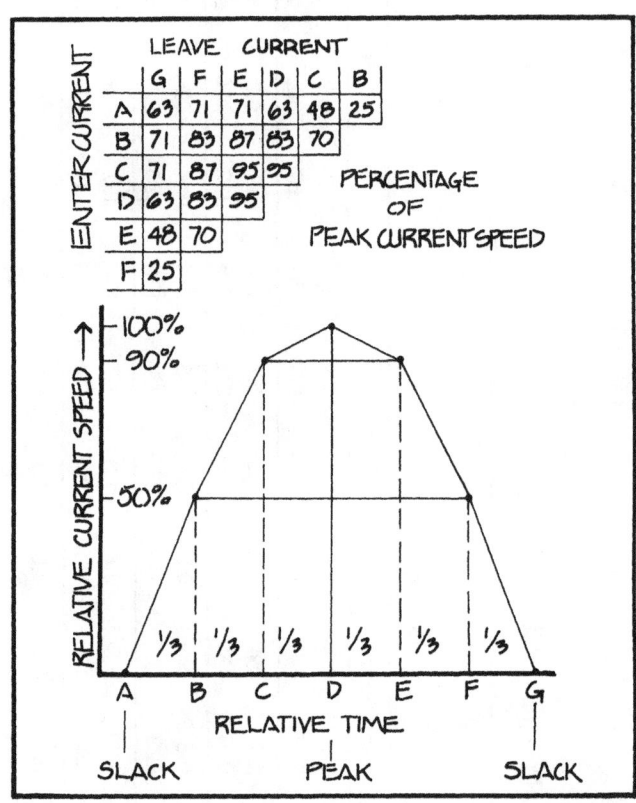

Divide the duration of the cycle into six parts, then use data from the inset to find the constant current speed that is equivalent to the changing current of the cycle. Sailing in a current with a peak speed of 3 knots from relative point B to point E, the current would be increasing from 1.5 knots to 3 knots and then decreasing to 2.7 knots during this time. From the inset, you can assume that this will move the boat as if in a constant current of 0.87 times 3, or 2.6 knots. Note that staying in a current from slack to peak (A to D) or slack to slack (A to G) is equivalent to sailing in a constant current of 0.63 times the peak current speed.

These three resources are from the text *Inland and Coastal Navigation*, 2nd edition (Starpath Publications, 2013)

Light List

U.S. Department of Homeland Security

United States Coast Guard

LIGHT LIST

Volume I

ATLANTIC COAST

St. Croix River, Maine to Shrewsbury River, New Jersey

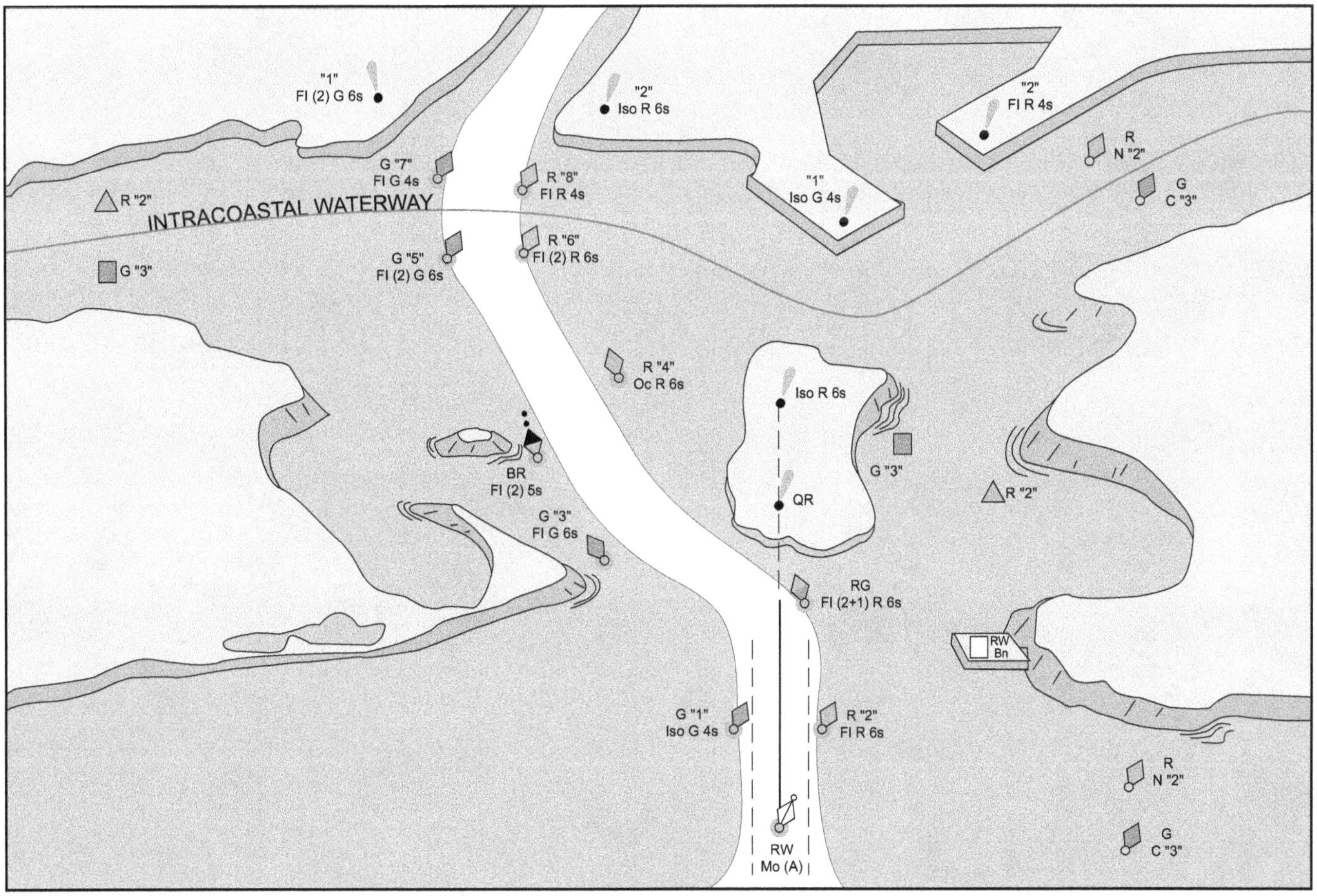

Fictitious chart from the Light List used to illustrate standard buoy, daymark, and light placement and labeling.

Light List corrected through LNM week: 01/13

(1) No.	(2) Name and Location	(3) Position	(4) Characteristic	(5) Height	(6) Range	(7) Structure	(8) Remarks
\multicolumn{8}{c}{**MASSACHUSETTS - First District**}							

MARTHA'S VINEYARD TO BLOCK ISLAND (Chart 13218)
Vineyard Sound
Main Channel

(1) No.	(2) Name and Location	(3) Position	(4) Characteristic	(5) Height	(6) Range	(7) Structure	(8) Remarks
15550	Middle Ground East End Buoy	41-29-09.163N 070-36-25.764W				Green can with red bands.	
15555	*Nobska Point Lighted Bell Buoy 26*	41-30-19.384N 070-38-43.046W	Fl R 4s		4	Red.	Replaced by nun when endangered by ice.
15560	**Nobska Point Light**	41-30-56.816N 070-39-18.398W	Fl W 6s	87	W 13 R 11	White tower. 87	Obscured from 125° to 195°. Red from 263° to 289°, covers Hedge Fence and L`Hommedieu Shoal. Lighted throughout 24 hours. Floodlighted sunset to sunrise. HORN: 2 blasts ev 30s (2s bl-2s si-2s bl-24s si).
15575	*Middle Ground Lighted Bell Buoy 27*	41-28-27.983N 070-41-07.919W	Fl G 4s		4	Green.	Replaced by can when endangered by ice.
15577	*Vineyard Sound Lighted Whistle Buoy 29*	41-25-08.392N 070-48-04.979W	Fl G 4s		4	Green.	Replaced by can when endangered by ice.
15580	TARPAULIN COVE LIGHT	41-28-07.740N 070-45-26.991W	Fl W 6s	78	9	White tower; small white building attached to west side of tower.	
15590	Lucas Shoal Buoy LS	41-24-41.699N 070-45-52.216W				Green and red bands; can.	
15597	*Vineyard Sound Entrance Lighted Bell Buoy 30*	41-24-00.071N 070-50-11.004W	Fl R 4s		4	Red.	Replaced by nun when endangered by ice.
15605	*Gay Head Lighted Gong Buoy 31*	41-21-49.397N 070-51-47.615W	Fl G 4s		4	Green.	Replaced by can when endangered by ice.
15610 620	**Gay Head Light**	41-20-54.402N 070-50-05.838W	Al WR 15s 0.2s W fl 7.3s ec. 0.2s R fl 7.3s ec.	170	W 24 R 20	Red brick tower. 170	Obscured from 342° to 359° by Nomans Land; light occasionally visible through notches in hilltop. Emergency light (Fl W 6s) of reduced intensity when main is extinguished. Lighted throughout 24 hours.
15613	*Vineyard Sound Entrance Lighted Whistle Buoy 32*	41-22-04.917N 070-57-25.091W	Fl R 2.5s		4	Red.	Replaced by nun when endangered by ice.
15617	Sow and Pigs Buoy 34	41-23-45.728N 070-57-46.360W				Red nun.	
15618	*Sow and Pigs Lighted Bell Buoy 36*	41-23-48.386N 070-59-04.132W	Fl R 4s		4	Red.	

Great Harbor

15690	- DIRECTIONAL LIGHT	41-31-38.912N 070-40-32.962W	F R W G	45	R G W	On tower.	Shows red from 342.25 to 343.25, white from 343.25 to 344.75, green from 344.75 to 345.75.
15695	- Channel Entrance Gong Buoy 1 On south end of shoal.	41-30-31.200N 070-40-13.824W				Green.	

Light List corrected through LNM week: 01/13

(1) No.	(2) Name and Location	(3) Position	(4) Characteristic	(5) Height	(6) Range	(7) Structure	(8) Remarks
	MASSACHUSETTS - First District						
15700	- *Channel Entrance Lighted Bell Buoy 2* On southwest side of shoal.	41-30-34.202N 070-40-05.892W	Fl R 4s		4	Red.	Replaced by nun when endangered by ice.
15705	- Channel Buoy 4 Off west end of ledge.	41-30-42.594N 070-40-09.034W				Red nun	
15710	Great Ledge Buoy	41-30-49.275N 070-40-01.365W				White with orange bands and orange diamond.	Marked ROCKS.
15715	- *Channel Lighted Buoy 5*	41-30-56.360N 070-40-19.410W	Fl G 4s		4	Green.	Replaced by can when endangered by ice.
15720	- Channel Buoy 6	41-31-00.422N 070-40-06.658W				Red nun.	
15730	- Channel Buoy 8	41-31-15.071N 070-40-19.748W				Red nun.	
15745	- Channel Buoy 9 On north part of ledge.	41-31-22.091N 070-40-30.948W				Green can.	
15750	TIMBER PIER LIGHT	41-31-28.398N 070-40-23.008W	F R	14			Private aid.
	Broadway						
15755	- Buoy 1	41-31-02.196N 070-40-32.842W				Green can.	
15760	- Daybeacon 3	41-31-08.969N 070-40-47.825W				SG on pile.	
15765	- Buoy 2	41-31-06.458N 070-40-34.734W				Red nun.	
	Woods Hole Passage						
15773	WOODS HOLE PASS DIRECTIONAL LIGHT	41-31-17.218N 070-40-16.513W	Oc W 4s	30		NR on dolphin.	Visible on course to steer 077°T.
15774	Woods Hole Station Mooring Buoy A	41-31-16.832N 070-39-56.678W				White and blue.	
15774.2	Woods Hole Station Mooring Buoy C	41-31-18.792N 070-39-58.378W				White and blue.	
	Hadley Harbor						
15840	Hadley Rock Buoy North of rock.	41-31-03.501N 070-41-21.119W				White can with orange bands worded ROCK.	
15845	- Bouy 3	41-30-53.367N 070-41-52.503W				Green can.	
15850	- Bouy 2	41-30-54.323N 070-41-52.509W				Red. nun.	
15855	- Entrance Daybeacon	41-30-55.000N 070-41-57.000W				NW on spindle.	Ra ref. Private aid.
	MARTHA'S VINEYARD TO BLOCK ISLAND (Chart 13218)						
	Quicks Hole						
15910	- *Entrance Lighted Bell Buoy 1*	41-25-48.392N 070-50-22.116W	Fl G 4s		4	Green.	Replaced by can when endangered by ice.
15915	- *Ledge Lighted Buoy 2*	41-26-39.705N 070-50-41.426W	Fl R 4s		3	Red.	Replaced by nun when endangered by ice.
15920	Felix Ledge Buoy 3	41-26-46.910N 070-50-56.708W				Green can.	
	Canapitsit Channel						
15925	- Entrance Bell Buoy CC	41-25-00.779N 070-54-22.723W				Red and white stripes with red spherical topmark.	Removed when endangered by ice.

RESOURCES 53

Light List corrected through LNM week: 01/13

(1) No.	(2) Name and Location	(3) Position	(4) Characteristic	(5) Height	(6) Range	(7) Structure	(8) Remarks
			MASSACHUSETTS - First District				
15930	- Buoy 1	41-25-13.744N 070-54-24.656W				Green can.	
15935	- Buoy 2	41-25-20.253N 070-54-22.962W				Red nun.	
15940	- Buoy 3	41-25-21.232N 070-54-24.545W				Green can.	
15945	- Buoy 5	41-25-28.780N 070-54-31.679W				Green can.	
15947	Menemsha Bight CG Mooring Buoy	41-21-22.007N 070-47-10.115W				White with blue band.	
15985 630	**Buzzards Bay Entrance Light**	41-23-49.118N 071-02-04.866W	Fl W 2.5s	67	17	Tower on red square on 3 red piles with large red tube in center, worded BUZZARDS on sides. 68	Emergency light of reduced intensity when main light is extinguished. RACON: B (– •••). HORN: 2 blasts ev 30s (2s bl-2s si-2s bl-24s si)
16000	Buzzards Bay Lighted Buoy 1	41-25-50.491N 071-02-15.870W	Fl G 2.5s		3	Green.	
16005	Buzzards Bay Lighted Bell Buoy 2	41-26-08.432N 071-00-39.317W	Fl R 2.5s		3	Red.	
16010	Buzzards Bay Lighted Gong Buoy 3	41-27-15.000N 071-00-34.000W	Fl G 4s		4	Green.	
16015	Hen and Chickens Buoy 1 Off south part of ledge.	41-27-33.699N 071-01-48.341W				Green can.	
16025	Buzzards Bay Lighted Bell Buoy 4 West side of shoal.	41-27-01.882N 070-59-13.635W	Q R		3	Red.	
16030	Buzzards Bay Lighted Gong Buoy 5 Off southeast side of ledge.	41-28-58.101N 070-57-22.283W	Fl G 6s		4	Green.	Replaced by can when endangered by ice.
16035	Buzzards Bay Lighted Bell Buoy 6	41-28-04.000N 070-56-41.000W	Fl R 4s		4	Red.	
	MARTHA'S VINEYARD TO BLOCK ISLAND (Chart 13218)						
	Buzzards Bay Main Channel						
16040 16731	DUMPLING ROCKS LIGHT 7 On rock.	41-32-17.800N 070-55-17.100W	Fl G 6s	52	8	SG on skeleton tower.	
16045	Buzzards Bay Lighted Buoy 7	41-30-24.988N 070-54-18.883W	Fl G 2.5s		3	Green.	Replaced by can when endangered by ice.
16050	Buzzards Bay Lighted Gong Buoy 8	41-28-57.492N 070-53-50.027W	Fl R 2.5s		3	Red.	Replaced by LIB when endangered.
16055	Buzzards Bay Midchannel Lighted Bell Buoy BB	41-30-33.000N 070-49-54.000W	Mo (A) W		4	Red and white stripes with red spherical topmark.	Removed when endangered by ice.
16058	Buzzards Bay Lighted Bell Buoy 9	41-32-52.000N 070-46-27.000W	Fl G 4s		4	Green.	Replaced by LIB when endangered by ice.
16060	Buzzards Bay Lighted Gong Buoy 10	41-34-23.986N 070-43-11.943W	Fl R 4s		4	Red.	Replaced by LIB when endangered by ice.
16080	**Cleveland East Ledge Light**	41-37-51.470N 070-41-39.046W	Fl W 10s	74	15	White cylindrical tower and dwelling on red caisson. 74	Emergency light of reduced intensity when main light is extinguished RACON: C (– • – •). HORN: 1 blast ev 15 (2s bl).

Light List corrected through LNM week: 01/13

(1) No.	(2) Name and Location	(3) Position	(4) Characteristic	(5) Height	(6) Range	(7) Structure	(8) Remarks
			MASSACHUSETTS - First District				
	Cleveland Ledge Channel						
16085	- RANGE FRONT LIGHT On southern end of Abiels Ledge	41-41-32.941N 070-40-27.505W	Q G	27		KRW on white tower.	Visible 4° each side of rangeline.
16090	- RANGE REAR LIGHT 3,167 yards, 015° from front light.	41-43-03.299N 070-39-53.654W	F G	72		KRW on white skeleton tower.	Visible 1.5° each side of rangeline.
16095	- Lighted Bell Buoy 2 West of shoal.	41-36-38.662N 070-42-10.996W	Fl R 4s		3	Red.	Replaced by nun from Dec. 15 to Mar. 15.
16100	- Lighted Buoy 3	41-37-19.000N 070-42-10.000W	Q G		3	Green.	Replaced by LIB from Dec. 15 to Mar. 15.
16105	- Lighted Buoy 4	41-37-17.591N 070-41-56.553W	Q R		3	Red.	Maintained from Mar. 15 to Dec. 15.
16115	- Lighted Buoy 6	41-37-48.290N 070-41-45.350W	Fl R 2.5s		3	Red.	Replaced by nun from Dec. 15 to Mar. 15.
16120	- Lighted Gong Buoy 7 Marks shoal.	41-39-07.042N 070-41-27.496W	Fl G 4s		3	Green.	Replaced by LIB from Dec. 15 to Mar. 15.
16125	- Lighted Buoy 8	41-39-05.623N 070-41-17.181W	Fl R 4s		3	Red.	Replaced by nun from Dec. 15 to Mar.15.
	MARTHA'S VINEYARD TO BLOCK ISLAND (Chart 13218)						
	Cuttyhunk Harbor						
16260	Middle Ground Buoy MG	41-26-24.382N 070-55-43.143W				Red and green bands; nun.	
16265	- West Entrance Buoy 1W	41-26-40.386N 070-55-30.127W				Green can.	
16270	Whale Rock Danger Buoy	41-26-02.186N 070-55-12.626W				White with orange bands worded DANGER ROCK.	
16275	- West Entrance Buoy 3W	41-26-25.026N 070-54-51.745W				Green can.	
16280	- West Entrance Buoy 2W	41-26-04.758N 070-55-02.508W				Red nun.	
16285	Pease Ledge Buoy 4	41-25-46.247N 070-54-58.305W				Red nun.	
16290	- North Jetty Bell Buoy 6	41-25-34.448N 070-54-51.665W				Red.	
16295	- NORTH JETTY LIGHT 8	41-25-30.500N 070-55-00.900W	Fl R 6s	29	6	TR on gray skeleton tower on concrete base.	Obscured from 284° to 044°.
16300	- Buoy 9	41-25-29.713N 070-54-57.270W				Green can.	
	Cuttyhunk Harbor						
16305	- East Entrance Buoy 1E	41-26-13.099N 070-54-08.126W				Green can.	
16310	- East Entrance Buoy 2E	41-26-26.727N 070-54-12.114W				Red nun.	
	Cuttyhunk						
16315	- East Entrance Lighted Bell Buoy CH	41-26-34.071N 070-53-21.805W	Mo (A) W		5	Red and white stripes with red spherical topmark.	Replaced by can when endangered by ice.
	South Side						
16320	Lone Rock Lighted Buoy LR Southeasterly of rock.	41-27-39.346N 070-51-08.832W	Fl (2+1)G 6s		4	Green and red bands.	Replaced by can when endangered by ice.

RESOURCES 55

Light List corrected through LNM week: 01/13

(1) No.	(2) Name and Location	(3) Position	(4) Characteristic	(5) Height	(6) Range	(7) Structure	(8) Remarks
			MASSACHUSETTS - First District				
16325	Weepecket Rock Lighted Gong Buoy 8 On northeasterly end of shoal.	41-31-48.459N 070-43-26.391W	Fl R 2.5s		4	Red.	
	BUZZARDS BAY (Chart 13230)						
	New Bedford Harbor						
	Southwest Approach						
16780	- Buoy 10	41-33-42.979N 070-53-34.207W				Red nun.	
16786	Inez Rock Buoy 11 East of rock.	41-33-44.787N 070-54-25.913W				Green can.	
16791	- Buoy 12	41-34-26.006N 070-53-35.021W				Red nun.	
16796	Old Bartlemy Buoy 13	41-35-38.333N 070-53-43.805W				Green can.	
	MARTHA'S VINEYARD TO BLOCK ISLAND (Chart 13218)						
	New Bedford Harbor						
	New Bedford Channel						
16805	- Lighted Buoy 1	41-31-43.995N 070-50-45.992W	Q G		3	Green.	
16810	- Lighted Buoy 2	41-31-45.969N 070-50-32.020W	Q R		3	Red.	
16815	- Buoy 3	41-32-56.306N 070-51-47.965W				Green can.	
16817	Phinney Rock Lighted Buoy DP	41-33-03.942N 070-52-59.020W	Fl (2)W 5s		6	Black and red bands with two black spherical topmarks.	
16820	- Lighted Buoy 4	41-33-36.025N 070-51-41.959W	Fl R 4s		3	Red.	
16825	- Lighted Buoy 5	41-33-30.029N 070-51-54.057W	Fl G 4s		3	Green.	
16830	- Lighted Buoy 6 On southwest side of rock.	41-34-12.930N 070-52-15.901W	Fl R 2.5s		3	Red.	
16835	- Lighted Gong Buoy 7 East of rock.	41-34-09.268N 070-52-28.723W	Fl G 2.5s		3	Green.	
16845	- Lighted Buoy 8	41-35-12.954N 070-52-56.025W	Fl R 6s		3	Red.	
16851	- Lighted Buoy 9	41-35-11.511N 070-53-02.008W	Fl G 6s		3	Green.	
16853	BUTLER FLATS LIGHT	41-36-12.000N 070-53-40.000W	Fl W 4s	25		White conical tower on black cylindrical base.	Private aid.
16855	- Lighted Buoy 10	41-36-17.003N 070-53-31.925W	Fl R 2.5s		3	Red.	
16860	- Lighted Buoy 11	41-36-15.186N 070-53-36.489W	Fl G 2.5s		3	Green.	
16870	- Buoy 12	41-36-38.757N 070-53-47.030W				Red nun.	
16875	- Buoy 13	41-36-38.132N 070-53-51.912W				Green can.	
16880	- Lighted Buoy 14	41-36-57.384N 070-53-59.080W	Fl R 4s		3	Red.	
16885	- Lighted Buoy 15	41-36-58.049N 070-54-05.108W	Fl G 4s		3	Green.	

56 NAVIGATION WORKBOOK 1210 TR

Light List corrected through LNM week: 01/13

(1) No.	(2) Name and Location	(3) Position	(4) Characteristic	(5) Height	(6) Range	(7) Structure	(8) Remarks
			MASSACHUSETTS - First District				
16896	NEW BEDFORD EAST BARRIER LIGHT	41-37-28.900N 070-54-19.400W	Q R	48	5	On pile.	Higher intensity beam up channel.
MARTHA'S VINEYARD TO BLOCK ISLAND (Chart 13218)							
New Bedford Harbor							
New Bedford Channel							
16897	NEW BEDFORD WEST BARRIER LIGHT	41-37-27.200N 070-54-22.000W	Q G	48	8	On pile.	Higher intensity beam up and down channel. Emergency light of reduced intensity when main light is extinguished. HORN: 1 blast ev 10s (1s bl).

Light List Luminous Range Diagram

The nominal range given in this Light List is the maximum distance a given light can be seen when the meteorological visibility is 10 nautical miles. If the existing visibility is less than 10 NM, the range at which the light can be seen will be reduced below its nominal range. And, if the visibility is greater than 10 NM, the light can be seen at greater distances. The distance at which a light may be expected to be seen in the prevailing visibility is called its luminous range.

This diagram enables the mariner to determine the approximate luminous range of a light when the nominal range and the prevailing meteorological visibility are known. The diagram is entered from the bottom border using the nominal range listed in column 6 of this book. The intersection of the nominal range with the appropriate visibility curve (or, more often, a point between two curves) yields, by moving horizontally to the left border, the luminous range.

CAUTION

When using this diagram it must be remembered that:

1. The ranges obtained are approximate.

2. The transparency of the atmosphere may vary between observer and light.

3. Glare from background lighting will reduce the range that lights are sighted.

4. The rolling motion of a vessel and/or of a lighted aid may reduce the distance that lights can be detected or identified.

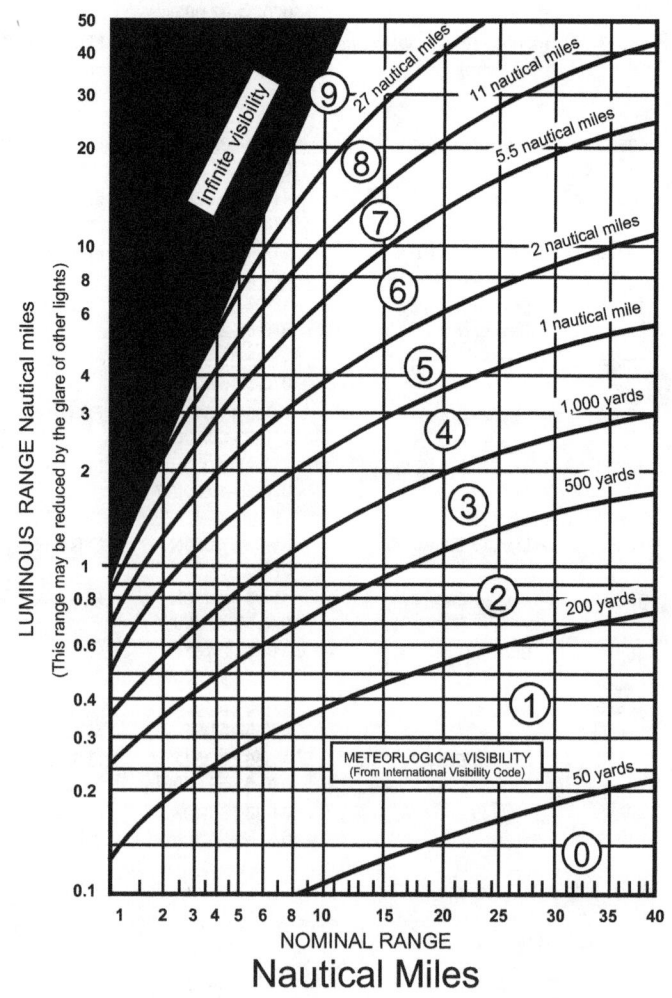

Light List Characteristics of Lights

Illustration	Type Description	Abbreviation
	1. FIXED. A light showing continuously and steadily.	F
	2. OCCULTING. A light in which the total duration of light in a period is longer than the total duration of darkness and the intervals of darkness (eclipses) are usually of equal duration	
	2.1 Single-occulting. An occulting light in which an eclipse is regularly repeated.	Oc
	2.2 Group-occulting. An occulting light in which a group of eclipses, specified in numbers, is regularly repeated.	Oc (2)
	2.3 Composite group-occulting. A light, similar to a group-occulting light, except that successive groups in a period have different numbers of eclipses.	Oc (2+1)
	3. ISOPHASE. A light in which all durations of light and darkness are equal.	Iso
	4. FLASHING. A light in which the total duration of light in a period is shorter than the total duration of darkness and the appearances of light (flashes) are usually of equal duration.	
	4.1 Single-flashing. A flashing light in which a flash is regularly repeated (frequency not exceeding 30 flashes per minute).	Fl
	4.2 Group-flashing. A flashing light in which a group of flashes, specified in number, is regularly repeated.	Fl (2)
	4.3 Composite group-flashing. A light similar to a group flashing light except that successive groups in the period have different numbers of	Fl (2+1)
	5. QUICK. A light in which flashes are produced at a rate of 60 flashes per minute.	
	5.1 Continuous quick. A quick light in which a flash is regularly repeated.	Q
	5.2 Interrupted quick. A quick light in which the sequence of flashes is interrupted by regularly repeated eclipses of constant and long duration.	I Q
	6. MORSE CODE. A light in which appearances of light of two clearly different durations (dots and dashes) are grouped to represent a character or characters in the Morse code.	Mo (A)
	7. FIXED AND FLASHING. A light in which a fixed light is combined with a flashing light of higher luminous intensity.	F Fl
	8. ALTERNATING. A light showing different colors alternately	Al RW

U.S. Department of Homeland Security

United States Coast Guard

LOCAL NOTICE TO MARINERS

District: 1   Week: 15/14

COASTAL WATERS FROM EASTPORT, MAINE TO SHREWSBURY, NEW JERSEY

The Local Notice to Mariners is available online at http://www.navcen.uscg.gov/?pageName=lnmDistrict&region=1
The 2013 Light List is available online at: http://www.navcen.uscg.gov/index.php?pageName=lightLists
Information on Private Aids to Navigation is available at: http://www.uscg.mil/d1/prevention/NavInfo/navinfo/paton.htm
Reports of Channel conditions can be found at the Army Corps of Engineers website at:
http://www.nan.usace.army.mil/Missions/Navigation/ControllingDepthReports.aspx .
NOAA Tides and Currents can be found at: http://tidesandcurrents.noaa.gov/ .

ABBREVIATIONS

A through H

ADRIFT - Buoy Adrift
AICW - Atlantic Intracoastal Waterway
Al - Alternating
B - Buoy
BKW - Breakwater
bl - Blast
BNM - Broadcast Notice to Mariner
bu - Blue
C - Canadian
CHAN - Channel
CGD - Coast Guard District

C/O - Cut Off
CONT - Contour
CRK - Creek
CONST - Construction
DAYMK/Daymk - Daymark
DBN/Dbn - Daybeacon
DBD/DAYBD - Dayboard
DEFAC - Defaced
DEST - Destroyed
DISCON - Discontinued
DMGD/DAMGD - Damaged
ec - eclipse
EST - Established Aid
ev - every
EVAL - Evaluation
EXT - Extinguished
F - Fixed
fl - flash
Fl - Flashing
G - Green
GIWW - Gulf Intracoastal Waterway
HAZ - Hazard to Navigation
HBR - Harbor
HOR - Horizontal Clearance
HT - Height

I through O

I - Interrupted
ICW - Intracoastal Waterway
IMCH - Improper Characteristic
INL - Inlet
INOP - Not Operating
INT - Intensity
ISL - Islet
Iso - Isophase
kHz - Kilohertz
LAT - Latitude
LB - Lighted Buoy

LBB - Lighted Bell Buoy
LHB - Lighted Horn Buoy
LGB - Lighted Gong Buoy
LONG - Longitude
LNM - Local Notice to Mariners
LT - Light
LT CONT - Light Continuous
LTR - Letter
LWB - Lighted Whistle Buoy
LWP - Left Watching Properly
MHz - Megahertz
MISS/MSNG - Missing
Mo - Morse Code
MRASS - Marine Radio Activated Sound Signal
MSLD - Misleading
N/C - Not Charted
NGA - National Geospatial-Intelligence Agency
NO/NUM - Number
NOS - National Ocean Service
NW - Notice Writer
OBSCU - Obscured
OBST - Obstruction
OBSTR - Obstruction
Oc - Occulting
ODAS - Anchored Oceanographic Data Buoy

P through Z

PRIV - Private Aid
Q - Quick
R - Red
RACON - Radar Transponder Beacon
Ra ref - Radar reflector
RBN - Radio Beacon
REBUILT - Aid Rebuilt
RECOVERED - Aid Recovered
RED - Red Buoy
REFL - Reflective
RRL - Range Rear Light

RELIGHTED - Aid Relit
RELOC - Relocated
RESET ON STATION - Aid Reset on Station
RFL - Range Front Light
RIV - River
RRASS - Remote Radio Activated Sound Signal
s - seconds
SEC - Section
SHL - Shoaling
si - silent
SIG - Signal
SND - Sound
SPM - Single Point Mooring Buoy
SS - Sound Signal
STA - Station
STRUCT - Structure
St M - Statute Mile
TEMP - Temporary Aid Change
TMK - Topmark
TRLB - Temporarily Replaced by Lighted Buoy
TRLT - Temporarily Replaced by Light
TRUB - Temporarily Replaced by Unlighted Buoy
USACE - Army Corps of Engineers
W - White
Y - Yellow

All bearings are in degrees TRUE - All times are in Local Time unless otherwise noted.

SECTION I - SPECIAL NOTICES
This section contains information of special concern to the Mariner.

REQUESTS FOR PUBLISHED INFORMATION-CAPTAIN OF THE PORT NEW YORK AREA OF RESPONSIBILITY

Coast Guard Sector New York is no longer accepting notifications through use of the "Request for Marine Activity Approval". Requests for Notices to Mariners must now be submitted directly to the First Coast Guard District Waterways Management Division at LNM@d1.uscg.mil as outlined on page one of the weekly Local Notice to Mariners at http://www.navcen.uscg.gov . Please remember that many mariners do not read the Local Notice to Mariners nor monitor VHF radio for Coast Guard Safety Broadcast Notice to Mariners and will not be aware of your project. Plan accordingly. The navigation rules at http://www.navcen.uscg.gov/?pageName=navRulesContent apply. Mariners are reminded, as per 33 CFR 110.155(l)(11), "Whenever the maritime or commercial interests of the United States so require, the Captain of the Port is hereby empowered to shift the position of any vessel anchored within the anchorage areas, of any vessel anchored outside the anchorage areas, of any vessel which is so moored or anchored as to impede or obstruct vessel movements in any channel or obstruct or interfere with range lights and of any vessel which, lying at the exterior end of a pier or alongside an open bulkhead, obstructs or endangers the passage of vessels in transit by, or to or from, adjacent wharf property or impedes the movements of vessels entering or leaving adjacent slips". It is recommended that you email the following information, at a minimum, to LNM@d1.uscg.mil, or fax to (617) 223-8291, at least 14 days prior to beginning operations:
Date of submission,
Name, phone number, and email address of project point of contact,
Company Name,
Type of Work,
Waterway and location where work will be done,
Latitude & Longitude of work area (Degrees, Minutes, Thousandths of seconds),
Work Start & Stop dates and Hours of Operation,
Equipment on scene,
Passing Arrangements / Time to move vessels to not impede navigation,
VHF Radio Channel monitored,
Disposal Site (if used),
NOAA Chart Number for the area.

LNM 15/14

RIGHT WHALES

NOAA Fisheries announces that a voluntary vessel speed restriction zone (Dynamic Management Area - DMA) has been established south of Nantucket to protect an aggregation of 7 right whales sighted in this area on April 7, 2014. This DMA is in effect immediately through April 22, 2014. Mariners are requested to route around this area or transit through it at 10 knots or less.

VOLUNTARY DYNAMIC MANAGEMENT AREAS (DMAs)
Mariners are requested to avoid or transit at 10 knots or less inside the following areas where persistent aggregations of right whales have been sighted. Please visit www.nmfs.noaa.gov/pr/shipstrike for a graphic depicting this area.

North of Nantucket DMA -- in effect through April 22, 2014
41 55N
41 11N
070 21W
069 21W

South of Nantucket DMA -- in effect through April 17, 2014
41 12N
40 29N
070 41W
069 45W

NOTICE TO ALL PRIVATE BOATS AT SEA

United States laws and regulations require that ALL private boats arriving from a foreign port or place MUST report to the Bureau of Customs and Border Protection IMMEDIATELY upon their arrival into the United States. Every person entering the United States must be seen in person for immigration purposes by a Customs and Border Protection officer, except those participating in the I-68 -Canadian Border Boat Landing Program-. However, holders of form I-68 are still required to report their arrival into the United States to the Bureau of Customs and Border Protection. Masters and passengers must provide proof of citizenship or legal immigration status, and be in possession of a valid passport and visa, if required. Citizens of countries that are participants in the Visa Waiver Program are not eligible to seek admission to the United States under that program via private vessel. Once your boat is anchored or tied, you are considered to have entered the United States. No one may leave the vessel until Customs and Border Protection grants permission. The only exception to this requirement is to report arrival. In order to fulfill the requirement to immediately report a private boat arrival, the master of the vessel must contact the nearest Customs and Border Protection Office, or if the arrival occurs after business hours, the nearest 24 hour port of entry. Upon reporting, you may be required to proceed to a staffed port for inspection by Customs and Border Protection. Failure to comply with these requirements could result in serious criminal and civil penalties, including seizure of the boat. International mariners are urged to report any suspicious or illegal activity to the Bureau of Customs and Border Protection at 1-800-BE-ALERT.

SECTION II - DISCREPANCIES

This section lists all reported and corrected discrepancies related to Aids to Navigation in this edition. A discrepancy is a change in the status of an aid to navigation that differs from what is published or charted.

DISCREPANCIES (FEDERAL AIDS)

LLNR	Aid Name	Status	Chart No.	BNM Ref.	LNM St	LNM End
95	Wood Island Light	SS INOP	13287	NONE	14/14	
520	Chatham Beach Lighted Whistle Buoy C	OFF STA	13248	SSENE-0060-14	13/14	
560	NOAA Data Lighted Buoy 44018	MISSING	13203	SSENE-0019-12	12/12	
725	NOAA Data Lighted Buoy 44065	LT EXT	12348	SNEW-0117-12	24/12	
825	NOAA Data Lighted Buoy 44011 (ODAS)	ADRIFT	13200	CGD1-0007-12	37/12	
16120	Cleveland Ledge Channel Lighted Gong Buoy 7	SS INOP	13236	SSENE-0050-14	11/14	
16125	Cleveland Ledge Channel Lighted Buoy 8	LT EXT	13236	SSENE-0050-14	11/14	
16220	**Hog Island Channel Lighted Bell Buoy 18**	**LT EXT**	**13236**	**SSENE-0074-14**	**15/14**	
16235	Hog Island Channel Bell Buoy 25	SS IMCH	13236	SSENE-0050-14	11/14	
16240	Hog Island Channel Lighted Bell Buoy 26	SS INOP	13236	SSENE-0050-14	11/14	
19450	**Point Judith Light**	**SS INOP**	**13219**	**SSENE-0073-14**	**15/14**	
19500	Point Judith Harbor of Refuge West Entrance Light 2	LT EXT	13219	SSENE-0250-13	50/13	
21115	**Saybrook Breakwater Light**	**SS IMCH**	**12375**	**SLIS-0180-14**	**15/14**	
22215	**Perche Rock Light 43**	**LT EXT**	**12372**	**SLIS-0183-14**	**15/14**	
22495	**Saybrook Breakwater Light**	**SS IMCH**	**12375**	**SLIS-0180-14**	**15/14**	
24675	Black Rock Harbor Entrance Light 2A	TRLB/LT EXT	12369	SLIS-0286-12	45/12	

DISCREPANCIES (PRIVATE AIDS)

LLNR	Aid Name	Status	Chart No.	BNM Ref.	LNM St	LNM End
368.1	Neptune LNG Deepwater Port Lighted Buoy North A2	MISSING	13274	SBOS-0162-13	52/13	
368.2	Neptune LNG Deepwater Port Lighted Buoy South B1	OFF STA	13274	SBOS-0171-13	53/13	
13260.2	Pamet River Entrance Lighted Buoy 2	LT EXT	13249	SSENE-0059-14	12/14	
14741.13	West Bay Entrance Buoy 7	MISSING	13237	SSENE-0120-13	26/13	
16853	Butler Flats Light	LT EXT	13232	SSENE-0081-13	17/13	
17891	Jamestown Harbor Channel Buoy 1	MSLD SIG	13223	SSENE-0131-11	29/11	

SECTION IV - CHART CORRECTIONS

This section contains corrections to federally and privately maintained Aids to Navigation, as well as NOS corrections.

This section contains corrective actions affecting chart(s). Corrections appear numerically by chart number, and pertain to that chart only. It is up to the mariner to decide which chart(s) are to be corrected. The following example explains individual elements of a typical chart correction.

```
Chart          Chart        Edition       Last Local Notice    Horizontal         Source of         Current Local
Number         Edition      Date          to Mariners          Datum Reference    Correction        Notice to Mariners
  |              |            |                 |                   |                  |                  |
12327          91st Ed.    19-APR-97     Last LNM: 26/97        NAD 83                                27/97
Chart Title: NY-NJ-NEW YORK HARBOR - RARITAN RIVER
         Main Panel 2245   NEW YORK HARBOR                                         CGD01
  (Temp)    ADD          NATIONAL DOCK CHANNEL BUOY 3                           at 40-41-09.001N   074-02-48.001W
    .        |              Green can        |                .                    |
  Corrective                Object of Corrective                                 Position
    Action                  Action
```

(Temp) indicates that the chart correction action is temporary in nature. Courses and bearings are given in degrees clockwise from 000 true. Bearings of light sectors are toward the light from seaward. The nominal range of lights is expressed in nautical miles (NM) unless otherwise noted.

LNM p4

RESOURCES 61

| 12354 | 44th Ed. | 01-MAY-12 | Last LNM: 12/14 | NAD 03 | | 15/14 |

ChartTitle: **Long Island Sound Eastern part**

Main Panel 2221 LONG ISLAND SOUND-EASTERN PART CONN-NY. Page/Side: N/A

| ADD | Rock in Feet; 10 Rk | Chart No. 1: K14.2 | (NOS NW-23679) | 41-05-21.280N NOS | 072-26-07.590W |
| ADD | Rock in Feet; 13 Rk | Chart No. 1: K14.2 | (NOS NW-23679) | 41-01-38.490N NOS | 072-32-59.730W |

SECTION VII - GENERAL

This section contains information of general concern to the Mariners. Mariners are advised to use caution while transiting these areas.

NY-MANHATTAN-EAST RIVER

Demolition and reconstruction of the East River Esplanade, from 38th St. to 41st St. (between 34th St. East River Ferry station and United Nations Headquarters), is being done until approximately May 31, 2014. The hours of operation are Monday - Friday, 6:00 am - 5:00 pm. On scene are divers, crane, barge & a scow. Mariners are requested to proceed with caution after passing arrangements have been made.

Chart 12327   LNM: 15/14

MA – VINEYARD SOUND-Vicinity of West Chop & Middle Ground

Submarine Power Transmission Cable Infrastructure Installation

A contractor for NSTAR electric utility, Caldwell Marine, will be conducing emergency submarine power transmission cable repair operations from approximately April 1 to April 20, 2014, in Vineyard Sound in the vicinity of 41° 29.21N /070° 36.37W and 41° 32.076N/070° 37.36W, an area between West Chop, Martha's Vineyard and Falmouth, MA. Operations will be conducted seven days per week, 24 hours per day, during this period. The vessels on location will be the tugs NAVIGATOR and PATRICK HUNT, the cable installation barge Rockland, also known as the Caldwell Cable Layer (AIS ID), and a 160 foot dive barge. The dive barge will be set on a four-point mooring with white surface buoys set out approximately ½ NM from the barge. The Caldwell Cable Layer will first conduct route clearance through the cable right of way, towing sets of grapnels and clearing the sea floor of debris. On or about April 6, 2014, the installation barge Caldwell Cable Layer will commence the cable install between West Chop, Martha's Vineyard and Falmouth, MA. The operations will be carried out on a 24-hour schedule. The barges, mooring buoys and the tugs will be properly lit for nighttime operations. During the operation the barges will be unable to move from their respective moorings under normal circumstances. All passing vessels are requested to maintain a minimum separation of ½ NM from the barges and tugs NAVIGATOR and PATRICK HUNT. Tugs NAVIGATOR and PATRICK HUNT will be monitoring VHF channels 16 and 13. The on-scene 24-hour point of contact is Paul Larrabee of Caldwell Marine who may be reached at 732-620-3938. Mariners are urged to use extreme caution when navigating in the vicinity of Vineyard Sound between West Chop, Martha's Vineyard and Falmouth, MA, during this submarine power transmission cable infrastructure installation. See enclosed chartlet.

SUMMARY OF GENERAL PROJECTS STILL IN EFFECT

Enclosure

LNM: 14/14

CT-NEW LONDON

Two research buoys are deployed within the anchorage area off Green Harbor Beach in (PA) 41° 19' 47.9994"N 72° 5' 16.7994" W from 4:00 pm April 11 until 10:00 am April 12, 2014. The buoys are to test onboard sensors (temperature & light, pH sensor, and hydrophone).

Chart 12366   LNM: 15/14
                                                                                       LNM: 15/14

RI-NARRAGANSETT BAY

Unmanned Underwater Vehicle (UUV) operation will be done from April 21 - 15, 2014 in the following positions. Primary area of operations will be in the East and West Passages of Narragansett Bay as far north as Hog Island and will continue south out of Narragansett Bay and into Rhode Island Sound. The test area will be bounded by the following four points:

NW Point: 41°35.00'N 71°24.000'W
SW Point: 41°14.000'N 71°34.000'W
NE Point: 41°38.000'N 71°15.000'W
SE Point: 41°20.000'N 71°02.000'W

The work will be done from 6:00 am - 7:00 pm. On scene will be a The UUV and research vessel Discovery that will be monitoring VHF-FM channels 13 & 16.

LNM: 15/14

SECTION VIII - LIGHT LIST CORRECTIONS

An Asterisk *, indicates the column in which a correction has been made to new information

(1) No.	(2) Name and Location	(3) Position	(4) Characteristic	(5) Height	(6) Range	(7) Structure	(8) Remarks	
625 15980	*Narragansett-Buzzards Bay Approach Lighted Whistle Buoy A*						Remove from list.	15/14
15495	Lagoon Pond Daybeacon 2	41-27-33.933N 070-35-25.458W				On pile.	* Private Aid.	15/14
15980 625	* *Narragansett-Buzzards Bay Approach Lighted Whistle Buoy A*	*				*	Remove from list.	15/14
19505	POINT JUDITH HARBOR OF REFUGE WEST ENTRANCE LIGHT 3	41-21-56.200N 071-30-53.000W	Fl G 6s	35	5	SG on post on concrete base.	* HORN: 1 blast ev 30s (3s bl). Fog signal is radio activated, during times of reduced visibility, turn marine VHF-FM radio to channel 83A/157.175Mhz. Key microphone 5 times consecutively, to activate fog signal for 45 minutes. *	15/14

UNITED STATES COAST GUARD
U.S. Department of Homeland Security

MARINE SAFETY ALERT
Inspections and Compliance Directorate

January 9, 2014
Washington, DC

Alert 01-14

Offshore Sailing
You must be prepared.

In a recent offshore regatta, numerous sailboats experienced steering system and other failures which required assistance and/or rescue by the U. S. Coast Guard when a weather system stalled offshore creating higher than expected sea states and winds. The Coast Guard responded using an array of assets to render assistance.

Offshore sailing requires special knowledge, skills, and abilities. Vessel equipment and components must be thoroughly checked <u>before</u> getting underway and periodically while at sea. The offshore domain's remoteness adds a negative dynamic to survivability concerns. <u>Preparation is key to minimizing misfortune.</u>

The Coast Guard **strongly recommends** that owner / operators of offshore sailboats ensure proper maintenance and repair of their critical mechanical systems to reduce the possibility of failure during stressed operating conditions.

- ✓ Operational limitations of the systems must be understood.
- ✓ Sailors should have the repair manuals associated with their important propulsion and steering systems onboard and be able to detect oncoming failures and perform emergency repairs.
- ✓ Adequate tools, hardware, and an array of fasteners should be kept onboard.
- ✓ Common spare parts that are known to fail on a particular system should be kept onboard.
- ✓ If mechanical ability is lacking, additional training should be taken to provide minimum skill sets.
- ✓ Regular inspection and prompt corrective action of all steering gear components including linkages, ram assemblies, controls and cables, in addition to engine systems, should be part of getting underway and day-to-day operations.
- ✓ Equipment should be tested before getting underway, noting variations in movement, feel, sound, and resistance.
- ✓ Flooding and damage control kits should be kept onboard.
- ✓ Sailors should contemplate and envision ways to fabricate a temporary emergency rudder using components (table tops, cabinet doors, spinnaker poles, etc.) already onboard.
- ✓ Make sure all EPIRBs, PLBs, are registered, operational and available. Ensure your VHF radio is fully functional.
- ✓ Lastly, always file a float plan with family or friends ashore *before* getting underway. Float plans are simple tools that help rescuers locate stranded boaters in distress, and may be printed from the following site: http://www.floatplancentral.org/download/USCGFloatPlan.pdf

This alert is for informational purposes only and does not relieve any domestic or international safety, operational, or material requirement. Developed by the Fifth Coast Guard District, Portsmouth, VA.

Excerpts from NOAA Chart Catalog No. 1

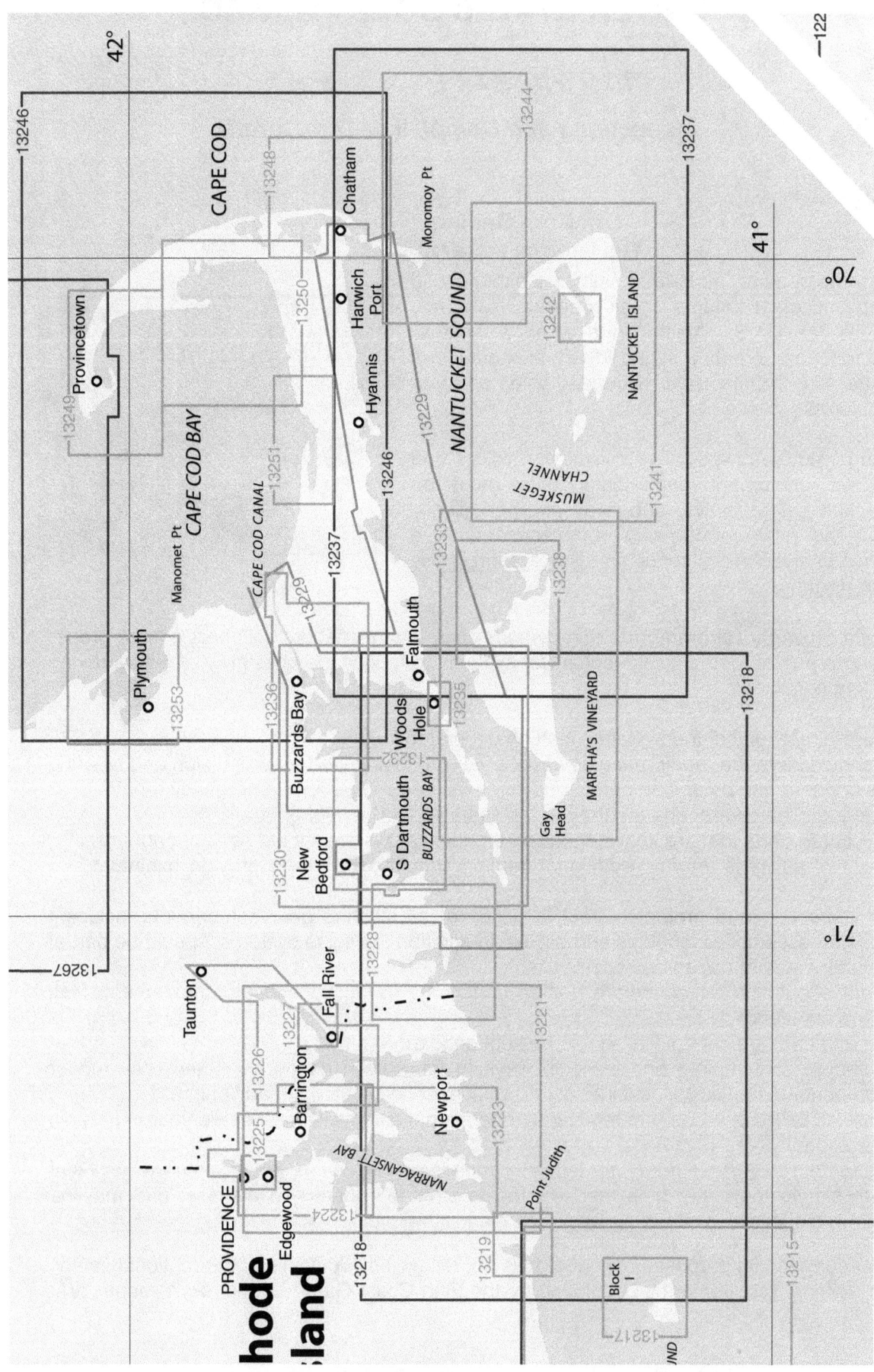

Chart Number	Title	Scale
12352 SC	Shinnecock Bay to East Rockaway Inlet	1:20,000, 1:40,000
12353	Shinnecock Light to Fire Island Light	1:80,000
12354	Long Island Sound—Eastern Part	1:80,000
12358	New York—Long Island, Shelter Island Sound and Peconic Bays	1:40,000
	Mattituck Inlet	1:10,000
12362	Port Jefferson and Mount Sinai Harbors	1:10,000
12363	Long Island Sound—Western Part	1:80,000
12364 SC	Long Island Sound—New Haven Harbor Entrance and Port Jefferson to Throgs Neck	1:40,000
12365	South Shore of Long Island Sound—Oyster and Huntington Bays	1:20,000
12366	Long Island Sound and East River—Hempstead Harbor to Tallman Island	1:20,000
12367	North Shore of Long Island Sound—Greenwich Point to New Rochelle	1:20,000
12368	North Shore of Long Island Sound—Sherwood Point to Stamford Harbor	1:20,000
12369	North Shore of Long Island Sound—Stratford to Sherwood Point	1:20,000
12370	North Shore of Long Island Sound—Housatonic River and Milford Harbor	1:20,000
12371	New Haven Harbor	1:20,000
	New Haven Harbor (Inset)	1:10,000
12372 SC	Long Island Sound—Watch Hill to New Haven Harbor	1:40,000
12373	North Shore of Long Island Sound—Guilford Harbor to Farm River	1:20,000
12374	North Shore of Long Island Sound—Duck Island to Madison Reef	1:20,000
12375	Connecticut River—Long Island Sound to Deep River	1:20,000
12377	Connecticut River—Deep River to Bodkin Rock	1:20,000
12378	Connecticut River—Bodkin Rock to Hartford	1:20,000
13205	Block Island Sound and Approaches	1:80,000
13209	Block Island Sound and Gardiners Bay	1:40,000
	Montauk Harbor	1:7,500
13211	North Shore of Long Island Sound—Niantic Bay and Vicinity	1:20,000
13212	Approaches to New London Harbor	1:20,000
13213	New London Harbor and Vicinity	1:10,000
	Bailey Point to Smith Cove	1:5,000
13214	Fishers Island Sound	1:20,000
13215	Block Island Sound—Point Judith to Montauk Point	1:40,000
13217	Block Island	1:15,000
13218	Martha's Vineyard to Block Island	1:80,000
13219	Point Judith Harbor	1:15,000
13221 MF	Narragansett Bay	1:40,000
13223	Narragansett Bay, Including Newport Harbor	1:20,000
13224	Providence River and Head of Narragansett Bay	1:20,000
13225	Providence Harbor	1:10,000

See also the following first two pages of the Coast Pilot excerpt. The Coast Pilot usually includes related sections of the Chart Catalog

Annotations in a Chart Catalog is a convenient way to index the charts you have onboard.

US Coast Pilot Vol. 2, Chapter 5

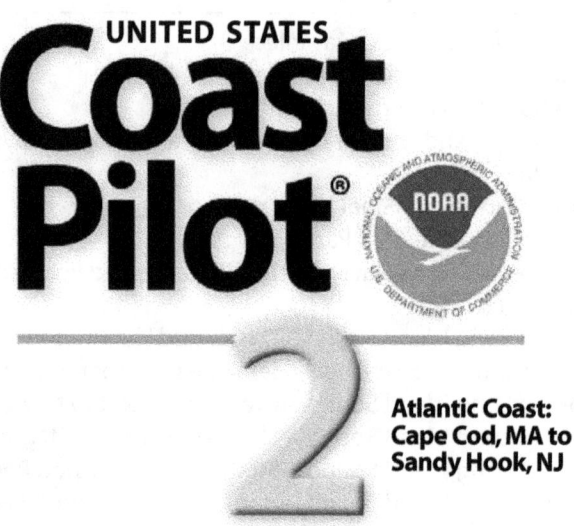

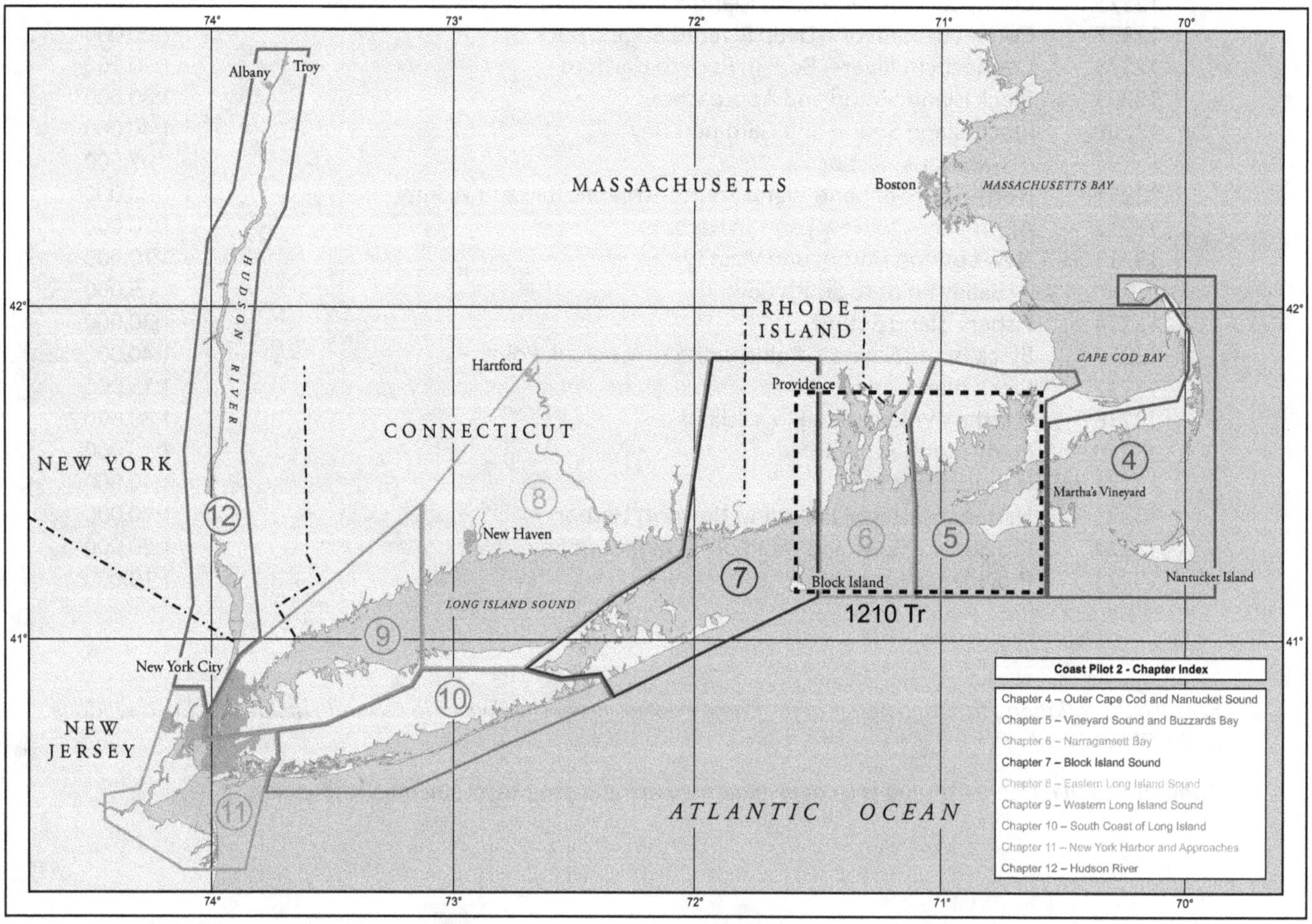

Regions covered by Chapters in US Coast Pilot Vol 2, with outline of chart 1210 Tr added.

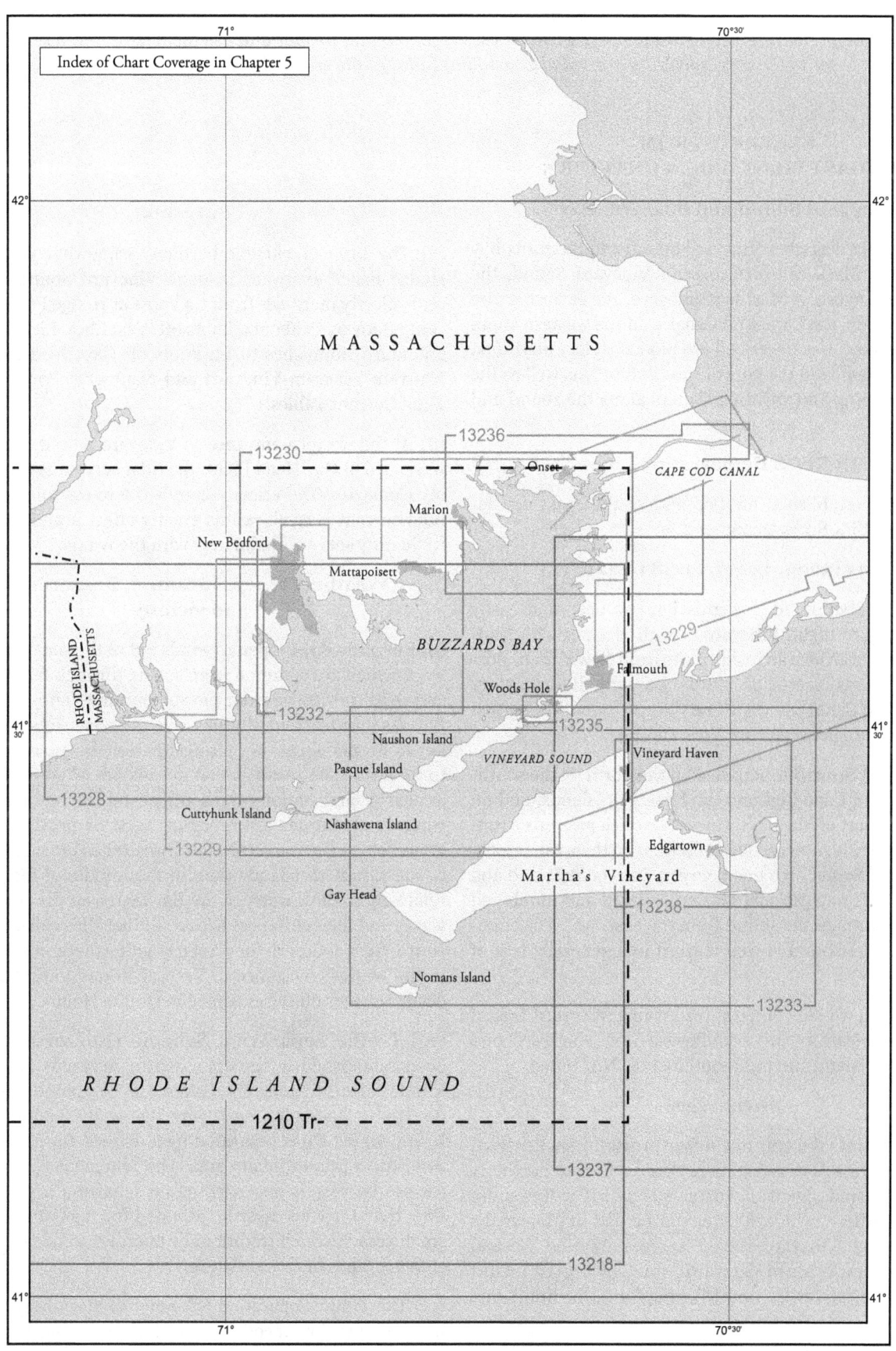

Charts covered in Chapter 5. Training chart 1210 Tr extends to the west, into Chapters 6 and 7.

Chart 1210 Tr is covered in Chapters 5, 6, and 7 of Volume 2. The following are excerpted parts of Chapter 5 (just a small part of the full chapter) to practice use of this important resource. Paragraphs are numbered in the original books, though not referred to in the books themselves. We follow that format and use them here to reference the answers. Refer to the corresponding excerpted Coast Pilot Index at the end to find specific references.

EXCERPTS FROM US COAST PILOT, VOL. 2 CHAPTER 5

Vineyard Sound and Buzzards Bay

(1) This chapter describes Vineyard Sound and Buzzards Bay following the Massachusetts coast of Vineyard Sound, the northwestern shore of Martha's Vineyard, the eastern shore of Buzzards Bay, the Cape Cod Canal, and the western shore of Buzzards Bay. Also described are Woods Hole, Cuttyhunk, Onset, Wareham, and the port of New Bedford, as well as the numerous fishing and yachting centers along the sound and bay.

COLREGS Demarcation Lines

(2) The lines established for this part of the coast are described in 33 CFR 80.145, chapter 2.

Charts 13230, 13237, 13218 (& 1210Tr)

(3) Vineyard Sound and Buzzards Bay are deep and easily navigated day or night. Vineyard Sound, together with Nantucket Sound, provides an inside route from New York to Boston which avoids Nantucket Shoals. Buzzards Bay, together with Cape Cod Canal and Cape Cod Bay, provides the shortest deep-draft route between New York and Boston.

(4) **Vineyard Sound** is bounded on the north by the southwestern part of Cape Cod and the Elizabeth Islands, and on the south by part of Martha's Vineyard, which presents a rugged and generally inaccessible shoreline. To the west, it joins Rhode Island Sound on a line between Cuttyhunk Island and Gay Head. The navigational aids are colored and numbered for passing through the sound from the eastward. The channel through the sound is well marked and generally free of dangers.

(5) Deep-draft vessels entering or leaving Vineyard Sound should stay at least 3.5 miles southward of the southwest end of Cuttyhunk Island and pass southeast of "NA" buoy.

Anchorages

(6) Woods Hole is the only anchorage providing shelter from all winds for vessels drawing more than 10 feet. In northerly and westerly winds, good anchorage may be had in Tarpaulin Cove. In southerly winds, shelter can be had in Menemsha Bight, although Vineyard Haven is generally used. Several general anchorages are in Vineyard Sound. (See 33 CFR 110.1 and 110.140(c)(1), (c)(2), and (d), chapter 2, for limits and regulations.)

Currents

(7) The time of current becomes somewhat earlier from Hedge Fence westward through Vineyard Sound. The current velocity increases from 1.4 knots at Hedge Fence Lighted Gong Buoy 22 to about 3 knots off West Chop Light, and then gradually diminishes to 1.2 knots off Gay Head Light. (See "Current Diagram-Vineyard and Nantucket Sounds" in the Tidal Current Tables.)

(8) At the western entrance to Vineyard Sound, west northwestward of Gay Head Light, the tidal current is rotary, turning clockwise. The velocity is only 0.2 to 0.5 knot. Since the tidal current is weak, winds greatly affect it and the current frequently sets approximately with the winds.

Weather: Vineyard Sound, Buzzards Bay and vicinity.

(9) Buzzards Bay is open to winds out of the south and southwest, which are common from spring through fall. Winds increase as they move from the surrounding land out over the Bay. Its northeast-southwest orientation causes southwesterlies to strengthen as they funnel up from the mouth of the Bay to its head. The result is that speeds are often double those at nearby land stations and southwesterlies may prevail even when land stations are reporting west or northwest winds. However, as a general rule southwesterlies blow harder close to the Elizabeth Islands than in the middle of the Bay. The relatively shallow water of the Bay increases the steepness of waves and their closeness to one another; this can cause a stiff chop. With southerly or westerly gales there is a heavy sea in the westerly entrance to Vineyard Sound and heavy seas occur at times off the entrance to Quicks Hole.

(10) **Traffic Separation Scheme (Buzzards Bay)** has been established in the approach to Buzzards Bay through Rhode Island Sound. The Scheme is composed basically of directed traffic lanes, each with one-way inbound and outbound traffic lanes separated by a defined traffic separation zone and a precautionary area. The Scheme is recommended for use by vessels approaching or departing from Buzzards Bay, but is not necessarily intended for tugs, tows, or other small vessels which traditionally operate outside of the usual steamer lanes or close inshore.

(11) The Traffic Separation Scheme has been designed to aid in the prevention of collisions at the approaches to the major harbors, but is not intended in any way to supersede or alter the applicable Navigation Rules. Separation zones are intend-

ed to separate inbound and outbound traffic lanes and be free of ship traffic, and should not be used except for crossing purposes. Mariners should use extreme caution when crossing traffic lanes and separation zones. (See 33 CFR 167.1 through 167.15 and 167.100 through 167.103, chapter 2, for limits and regulations and Traffic Separation Schemes, chapter 1, for additional information.)

(12) The precautionary area in the southwest part of Rhode Island Sound has a radius of 5.4 miles centered on 41°06'00"N., 71°23'18"W., excluding those areas of the circle bounded by imaginary lines extended between the outer limits of the inbound and outbound traffic lanes. (Note that this precautionary area is common to the Traffic Separation Schemes for the approaches to both Buzzards Bay and Narragansett Bay. The Traffic Separation Scheme for the approach to Narragansett Bay is described in chapter 6.)

(13) The separation zone is a 1-mile-wide zone centered in the following positions:

(i) 41°10'12"N., 71°19'06"W.,

(ii) 41°21'48"N., 71°07'06"W.

(14) The inbound traffic lane is a 1-mile-wide lane with a length of about 14.8 miles. Entering the traffic lane at a point in about 41°09'36"N., 71°18'00"W., a course of 038° follows the centerline of the traffic lane to its end, thence steer usual courses to destination.

(15) The outbound traffic lane is a 1-mile-wide lane with a length of about 14.8 miles. Entering the traffic lane at a point in about 41°22'25"N., 71°08'06"W., a course of 218° follows the centerline of the traffic lane to a junction with the precautionary area.

(16) The Traffic Separation Scheme is not buoyed.

Charts 13233, 13229 (& 1210Tr)

17) **Middle Ground**, covered 6 to 18 feet, is the easterly half of a narrow, somewhat shifting ridge in Vineyard Sound that extends for about 9 miles westward from a point about 0.5 mile northwestward of West Chop Light. A buoy is at the northeast end, and a lighted bell buoy off the southwestern end.

(18) **Lucas Shoal**, covered 17 to 30 feet, is the southwestern end of the ridge. It is separated from the Middle Ground by a natural channel with a depth of 31 feet. A buoy marks the southwestern end of the shoal.

(19) **Norton Point and Cape Higgon** are prominent bluffs on the northwest side of Martha's Vineyard about 3 and 8 miles, respectively, southwestward of West Chop Light.

(20) **Menemsha Bight**, on the northerly side of the western end of Martha's Vineyard 2.5 miles east of Gay Head, affords shelter from southerly and easterly winds in depths of 25 to 60 feet, sticky bottom. There are no dangers in the bight if the shore is given a berth of 0.3 mile.

(21) **Menemsha Creek**, on the northwestern shore of Martha's Vineyard and about 3 miles eastward of Gay Head Light, is entered from Menemsha Bight through a dredged channel that leads southeastward to Menemsha Basin, on the north shore just inside the entrance. From the basin, the dredged channel continues southward through the creek to Menemsha Pond, about 1 mile above the entrance. The entrance to the creek is protected by jetties. The east jetty is marked by a light. A bell buoy, about 300 yards northwestward of the light, marks the channel approach, and buoys and daybeacons mark the channel. The channel south of Menemsha Basin is reported to shoal rapidly after dredging; mariners are advised to seek local knowledge before attempting to go beyond Menemsha Basin.

(22) **Menemsha** is a small fishing village on Menemsha Basin. Menemsha Pond, a rectangular basin about 1 mile long and 0.7 mile wide, has general depths of 2 to 18 feet, with the deepest water in the southern half of the pond.

(23) **Gay Head**, the westerly end of Martha's Vineyard, is a prominent high bluff. It is marked by Gay Head Light (41°20'54"N., 70°50'06"W.), 170 feet above the water, shown from a 51-foot red brick tower on the head. A lighted gong buoy is 1.6 miles northwestward of the light. Several rocks exist between Gay Head and the lighted gong buoy.

(24) **Devils Bridge** is a reef making off 0.8 mile northwestward of Gay Head. The reef has a depth of 2 feet about 0.4 mile offshore and 17 feet at its end.

(25) **Nomans Land**, about 5.5 miles southward of Gay Head, is a prominent, high, and rocky island. Except for a small section on its northwestern side, the shore consists of clay and gravel cliffs 10 to 18 feet high with boulders lining the shores. In the interior of the island are many hills, the highest over 100 feet high, with considerable marshy area between the hills. A Prohibited Area surrounds Nomans Land. (See 33 CFR 334.70, chapter 2, for limits and regulations.)

(26) Several sunken rocks and ledges are in the passage between Nomans Land and Martha's Vineyard. **Lone Rock**, covered 8 feet, and **Old Man**, a ledge covered 4 feet, are marked by buoys. A buoyed channel about 0.7 mile wide between the islands may be used by small vessels in the daytime. Shoal water extends 0.5 mile southward of **Squibnocket Point**, the southernmost point of Martha's Vineyard.

Charts 13230, 13229 (& 1210Tr)

(27) **Elizabeth Islands**, including Nonamesset, Uncatena, Weepecket, Naushon, Pasque, Nashawena, Penikese, and Cuttyhunk Islands, extend about 14 miles west southwest from the southwest end of Cape Cod. The islands, forming part of the northern shore of Vineyard Sound, separate the sound from Buzzards Bay. They are hilly and partly wooded; the shores are, in general, low bluffs. Westward of Woods

Woods Hole, Massachusetts
Image courtesy of Marblehead Power Squadron (2009)

Hole are several buoyed channels between the islands, but Quicks Hole is the only one recommended for strangers.

Charts 13235, 13229 (& 1210Tr)

(28) **Woods Hole** is that water area lying between the southwest tip of Cape Cod and Uncatena and Nonamesset Island, the easternmost of the Elizabeth Islands, with Buzzards Bay on the northwest and Vineyard Sound on the southeast; it includes Great and Little Harbors in the eastern part, and Hadley Harbor in the western part. Woods Hole is also the approach to the town of Woods Hole on the northeastern shore of Great Harbor. The town is a busy commercial center and a transshipping point for passengers and freight to and from Nantucket and Martha's Vineyard. During the summer it is an active resort and frequently a port of call by yachts passing through to Vineyard Sound or Buzzards Bay. There is considerable waterborne commerce in seafood products and general cargo.

Prominent features

(29) The most prominent landmark approaching Woods Hole is Nobska Point and light. A light marks the south end of **Juniper Point**, the finger of land separating Little and Great Harbors. Also prominent is the house high on Juniper Point, a standpipe 0.7 miles north-northwestward of Nobska Point, a water tower and stacks in the town, the dome of the Woods Hole Oceanographic Institution, and the buildings of the National Marine Fisheries Service and the Marine Biological Laboratory.

Channels

(30) Woods Hole Passage, a dredged section through the northern part of Woods Hole, connects Vineyard Sound and Great Harbor with Buzzards Bay, and consists of **The Strait** and a spur channel known as the **Branch** at the western end of The Strait, and **Broadway**, the southerly entrance to The Strait from Vineyard Sound. A Federal project provides for channel depths of 13 feet. (See Notice to Mariners and latest edition of charts for controlling depths.) The northerly entrance from Great Harbor into The Strait is preferred over Broadway with its sharp turn, which is difficult in strong currents, especially for low-powered vessels and vessels under sail.

(31) The passage through Woods Hole, between numerous ledges and shoals, is marked by navigational aids. However, tidal currents are so strong that the passage is difficult and dangerous without some local knowledge. Buoys in the narrowest part of the channel sometimes are towed under, and a stranger should attempt passage only at slack water.

(32) The entrance to **Great Harbor** from Vineyard Sound, between Great Ledge and Nonamesset Shoal, has depths of over 20 feet. A lighted bell buoy marks the entrance to the

harbor from Vineyard Sound and a directional light with a 343.25 deg-344.75 deg white sector and lighted and unlighted buoys mark the channel. Mariners should guard against the current from Buzzards Bay, which has a tendency to set vessels eastward.

(33) These channels are marked by buoys and lights, but extreme caution and slack water are required to safely navigate them with drafts greater than 8 feet. Mariners entering from Buzzards Bay should keep in mind that the buoys are colored and marked for passage from Vineyard Sound to Buzzards Bay.

Anchorages

(34) An anchorage about 0.2 mile square, with poor holding ground and irregular depths ranging from 19 to 62 feet, is at the head of Great Harbor. Shoals covered 5 to 9 feet are northwest of the anchorage. Good anchorage in depths of 29 to 36 feet is also available about 200 yards northwest of the National Marine Fisheries Service's wharf. Small craft can find good anchorage in Little Harbor and Hadley Harbor.

Dangers

(35) Numerous ledges and shoals border the channel through Woods Hole. Great Ledge, an extensive rocky shoal awash at low water with a full northwest gale, lies between the entrances to Little and Great Harbors; it is marked by a buoy. **Coffin Rock**, eastward of Great Ledge and covered 5 feet, is marked by a lighted buoy 120 yards eastward of the rock. **Nonamesset Shoal**, covered 10 feet, extends about 0.2 mile eastward from Nonamesset Island, at the entrance to Great Harbor. **Parker Flats** extend as much as 200 yards off the eastern shore of Great Harbor northward of Juniper Point. Most of these dangers are marked by buoys.

(36) Fringing the passage westward of Great Harbor are many other ledges and shoals. **Red Ledge**, grassy, and **Grassy Island**, with its surrounding ledge marked by a light, are on the western side of Great Harbor Channel.

(37) **Middle Ledge**, which uncovers 1 foot in places and is marked by buoys, is on the south side of The Strait. A ledge, awash at low water and marked by a light, is about 250 yards westward of Middle Ledge. **Hadley Rock**, covered 5 feet, is some 500 yards west-southwestward of the light west of Middle Ledge. A rocky shoal area extends more than 0.3 mile westward of **Penzance Point**, the southern extremity of **Penzance**, which is the curving peninsula sheltering the west and northwest sides of Great Harbor. Most of the dangers adjoining the passage channel are marked by navigational aids.

Currents

(38) The current velocity at times exceeds 4.5 knots in the narrow part of Woods Hole Passage. Velocities as high as 5.0 knots have been reported by the U.S. Coast Guard. For daily predictions of the current, see the Tidal Current Tables.

(39) The velocity of the current is about 3.5 knots in The Strait southward of Penzance Point. Both the velocity of the current and time of slack water are affected by strong winds. At the north entrance to Woods Hole in Buzzards Bay, the velocity of the tidal current is 0.8 knot, whereas at the eastern entrance to The Strait in Great Harbor, it is about 1.3 knots. In the upper part of Great Harbor, near the National Marine Fisheries Service's wharf, the currents are barely perceptible, and vessels at anchor lie head to wind.

(40) Drift ice is brought through from Buzzards Bay, but seldom interferes with navigation except in unusually severe winters, when it may close the entrance from the bay. Small craft may experience difficulty in severe winters, but powered vessels usually proceed through the ice. The strong tidal currents usually keep Great Harbor open.

Routes

(41) The following directions are good for medium-draft vessels entering Woods Hole at slack water. Approaching from the eastward, pass about 0.3 mile southward of Nobska Point on a west southwesterly course until in the white sector of the Great Harbor Directional Light, or from a point close to Nobska Point Lighted Bell Buoy 26, steer 279° until in the white sector. Approaching from the westward in Vineyard Sound, give the south side of the Elizabeth Islands a berth of about 0.5 mile and steer for Nobska Point Light on any bearing between 045° and 051° until in the white sector.

Wharves

(42) The ferry pier of the Woods Hole-Martha's Vineyard and Nantucket Steamship Authority is on the eastern side of Great Harbor. When a ferry is approaching in fog, a private sound signal is sounded, a private quick flashing white light is shown from the southwest corner of the pier, and a private quick flashing yellow light is shown from the southwest corner of the ferry slip. The ferry to Naushon Island lands at the service wharf about 60 yards north of the ferry pier. The buildings and wharf of the Woods Hole Oceanographic Institution are northwestward of the ferry pier. Northwestward of the Oceanographic Institution are the wharves of the Marine Biological Laboratory; the wharf, basin, and buildings of the National Marine Fisheries Service; the town pier; and several private buildings.

(42) Depths at the principal piers vary from 11 to 30 feet. A breakwater extends about 90 yards southwestward from the south end of the National Marine Fisheries Service wharf. Foul ground extends about 50 yards northwestward of the outer end of the breakwater.

(43) **Eel Pond**, an extension of Great Harbor to the northeastward, is a basin with depths of 10 to 20 feet. In 2001, the narrow entrance to the pond had a reported controlling depth of 6 feet. A highway bridge over the entrance channel has a 31-foot bascule span with a clearance of 5 feet. (See 33 CFR117.1 through 117.59 and 117.598, chapter 2, for drawbridge regulations.) The piers of the Marine Biological Laboratory are

along the southwest side of the pond. The harbormaster has an office in Falmouth.

(44) **Woods Hole Coast Guard Station** is on the west side of **Little Harbor** about 450 yards northward of Juniper Point. A Federal project provides for a depth of 12 feet from Vineyard Sound through a turning basin off the Coast Guard wharf on the west shore. (See Notice to Mariners and latest editions of charts for controlling depths.) The channel is marked by lighted buoys. The east side of the harbor is used as a mooring area for local craft. Numerous rocks awash are in this part of the harbor; extreme caution is advised. A 6 mph speed limit is enforced in the harbor by the Falmouth Harbormaster.

(45) **Hadley Harbor**, in the western portion of Woods Hole at the northwest end of Nonamesset Island, is suitable only for small craft. It is reached by a narrow, crooked channel. The deeper entrance, marked by buoys, is between ledges on both sides; the northern ledge is marked by a private daybeacon. The inner harbor forms a well-sheltered anchorage for small craft. Two wharves, with depths of about 9 feet at their ends, are on the western side of Hadley Harbor. A private wharf, with a depth of about 7 feet at its end, is at the western end of Nonamesset Island.

Charts 13233, 13230, 13229 (& 1210Tr)

(46) **Naushon Island**, the largest of the Elizabeth Islands, extends west-southwestward from Uncatena and Nonamesset Islands.

(47) **Weepecket Islands**, in Buzzards Bay off the northeastern part of Naushon Island, are bare and rocky.

(48) **Weepecket Rock**, on a rocky ledge about 0.7 mile northeastward of the northernmost of the Weepecket Islands, is covered 8 feet, and is marked by a lighted gong buoy.

(49) **Lackeys Bay**, between Nonamesset Island and Jobs Neck, the southeastern extremity of Naushon Island, is shoal with numerous bare rocks.

(50) **Tarpaulin Cove**, about 5 miles west-southwest of Nobska Point, is a bight about 0.5 mile in diameter, in the south shore of Naushon Island. The cove affords shelter from northerly and westerly winds, and is frequently used. A light is on the southwest side of the cove. Anchorage in depths of 14 to 18 feet, good holding ground, is in the cove with the light bearing between 212° and 189°. Deep-draft vessels should anchor farther out in depths of 36 feet or more. The eastern and northern shores should be given a berth of 200 yards. Rocks are near the western shore and should be given a berth of over 300 yards; buoys mark the dangers.

(51) **Robinsons Hole** is a narrow buoyed passage from Vineyard Sound to Buzzards Bay between the western end of Naushon Island and the eastern end of Pasque Island. It has numerous rocks and ledges, and strong tidal currents. The buoys often tow under, and the passage should never be attempted by strangers; it is used occasionally by local fishermen. It has been reported that currents sometimes reach a velocity of 5 knots in the passage. The velocity in the narrow part is about 3 knots. The flood sets southeastward and the ebb northwestward into Buzzards Bay. (See the Tidal Current Tables for predictions.)

(52) **Quicks Hole**, between Pasque Island and **Nashawena Island**, is the only passage between Vineyard Sound and Buzzards Bay eastward of Cuttyhunk available for vessels of over 10-foot draft. The clearly defined entrance from Vineyard Sound, about 0.6 mile wide, is about 4 miles southwestward of Tarpaulin Cove and about 5 miles north of Gay Head. The passage is used considerably by tows, especially during westerly or southerly winds, to avoid the very heavy sea in the entrance to Vineyard Sound, and also because a secure anchorage from these winds can be had, if necessary, on the north side of Nashawena Island. The passage is considered unsafe for a long tow at night, but otherwise it may be used by steamers either night or day.

(53) Vessels should follow a midchannel course through the passage. The channel is nearly straight with a width of about 0.2 mile. General depths are 30 feet or more, but there are several shoaler spots. Rocks covered 27 to 37 feet are near the center of the channel. Because of the broken nature of the bottom, the passage is not recommended for a stranger drawing more than 21 feet. Buoys mark the channel.

(54) The aids in Quicks Hole are colored and numbered for passage from Vineyard Sound to Buzzards Bay. The eastern side of Quicks Hole is foul, and no attempt should be made to pass eastward of the lighted buoy. **Felix Ledge**, 0.2 mile off the eastern shore of Nashawena Island, is covered 15 feet and marked by a buoy. A sunken wreck, covered 30 feet, is on the west side of the passage in about 41°26.6'N., 70°51.1'W.

(55) **Lone Rock**, covered 8 feet and marked by a lighted buoy, is off the northern entrance, about 0.7 mile northward of North Point, the northeastern extremity of Nashawena Island. Tide rips have been observed between North Point and Lone Rock during spring tides.

(56) **Penikese Island**, grassy and hilly, is about 1.3 miles northwestward of **Knox Point**, the northwestern extremity of Nashawena Island. Shoal water extends from Penikese Island to **Gull Island**, a small islet 0.5 mile southeastward. No attempt should be made to pass between them. Rocky ledges extend southward and westward from Gull Island; buoys are on the southern edge of this area. The channels to Cuttyhunk Harbor from Buzzards Bay are southward of the ledges.

(57) **Cuttyhunk Harbor** is formed by the bight between Nashawena Island and **Cuttyhunk Island**, the westernmost of the Elizabeth Islands. Northward of the harbor are Penikese and Gull Islands and several ledges, which shelter the harbor from winds from that direction. The harbor is exposed to winds from the northeastward. Weather-bound coasting vessels and fishermen sometimes use the anchorage in the harbor. Prominent from offshore is a 50-foot-high monu-

ment on an island in **Westend Pond** on the western end of Cuttyhunk Island. Vessels bound for Cuttyhunk Harbor generally approach from Buzzards Bay. The principal dangers are marked by buoys. Strangers should not enter except in the daytime with clear weather. If entering from the northwestward, a greater draft than 10 feet should not be taken in. The approach from northeastward is deeper.

(58) **Canapitsit Channel**, between the east end of Cuttyhunk Island and Nashawena Island, is used by small boats and is partially marked by buoys. In 2012, the channel had a controlling depth of 4 feet. The buoys at this entrance are often dragged off station by strong currents and heavy seas. The channel should never be used during a heavy ground swell. With southerly winds, heavy seas will break across the entrance.

Channels

(59) A Federal project provides a 10-foot channel from Cuttyhunk Harbor into Cuttyhunk Pond to a turning basin at the western terminal in the pond and a 10-foot anchorage basin in the eastern part of the pond north of the channel. The jettied entrance is marked by a light on the north jetty and by a buoy off the end of the submerged south jetty. A bell buoy marks the entrance to the channel.

Anchorage

(60) Limited anchorage with reported poor holding ground may be found in depths of 10 to 24 feet in Cuttyhunk Harbor. The shores on both sides of the harbor are foul, and the anchorage is in the middle.

Dangers

(61) Shoals extend 0.6 mile northeastward of Cuttyhunk Island. **Whale Rock** and **Pease Ledge** uncover at low water. **Middle Ground**, covered 9 feet, is 0.5 mile north of **Copicut Neck** in the northwestern approach to the harbor. **Middle Ledge**, covered 15 feet, is about 0.4 mile east of **Middle Ground**. **Edwards Rock**, covered 7 feet, is 250 yards northeastward of Whale Rock. These dangers, except for Middle Ledge, are buoyed. An unmarked rocky shoal, covered 12 feet, is in the middle of the northwestern approach about 0.2 mile southeastward of Middle Ledge. Numerous other rocks and ledges covered 4 to 12 feet are between Cuttyhunk Island and the ledges southwestward of Penikese and Gull Islands. The eastern point at the entrance and the eastern shore of the harbor should be given a berth of over 300 yards.

Charts 13218, 13228, 13230, 13229 (& 1210Tr)

(62) **Buzzards Bay** is the approach to New Bedford, many small towns and villages, and the entrance of Cape Cod Canal. The bay indents the south shore of Massachusetts, extending in a northeasterly direction from **Rhode Island Sound**. The bay is enclosed on the south side, and separated from Vineyard Sound, by the Elizabeth Islands.

(63) The shores are irregular, rocky in character, and broken by many bays and rivers. Large boulders are common, in places extending a considerable distance from shore, thus making close approach to the shore dangerous.

(64) The bottom in the main part of the bay and approach is very broken with boulder reefs in places. Vessels should proceed with caution when crossing shoal areas in the tributaries of the bay where the depths are not more than about 6 feet greater than the draft. Caution must also be exercised in the vicinity of the wrecks shown on the chart. Deep water prevails as far as Wings Neck, above which the bay is full of shoals.

(65) **Buzzards Bay** has six entrances, but two of these are so narrow and dangerous as to exclude their use except by small craft with local knowledge. The four major entrances are the main channel, from westward, passing north of Cuttyhunk Island; Cape Cod Canal from northeastward; and Quicks Hole and Woods Hole from the southward. The two hazardous entrances are Canapitsit Channel, between Cuttyhunk and Nashawena Islands, and Robinsons Hole, between Pasque and Naushon Islands.

(66) The western entrance has a clear width of 4.3 miles between Sow and Pigs Reef and Hen and Chickens. The bottom in this entrance is irregular and rocky, and there are spots with depths of 17 to 34 feet. Because these shoal areas are surrounded by deeper water, vessels of 16-foot draft or more must exercise extra caution when entering the bay. In heavy southwest gales the sea breaks over some of these spots.

(67) The best guides for entering the bay from westward are Buzzards Bay Entrance Light and the lighted buoys in the entrance. Gay Head Light and Buzzards Bay Entrance Light are the guides for vessels approaching from the southward.

(68) **Buzzards Bay Entrance Light** (41°23'49"N., 71°02'05"W.), 67 feet above the water, is shown from a tower on a red square superstructure on red piles about 4 miles 255° from the southwest corner of Cuttyhunk Island. The name BUZZARDS is painted in white on the sides. A sound signal and racon are at the light.

Anchorages

(69) New Bedford Inner Harbor affords anchorage for vessels of 25-foot draft. Cuttyhunk Harbor affords anchorage in depths of 10 to 24 feet; except for the smallcraft inner harbor, it is exposed to northerly winds. A good anchorage sheltered from all southerly winds may be had off the north shore of Nashawena Island eastward of Penikese and Gull Islands in depths of 40 to 48 feet. This anchorage, frequently used by tows, is available for vessels of any draft; however, care must be taken to stay clear of the fishtrap area in the vicinity. Two general anchorages are off the western entrance to Cape Cod Canal.

Dangers

(70) Hen and Chickens, extending 1.4 miles southward of Gooseberry Neck, is a reef consisting of many large boulders, most of them baring a foot or less. The reef is in two large

groups; the southerly group is the larger. Numerous covered rocks are well away from the visible part of the danger. A narrow ledge covered 5 to 14 feet extends about 0.4 mile northward from the visible part of Hen and Chickens. A buoy is north of the ledge. Old Cock, a rock awash, and The Wildcat, covered 5 feet and unmarked, are in the southern shoal area. The south edge of the shoal is marked by a buoy. Strangers are advised to stay outside the 5-fathom curve in this vicinity.

(71) **Sow and Pigs Reef**, much of which is dry or awash, extends about 1.5 miles west-southwestward from Cuttyhunk Island. Its outer end is marked by a lighted bell buoy. An unmarked rock strewn shoal, covered 20 feet, is 0.9 mile westward of Cuttyhunk Island. Numerous obstructions and rocks were reported to extend as much as 3 miles southward of Sow and Pigs Reef.

(72) **Ribbon Reef**, a detached ledge covered 18 feet, is about 1.5 miles northwestward of Cuttyhunk Island.

(73) **Mishaum Ledge**, a group of several rocky spots with a least depth of 8 feet, extends about 1.7 miles southward of Mishaum Point. It is marked by a lighted gong buoy off its southeast end. A lighted bell buoy marks a rocky shoal covered 22 feet about 1 mile north-northwestward of the north end of Penikese Island. An unmarked rocky shoal covered 18 feet is 0.5 mile north of the island.

Currents

(74) The tidal currents in the passages between Buzzards Bay and Vineyard Sound have considerable velocity and require special attention. At Buzzards Bay Lighted Gong Buoy 3, the tidal current is rotary, turning clockwise. Tide rips occur when a sea is running against the current. Maximum velocities are about 0.5 knot. Minimum velocities average about 0.2 knot.

Charts 13236, 13229 (& 1210 Tr)

(75) **Onset Bay**, between **Sias Point** on the north and **Hog Neck** on the south, is the approach to the village of Onset. A dredged marked channel leads westward from Cape Cod Canal along the southerly side of the bay to a turning basin off the village. Two anchorage areas, one on each side of the channel, are at the head of the channel.

(76) **Wickets Island** is a high and wooded islet in the middle of the bay. The buoys in the entrance channel are frequently towed under because of the strong currents. A rock, covered 9 feet, is near the channel entrance about 75 yards northeast of Hog Island Channel Light 21. In 1981, two rocks, covered 4 to 5 feet, were reported on the north edge of the channel between Buoys 2 and 4; caution is advised.

(77) **East River** empties into Onset Bay southeast of Onset. A draft of 4 feet can be taken to **Broad Cove** above the highway bridge which connects Onset and Long Neck. The bridge has a fixed span with a clearance of 11 feet.

Coast Pilot Chapter 5 Index

Anchorage 79, 81
Branch 78
Broad Cove 82
Broadway 78
Buzzards Bay 81
Canapitsit Channel 81
Cape Cod Canal 76, 81
Cape Higgon 77
Channels 81
Charts 13233, 13230, 13229 (& 1210Tr) 80
Charts 13235, 13229 (& 1210Tr) 78
Charts 13236, 13229 (& 1210 Tr) 82
Coffin Rock 79
COLREGS Demarcation Lines 76
Copicut Neck 81
Currents 76, 79, 82
Cuttyhunk Harbor 80
Cuttyhunk Island 80, 81
Cuttyhunk Pond 81
Dangers 79, 81

Devils Bridge 77
East River 82
Edwards Rock 81
Eel Pond 79
Elizabeth Islands 77, 81
Falmouth Harbormaster 80
Felix Ledge 80
Gay Head 77
Grassy Island 79
Great Harbor 78
Gull Island 80
Hadley Harbor 80
Hadley Rock 79
Hog Neck 82
Juniper Point 78
Knox Point 80
Little Harbor 80
Lone Rock 77, 80
Lucas Shoal 77
Menemsha Bight 77
Middle Ground 77, 81
Middle Ledge 79, 81
Mishaum Ledge 82
Nantucket Shoals 76

Nantucket Sound 76
Nashawena Island 80
Naushon Island 80
Nobska Point 78
Nomans Land 77
Nonamesset Island 80
Nonamesset Shoal 79
Norton Point 77
Old Man 77
Onset Bay 82
Parker Flats 79
Pasque Island 81
Pease Ledge 81
Penikese Island 80
Penzance 79
Penzance Point 79
Quicks Hole 80
Red Ledge 79
Rhode Island Sound 81
Ribbon Reef 82
Robinsons Hole 80
Routes 79
Sias Point 82
Sow and Pigs Reef 82

Squibnocket Point 77
Tarpaulin Cove 80
The Strait 78
Traffic Separation Scheme 76, 77
Vineyard Sound 76
Weather 76
Westend Pond 81
Whale Rock 81
Wharves 79
Wickets Island 82
Woods Hole 78
Woods Hole Coast Guard Station 80

Coast Pilot Climate Data (Appendix B)

CLIMATOLOGICAL DATA – NEWPORT, RI (41°32'N, 71°21'W) 10 feet (3 m)														
WEATHER ELEMENTS	JAN	FEB	MAR	APR	MAY	JUN	JUL	AUG	SEP	OCT	NOV	DEC	YEAR	YEARS OF RECORD
SEA LEVEL PRESSURE (station pressure reduced to sea level)														
Mean (millibars)	1019.6	1018.2	1017.3	1017.8	1017.8	1015.7	1016.2	1017.7	1019.8	1018.7	1017.0	1018.3	1017.9	2
TEMPERATURE (°F)														
Mean	30.8	31.6	38.2	47.0	56.2	65.0	71.1	70.9	64.6	55.2	45.9	35.3	51.1	34
Mean daily maximum	38.1	38.9	45.6	55.1	64.4	72.9	78.6	78.1	72.1	62.8	53.0	42.4	58.6	34
Mean daily minimum	23.0	23.8	30.3	38.4	47.4	56.6	63.1	63.2	56.6	47.1	38.3	27.6	43.1	34
Extreme (highest)	65	65	74	86	89	93	96	98	93	81	75	65	98	34
Extreme (lowest)	-9	-3	3	10	25	37	41	41	35	26	11	-5	-9	34
CLOUD COVER														
Percent of time clear	11.7	10.6	6.6	10.2	10.1	10.3	18.6	13.9	15.7	15.6	12.4	11.3	12.3	3
Percent of time scattered	26.0	29.0	27.5	26.1	29.5	22.4	15.0	17.5	19.1	19.9	22.2	31.9	23.7	3
Percent of time broken	24.0	21.2	22.4	19.9	26.7	26.9	29.4	26.6	23.6	26.2	29.7	17.1	24.5	3
Percent of time overcast	38.3	39.2	43.5	43.8	33.8	40.4	37.0	42.0	41.6	38.3	35.7	39.7	39.5	3
PRECIPITATION (inches)														
Mean amount	3.8	3.6	4.4	4.2	3.5	3.0	2.9	3.2	3.6	3.3	4.5	4.3	45.0	35
Greatest amount	11.8	6.5	10.6	10.5	8.9	9.2	6.4	12.9	10.6	6.4	9.8	8.9	63.4	35
Least amount	0.9	0.8	1.1	1.1	0.8	0.6	0.8	0.4	0.2	1.5	0.8	0.9	27.6	35
Maximum amount (24 hours)	2.7	2.6	4.4	3.7	4.8	3.0	3.2	4.4	7.8	2.7	3.9	3.1	7.8	35
Mean number of days	16	15	16	16	16	14	14	14	13	12	15	17	178	14
SNOW														
Mean amount	7.2	6.6	2.5	0.2	0.0	0.0	0.0	0.0	0.0	T	0.5	3.4	20.3	32
Greatest amount	30.5	28.0	15.0	5.0	0.0	0.0	0.0	0.0	0.0	T	6.0	13.6	44.5	32
Least amount	0.0	0.0	0.0	0.0	0.0	0.0	0.0	0.0	0.0	0.0	0.0	0.0	1.5	32
Maximum amount (24 hours)	10.0	20.0	6.5	5.0	0.0	0.0	0.0	0.0	0.0	T	6.0	11.0	20.0	32
Mean number of days	7	8	4	1	0	0	0	0	0	Miss	1	5	26	14
WIND														
Percentage with gales	0.47	0.00	0.16	0.00	0.00	0.00	0.00	0.15	0.00	0.17	0.00	0.19	0.10	2
Mean wind speed (knots)	8.9	9.4	8.7	8.4	7.1	6.1	5.1	5.6	6.2	7.3	9.2	9.0	7.5	2
Direction (percentage of observations)														
North	10.4	12.9	9.9	7.7	7.6	3.0	6.4	7.5	10.1	8.2	8.8	13.7	8.8	2
North Northeast	4.9	6.4	8.4	6.5	8.3	6.3	4.6	4.9	8.4	6.0	7.8	7.8	6.6	2
Northeast	8.0	10.1	8.7	13.7	12.0	6.4	8.0	8.5	9.9	10.8	6.3	5.5	9.0	2
East Northeast	1.9	3.3	2.3	1.7	1.2	0.5	1.6	2.1	2.6	2.2	1.3	0.6	1.8	2
East	2.8	3.3	5.4	2.9	4.9	3.4	3.6	2.4	1.8	1.8	1.5	1.3	3.0	2
East Southeast	0.8	0.8	1.9	2.6	2.3	1.4	1.0	1.9	1.9	2.0	1.0	1.5	1.6	2
Southeast	2.7	1.3	5.4	7.2	6.3	5.5	6.2	4.3	4.7	6.8	2.9	2.8	4.7	2
South Southeast	0.6	1.5	2.0	3.1	2.5	1.1	3.3	1.9	3.7	2.0	1.9	0.8	2.0	2
South	3.9	3.1	6.2	6.5	6.3	8.8	10.7	9.3	10.2	7.0	3.1	2.1	6.6	2
South Southwest	5.4	4.3	6.8	10.2	11.4	14.6	12.7	13.0	9.4	8.0	4.8	3.6	8.8	2
Southwest	15.7	20.6	12.2	20.5	20.6	28.9	21.2	21.1	18.5	21.3	20.3	13.3	19.6	2
West Southwest	7.4	5.1	4.2	3.2	4.8	6.7	4.6	6.7	3.7	6.7	10.9	10.8	6.1	2
West	14.3	7.8	8.7	4.1	3.5	2.7	3.4	3.3	4.7	5.2	8.4	12.0	6.4	2
West Northwest	3.9	3.8	4.8	2.4	2.1	3.9	3.1	1.9	2.3	2.3	6.1	6.8	3.5	2
Northwest	15.3	11.2	10.9	4.4	4.0	5.1	5.9	8.1	6.0	6.8	12.2	14.0	8.6	2
North Northwest	1.9	4.5	2.0	2.7	2.1	1.3	3.3	2.8	1.5	2.8	2.7	3.2	2.6	2
Calm	0.0	63.7	0.2	0.7	57.9	0.3	0.7	0.1	0.5	56.8	80.7	0.2	20.3	2
Direction (mean speed, knots)														
North	8.2	9.3	8.8	7.4	6.2	5.7	5.5	4.7	6.9	6.9	6.7	9.7	7.5	2
North Northeast	9.6	8.7	10.5	7.4	6.5	4.6	5.3	5.1	6.2	11.7	11.3	8.5	8.0	2
Northeast	8.5	8.4	8.0	9.6	6.8	5.3	5.0	5.2	5.2	7.1	7.3	7.0	7.1	2
East Northeast	6.7	10.1	8.5	7.4	6.7	6.0	4.9	6.1	3.6	4.3	4.5	5.7	6.5	2
East	7.5	6.6	7.2	6.5	6.4	5.4	5.1	5.1	4.8	4.4	5.4	4.3	6.0	2
East Southeast	4.6	7.6	6.7	8.7	6.2	4.9	6.0	5.8	4.2	3.8	9.0	9.9	6.3	2
Southeast	8.0	7.6	6.3	8.2	6.8	5.7	4.9	5.7	3.9	5.8	9.4	9.5	6.4	2
South Southeast	4.0	10.8	8.9	6.9	7.0	4.3	4.6	5.7	5.1	6.2	9.8	5.2	6.5	2
South	8.7	7.5	8.5	7.0	7.0	5.5	5.1	5.4	7.7	7.0	8.7	8.8	6.8	2
South Southwest	8.2	7.5	9.2	9.3	7.0	5.7	5.2	6.1	6.9	7.6	9.7	10.3	7.2	2
Southwest	10.2	11.4	11.2	9.5	8.2	6.6	5.7	6.2	7.1	7.9	10.5	9.3	8.4	2
West Southwest	9.9	10.0	9.1	10.1	6.9	6.7	4.9	5.7	5.7	7.1	9.4	10.1	8.1	2
West	9.2	9.7	7.4	7.9	7.2	7.4	5.3	5.0	5.2	7.7	10.8	9.3	8.2	2
West Northwest	7.3	7.8	9.0	8.7	7.9	6.9	3.6	4.5	4.0	5.4	8.2	9.1	7.3	2
Northwest	9.3	9.2	7.7	6.4	7.4	7.6	4.6	5.1	6.4	8.0	8.4	8.8	7.8	2
North Northwest	7.1	9.6	8.7	7.9	7.6	6.9	4.6	5.3	7.8	7.4	8.7	7.4	7.4	2
VISIBILITY														
Mean number of days with fog	3	4	5	6	9	10	12	9	7	6	4	2	77	14

Coast Pilot Marine Weather Statistics (Appendix B)

METEOROLOGICAL TABLE – COASTAL AREA SOUTH OF MARTHA'S VINEYARD, MA Between 40°N to 42°N and 70°W to 72°W													
WEATHER ELEMENTS	**JAN**	**FEB**	**MAR**	**APR**	**MAY**	**JUN**	**JUL**	**AUG**	**SEP**	**OCT**	**NOV**	**DEC**	**ANNUAL**
Wind > 33 knots [1]	5.9	5.0	3.8	1.9	0.9	0.3	0.1	0.3	1.2	2.3	4.0	5.8	2.4
Wave Height > 9 feet [1]	10.8	12.4	8.5	5.6	2.1	1.0	0.5	0.8	2.6	3.3	5.4	6.6	4.9
Visibility < 2 nautical miles [1]	6.6	7.2	9.9	11.6	17.2	19.0	19.6	10.9	7.5	4.6	4.2	4.9	10.7
Precipitation [1]	12.4	12.2	9.4	8.6	7.2	4.5	4.0	4.8	6.2	5.8	9.3	12.3	7.8
Temperature > 69° F	0.1	0.1	0.0	0.0	0.4	6.3	42.6	51.6	18.5	1.8	0.2	0.2	11.1
Mean Temperature (°F)	37.5	36.3	40.0	45.2	52.5	62.1	69.5	70.5	65.6	58.1	49.6	41.9	53.3
Temperature < 33° F [1]	27.0	29.8	11.1	0.6	0.1	0.0	0.0	0.0	0.0	0.1	1.7	12.5	6.1
Mean RH (%)	80	80	81	82	84	86	85	84	82	78	78	77	82
Overcast or Obscured [1]	40.1	37.9	36.0	35.4	34.9	31.2	31.6	25.9	27.8	24.4	32.1	37.3	32.7
Mean Cloud Cover (8ths)	5.4	5.2	4.8	4.6	4.8	4.6	4.8	4.3	4.4	4.2	5.0	5.4	4.8
Mean SLP (mbs)	1016	1017	1016	1016	1016	1015	1016	1017	1018	1018	1017	1018	1016
Ext. Max. SLP (mbs)	1050	1049	1050	1040	1040	1038	1042	1046	1046	1044	1046	1050	1050
Ext. Min. SLP (mbs)	962	958	975	975	976	985	987	987	982	982	973	981	958
Prevailing Wind Direction	NW	NW	W	W	SW	SW	SW	SW	SW	W	W	NW	SW
Thunder and Lightning [1]	0.2	0.2	0.2	0.3	0.5	0.6	1.1	0.8	0.4	0.4	0.2	0.2	0.5

[1] Percentage Frequency

These data are based upon observations made by ships in transit. These ships tend to avoid bad weather when possible thus biasing the data toward good weather samples.

ANSWERS

CHAPTER 1 – THE ROLE OF NAVIGATION

1-1. (A) Determining a best guess for your position based on continuing measurement of Course, Distance and Time.

1-2. (B) By reference to nearby landmarks and buoys.

1-3. (B) "The Rules do not apply to kayaks, rowboats or jet skis." is a false statement.

1-4. (D) Magnetic bearing, if the value is referenced to Magnetic North.

1-5. (B) The Navigation Rules.

1-6. (C) A fix.

1-7. 6,000 ft [exact is 1852 m, which is also exactly 1852 × (100/2.54) × (1/12), which is 6076.12... ft].

1-8. (D) Good seamanship calls for us to be prepared to navigate in any condition.

1-9. (C) There is no single definition; it depends on the circumstances.

1-10. We traveled 20 miles according to our vessel's odometer, which I wrote into the book we use for keeping records of our voyage.

1-11. You can buy an instrument that tells you where you are, but you cannot buy one that tells you the safest and most efficient way to get to where you want to go.

1-12. (B) For safe navigation I need nautical charts and at least 3 books (Coast Pilot, Navigation Rules, then at least either: Chart No. 1, Tides, Currents, Light List, depending on the route.)

1-13. One example is rounding an island with near shore dangers. We set a radar range ring around our vessel that we watch on the screen compared to the shoreline, and not let it touch as we proceed, which guarantees we are that far off. We know we are safe, but we do not know where we are. Or use a maximum or minimum compass danger bearing to be certain you do not enter into dangerous waters. Or just watch the depth sounder (corrected for tide and draft) to be sure you stay in water deep enough to pass known hazards. There are many more such instances. We do not care if the GPS is right or wrong, we know we are safe.

1.14. (A) Red. (B) Green.

1-15. boy.

CHAPTER 2 – NAUTICAL CHARTS AND CHART READING

2-1. (A) 7th Edition, May 28/62; Revised May 5/90. [*This chart is frozen at this issue for training purposes.*] (B) Vineyard to Block Island including Western Approach to Cape Cod Canal (C) Mercator (D) 1:80,000 at Lat 41° 27' (E) Feet (F) MLW, Mean Low Water [*This region now uses MLLW.*] (G) MHW [*This remains the same.*] (H) 41° 09.0'N to 41° 45.0'N and 70° 36.0'W to 71° 35.0'W. (I) 36' Lat = 36.00 nmi, Lon 59' = 44.22 nmi [*Measure it or use 59 × cos (41.45). 41.45° is the mid latitude of the chart.*] (J). This note explains the three sets of colored lines on the chart, which are the LORAN time lines no longer used for navigation. This electronic nav system has been replaced by GPS so we do not see these lines on modern charts. (K) 13218.

2-2. Torpedo range.

2-3. No. It refers us to the applicable section of Chapter 2, Coast Pilot 2.

2-4. Block Island.

2-5. Sow and Pigs Reef.

2-6. Middle Ground.

2-7. Quicksand Point.

2-8. WADK.

2-9. 90 feet below chart datum.

2-10. Because this chart refers the user to another chart: Use Large Scale Charts (See Index Diagram).

2-11. 1985.

2-12. ½ degree (30 arc minutes).

2-13. An increase of 3' per year at each compass rose. Note that in spite of the wording of this question, this annual number is an observed trend, not a forecast. It is impossible to forecast any changes in the location of magnetic north.

2-14. Cleveland Ledge Channel.

2-15. Hog Island Channel.

2-16. Schuyler Ledge.

2-17. Elisha Ledge.

12-8. COLREGS, Demarcation Line.

2-19. Inside the line Inland Rules apply; outside the line International Rules apply.

2-20. A monument.

2-21. Designated anchorages, intended to keep the main channel clear of anchored vessels.

2-22. Note C states the project depth is 30 feet, and refers the user to local charts.

2-23. It refers to the channels shown by broken lines and warns of possible shoaling, especially at the edges.

2-24. We find five.

2-25. Penikese Island.

2-26. Chappaquiot Point.

2-27. A traffic light.

2-28. RACON.

2-29. Bell, gong, and whistle are on buoys, usually wave activated in all visibility, and have no standard characteristic Bells have one tone, gongs have multiple tones. Horns are usually on fixed structures, only heard in the fog, or can be triggered by keying a VHF radio. Horns have a charted characteristic sound pattern. Whistles have been described as a moaning sound, as compressed air is forced into bell chamber that fades in and out.

2-30. Parts of an early version of Chart No.1. [*Though most of what is shown remains valid, this booklet has been updated several times since then.*]

2-31. Two major changes are: (A) the soundings datum is now Mean Lower Low Water, and (B) today there are Traffic Lanes for Narragansett Bay and Buzzards Bay. Lesser distinctions are LORAN lines are gone, the variation is now different, and the new chart does not reach as far north.

2-32. 4 miles.

2-33. 8 miles.

2-34. LARGER. The 1:10,000 harbor chart is a large scale chart. A specific island would appear larger on a large scale chart than on a small scale chart.

2-35. Large scale charts would be better.

2-36. A raster chart.

2-37. (1) RNC are raster files (graphic images); ENC are vector files (they compute the chart data on display). (2) RNC are true replications of what the corresponding paper chart shows, ENC are mathematical approximations to the key data shown on the paper chart. (3) RNC file sizes are typically much larger than corresponding ENC (though there can be exceptions if the ENC brings with it a great deal of metadata). (4) The RNC are by definition correct charts (ie they are identical copies), whereas the ENC can include data which do not agree with the printed chart, sometimes as an improvement, more often as simple errors, or invalid approximations. (5) Almost all free and commercial echart viewers will display the RNC, although only a few display both RNC and ENC. (6) RNC display options are very uniform from one viewer to the next, whereas typical viewer options for ENC (other than ECDIS sanctioned viewers) have different options and even conventions, though must do try to emulate the ECDIS standards. (7) Navigators accustomed to using paper charts adapt easily to using the RNC, whereas the ENC look quite different and take getting used to.

2-38. (C) Local Notice to Mariners

2-39. Hard sand.

2-40. 61 feet.

2-41. Rocky.

2-42. Soft.

2-43. Mud.

2-44. Spire.

2-45. 30 feet.

2-46. The rotating white and green beacon indicating an airport. (Trivia: if the light flashes white-green-green it is a civilian airport; if it flashes white-green it is a military airport. If an airport beacon operates between sunrise and sunset it indicates that the airport is under Instrument Meteorological Conditions visibility less than 3 miles and/or ceiling less than 1,000 ft—and IFR rules apply to aircraft.)

2-47. It indicates that the area was swept by a wire drag confirming that the depth is at least 35 feet relative to chart datum.

2-48. A white light, Interrupted Quick Flashing

2-49. It is a bifurcation mark (a junction buoy) also called a preferred channel marker, which indicates the navigator is faced with a choice of routes. If the navigator wishes to take the preferred route, then he/she imagines the color of the buoy to be entirely the top color; if the alternate, or secondary, route is desired, then he or she imagines the buoy to be entirely the second color. In this situation, the mark has red as its top color; therefore, the rule being Red Right Return, the route defined as the preferred route leads into Buzzards Bay, while the alternate route leads into Vineyard Sound.

2-50. It is an intertidal area, which means it covers and uncovers.

2-51. (A) A rock awash ("asterisk rock"), which covers and and uncovers with the tide height. Its drying height at 0 tide level may or may not be given. (B) A submerged rock ("plus sign rock"), covered at zero tide height. Its depth may or may not be given.

2-52. An especially dangerous rock ("plus sign 4 dots rock"), that is at or just below the surface at 0 tide height. Every type of vessel of any draft can hit this rock.

2-53. Probably a steep cliff.

2-54. (A) 41° 37.4' N, 70° 55.0' W. (B) 41° 31.5' N, 70° 39.7' W. (C) 41° 31.8' N, 71° 24.3' W. (D) 41° 29.8' N, 71° 16.6' W. (E) 41° 27.2' N, 71° 12.2' W. (F) 41° 25.6' N, 70° 52.6' W. (G) 41° 23.3' N, 71° 20.3' W. (H) 41° 20.2' N, 70° 55.0' W.

2-55. (A) 0.75 nmi. (B) 5.9 nmi. (C) 8.1 nmi. (D) 9.0 nmi. (E) 11.3 nmi. (F) 23.0 nmi.

2-56. (A) 233 M (B) 347 M (C) 015 M (D) 043 M (E) 247 M (F) 313 M. *Working the problems the wrong way, finding reciprocal courses is a common mistake.*

2-57. (A) Red and White buoy, with the letters NA painted on it, and a white light flashing the Morse code for the letter A (dit-dah, 'short long'), and with a whistle. (B) Buoy with flashing green light, period 4 seconds, with a bell. (C) Green buoy, with numbers 31 painted on it, green light flashes on every 4 seconds, with a gong. (D) Red light always on (fixed), 25 ft above MHW, with an 8 painted on it. (E) Flashing light (usually white when not specified) 4 seconds period, 30 ft above MHW, nominal range of 8 nautical miles, with a 2 pained on the structure. (F) WHISTLE is now noted WHIS and sec (seconds) is now just plain s.

2-58. Port.

2-59. (B) Is usually sequential, but may occasionally be missing numbers of the sequence.

2-60. The lower is the nearer set.

2-61. We must look over our shoulder and follow their alignment outbound.

2-62. Either side, as it is a safe water buoy; also called a mid-channel marker.

2-63. Prohibited area.

2-64. MHW, Mean High Water.

2-65. (A) Course (B) Heading (C) Range and Bearing (D) Course Over Ground (E) Course Made Good (F) Track

2-66. (A) Direction you want to go, (B) Direction the boat is pointed toward, (C) Direction to a landmark or other vessel, (D) the instantaneous value of your CMG read from the GPS, (E) Direction from one position to a later position, regardless of the track between them, (F) The record or trail of your past positions.

2-67. An isolated danger.

2-68. (A) Navigable water to their named side.

2-69. (C) Navigable water to the west.

2-70. (A) Navigable water to the south.

2-71. The brightness of a navigation light expressed as clear-weather visible range in nautical miles. Clear is defined as visibility of 10 nmi.

CHAPTER 3 – OTHER NAVIGATION AIDS

In these answers CP23 refers to paragraph 23 of the Coast Pilot excerpt, and LL#15774 refers to aid no. 15774 in the Light List, and LNM p.6 is page 6 of the Local Notice to Mariners excerpt of the Resources.

3-1. (CP31, CP51, and CP57) (D) All of the above.

3-2. (CP27) (C) The islands stretching from Nonamesset to Cuttyhunk.

3-3. (CP Appendix B) (A) July, 12 days, bottom line of table. (B) 1019.6 mb, top line. (C) SW, 52.6%. (D) Nov., 80.7% of observations were calm. (E) About 0.17 mi west of Gould Island, which is 2.8 mi N-NW of Newport. These data must be an average of locations with archived data, and they use "Newport" as a well recognized name somewhere in the region. Other cities or towns are closer. Message, it always pays to check the location of places we have data for. This is especially important for current data since they round the Lat-Lon to the nearest mile, thus having reference stations sometimes on land. This is not the issue here since the Lat-Lon they give is much more than a mile away from Newport.

3-4. (B) Radar, together with an operator who has been trained to use it properly.

3-5. (CP Appendix B) (A) 0.124 × 28 = 3.5 days per average February with waves > 9 ft. (B) Calling "fog" < 2-mi visibility we get 0.196 × 28 = 5.5 days in coastal waters, whereas inland (Newport) they say fog for July is 12 days on average. There must be more radiation fog spilling down onto the inland waters to account for this difference. Also "fog" can include incidents of over 2 mile visibility. In any event, fog appears more likely inland than offshore. (C) These are underestimates. See Table footnote explaining observations made from vessels are biased in that bad weather is avoided. (D) 1016.0 mb. This is notably less than the 1019.6 listed for the inland waters just north of there. It could be that the average reported for mariners in the Coast Pilot in the Climate table is actually an average from airports, all on land, which would tend to have a higher pressure in the winter than over water, but even this effect seems not enough to account for this reported difference. The 1016 mb agrees with the Navy Climatic Atlas. (E) The table is called "Coastal Area *South of* Martha's Vineyard" and they give the Latitude range of the table 40 N to 42 N, whereas the southern boundary of Martha's Vineyard is about 41° 20' N.

3-6. (CP27) Quicks Hole.

3-7. (CP29) The Woods Hole Oceanographic Institution, and the buildings of the National Marine Fisheries Service and the Marine Biological Laboratory.

3-8. (CP30) The northerly entrance from Great Harbor into The Strait is preferred over Broadway - with its sharp turn - which is difficult in strong currents, especially for low-powered vessels and vessels under sail.

3-9. (CP31) Tidal currents are so strong that the passage is difficult and dangerous without some local knowledge, and buoys in the narrowest part of the channel sometimes are towed under. A stranger should attempt passage only at slack water.

3-10. (CP33) South to north, from Vineyard Sound to Buzzards Bay.

3-11. (CP58) The buoys at this entrance are often dragged off station by strong currents and heavy seas. The channel should never be used during a heavy ground swell. With southerly winds, heavy seas will break across the entrance.

3-12. (CP69) Vessels of up to 25 ft draft may anchor in New Bedford's Inner Harbor.

3-13. (LL#15690) Shows red from 342.25 to 343.25, white from 343.25 to 344.75, green from 344.75 to 345.75.

3-14. (LL#15555) The buoy could be affected by ice. When there is a risk of that happening, the lighted buoy is replaced by a simple unlighted can. Our guess is that the unlighted can is far less expensive to risk to ice than the lighted buoy.

3-15. (LL#15560) White and Red. White's nominal range is 13 miles, red's nominal range is 11 miles.

3-16. (LL#15560) 2 blasts every 30 seconds (2s blast – 2s silence – 2s blast – 24s silence).

3-17. (LL#15610) White 24 miles, red 20 miles.

3-18. (LL#15610) Alternating white and red, 0.2 sec white flash, 7.3 sec eclipse, 0.2 sec red flash, 7.3 sec eclipse.

3-19. (LL#15774) White and blue.

3-20. (LL#15985) Flashing white 2.5 sec.

3-21. (LL#15985) 67 feet.

3-22. (LL#15985) 17 miles.

3-23. (LL#15985) 2 blasts every 30 seconds.

3-24. (LL#15985) Radio beacons have been decommissioned. Today this light is equipped with RACON, transmitting Morse code B, (dah-dit-dit-dit; or long, short, short, short).

3-25. (LL#16050) The replacement is a LIB Searching a Light List glossary reveals that a LIB is a Lighted Ice Buoy.

3-26. (LL#16085 and #16090) A range light KRW indicates a rectangular red dayboard bearing a central white stripe.

3-27. (LL#16853) 25 feet.

3-28. (LL#16817) The Phinney Rock Lighted Buoy DP is now on station. It has black and red bands with two spherical topmarks, with DP painted on it, and a double flash white light that flashes every 5 seconds.

3-29. (LL#15855) A sign referred to as NR, which indicates a diamond-shaped white dayboard with an orange reflective border and black letters describing the information or regulatory nature of the mark.

3-30. (LL#15855) A radar reflector.

3-31. (LL#15947) White with blue band.

3-32. You have "bobbed the light," so must be near the geographic range, since this is a very bright light with nominal range of 22M. ie sqrt(101) + sqrt(15) = 13.9 nmi (visible) compared to sqrt(101) + sqrt(6) = 12.8 nmi (not visible). You must be about 13±1 nmi off the light.

3-33. (A) about 16 nmi (recall this is a log scale). (B) about 4 nmi. and (C) about 1.5 nmi. The quick estimates give: 15.3, 3.6, and 1.0, which shows they are pretty good since we rarely know the visibility very accurately.

3-34. Luminous range = (5.5/10) × 16 + 1 = 9.8 nmi. Geographic range = sort (65) + sqrt(10) = 8.1 + 3.1 = 11.2 mmi, so this light shines out into the fog for a distance of 9.8 mmi and the light is over the horizon from the cabin top at 11 miles off, so it will come into view somewhere about 10 miles off. These are all about ±10% computations.

3-35. (A) Nominal range is 8 mi. Height is 52 ft, so geographic range is sqrt(52) +sqrt(9) = 7.2 + 3 = 10.2. So in clear weather the light is over the horizon at 10.2 miles off, but it only shines out 8 miles, so it would first be seen about 8 miles off (regardless of eye height). (B) in 3 miles visibility, the 8 miles nominal range is reduced to about (3/10) × 8 + 1 = 3.4 mmi. Again it is the brightness of the light that determines its range.

3-36. The elevation of Nomans Land is not charted, but the Coast Pilot tells us it rises to about 100 ft. The geographic range is then sqrt(100) + sqrt(9) = 10+3 = 13 nmi. This is when the tip of the land is right on the horizon, so unlighted you would have to get rather closer, maybe about 10 mi off. At 10 miles off the land is above the horizon by an angle of arctan(100/60000) = 0.095° = 5.7'. This is a very small angle, but definitely visible in clear skies. You would likely see this by eye in clear weather before you could pick it up on radar. (B) This is almost a trick question, i.e. if the visible range of the land is 4 miles how far can you see it (assuming it is above the horizon)? Answer 4 miles. This is the definition of visibility.

3-37. Using our estimate of luminous range: (5/10) × 5 + 1 = 3.5 nmi.

3-38. (A) One approach to this is to just skim through the Light List and look at a lot of buoys to see what they average. Typical values are 4 to 6 nmi, with a few at 3 and 7. Thus we can call 5 nmi an average buoy nominal range. (B) Heights of buoys vary quite a bit, but 12 ft might be an average for the typical lighted buoy. So from an eye height of 9 ft we have a geographic range of about sqrt(9) +sqrt(12) = 6.5 or so, which shows that it is the light brightness that is usually the limit, which would be about 5 miles. In practice this would likely take binoculars to spot them on this limit on a clear night.

3-39. This is another example of bobbing a light, which works remarkably well for bright lights that are not very high. It means we are located very near the geographic range of the light. In this case sqrt(27) + sqrt(12) = 8.7 nmi visible, but sqrt(27) +sqrt(7) = 7.8 not visible. We are about 8 miles off with this light is shining out very brightly to 19 miles just over our head.

3-40. Woods Hole chart is number 13235.

3-41. (LL#16055) (A) 41° 30.8' N, 70° 50.1' W (B) 41° 30.55' N, 70° 49.9' W (C) About a quarter of a mile.

3-42. International.

3-43. (CP15) The Traffic Separation Scheme is not buoyed.

3-44. (LNM p2) Avoid the area or transit at 10 knots or less.

3-45. (LNM p2) (B) Immediately upon arrival into the United States.

3-46. (LNM p3) None; the sound signal is inoperative.

3-47. (LNM p3) None; the light is extinguished.

3-48. (LNM p4) A minimum separation of 0.5 nmi.

3-49. (LNM p4) The buoy no longer exists; it has been removed from the Light List.

3-50. (LNM p5) Samples of things to check for safe nav prep: (1) charts, (2) crucial pubs, (3) manuals of all nav instruments, (4) spare light bulbs, (5) waypoints entered into handheld GPS as back up, (6) printed course plan, (7) check of all radios, (8) teach others to use the radios, (9) good binoculars, (10) radio schedule of weather broadcasts, (11) some equivalent of Marine Weather Services Charts... amongst others.

3-51. (CP 77) 4 ft.

3-52. Navigation Rules, Tide Tables, Current Tables, Coast Pilot, and Light List.

3-53. It depends on the light. Check the *Light List*. Those on 24 hours are described as: "Lighted throughout 24 hours." Check an example Nobska Point Light, whereas a comparable light at Gay Head is not on all the time.

CHAPTER 4 – COMPASS USE

4-1. (A) The correcting direction is C to M using deviation or M to T using variation. If deviation is east, then it is added to C to get M, If variation is east, then it is added to M to get T. The rule is meant to remind us that if the correction is west, we subtract it when correcting. (B) Can Dead Men Vote Twice (at elections, for add east correcting), or going the other way: TV makes dull companion (add whiskey, for add west uncorrecting.)

4-2.

	A	B
T	330	330
V	15 W	15 W
M	345	345
D	0	4 E
C	345	341

4-3. The inner ring is magnetic bearing marked off in compass points, 11.25° = 1 point. This bearing system and feature of nautical charts is rarely, if ever, used these days.

4-4. This natural range is 113 T = 128 M, so 125 C means a deviation of 3° E.

4-5. (A) deviation = 0°. (B) You can say nothing at all. It might be zero as well, but could be 5 or 10° E or W. Deviation has to be measured on all headings. You might say, "It is probably zero because I just had the compass adjusted last week and it was zero on all headings," but even that could be wrong if one of the adjustment magnets fell out, which is a not unheard of Murphy's-Law possibility.

4-6.

#	Comp	Dev	Mag	Var	True
1	296	**0°**	**296**	16° W	280
2	**009**	5° E	014	21° E	**035**
3	354	8° W	**346**	**21° E**	007
4	276	**0°**	276	10° W	**266**
5	**098**	5° W	093	**21° E**	114
6	138	**4° W**	**134**	4° E	138
7	**006**	0°	006	21° W	**345**
8	028	0°	**028**	21° E	049
9	351	**4° E**	355	17° E	**012**

4-7. (A) Yes. (B) Approx 66 ft. (C) 41° 12.9' N, 70° 47.9' W. (D) C 039 M, 3.0 nmi.

4-8. (A) 41° 24.4' N, 71° 05.8' W. (B) 70 feet. (C) 2.9 nmi, 118 M.

4-9. 41° 30.4' N, 70° 55.5' W.

4-10. Distance is 16 nmi., so halfway bearing is 025 M.

4-11. (A) The sun is setting 245 T, or 25 degrees left of due west; must be winter if the sun is setting south. During fall and winter sunrise and sunset are south; spring and summer they are north.

4-12. (A) 41° 21.2' N, 70° 58.2' W. (B) 85 ft. (C) First, the 155 M course you are maintaining is not a LOP; And second, while the radar range is very accurate, a radar bearing is subject to error due to equipment alignment and inaccuracy due to beam width. Nevertheless, we can call this a radar bearing/range fix.

4-13. (A) 41° 21.0' N, 70° 54.4' W. (B) 035 R.

4-14. Something magnetic may have been placed near the binnacle compass. It turns out a crewmember has placed the handheld VHF radio in the drink holder at the helm.

4-15. (A) Var 15° 15' W increasing at 3' year. In 2014, 29 years × 3' = 87' = +1° 27' or Var = 16° 42'. (B) Latest chart shows 2013 value of 14° 45' W, decreasing at 3' year, so our prediction would be 2° wrong. (C) The message is that the rate of change is an observed trend, not a forecast. No one has any idea where magnetic north will be next year, or even tomorrow. Such change trends can be much larger at higher latitudes.

4-16. (A) Interpolated deviation values are shown in Deviation Table 2 Answers.

Deviation Table 2 Answers		
Compass	Deviation	Magnetic
000°	10.5° E	010.5
015°	13.7° E	028.7
030°	16.8° E	046.8
045°	20.0° E	065.0
060°	17.2° E	077.2
075°	14.3° E	089.3
090°	11.5° E	101.5
105°	7.3° E	112.3
120°	3.0° E	123.0
135°	1.2° W	133.8
150°	2.6° E	152.6
165°	4.1° E	169.1
180°	5.5° W	174.5
195°	6.3° W	188.7
210°	7.2° W	202.8
225°	8.0° W	217.0
240°	9.5° W	230.5
255°	11.0° W	244.0
270°	12.5° W	257.5
285°	10.6° W	274.4
300°	8.7° W	291.3
315°	6.8° W	308.2
330°	1.0° W	329.0
345°	4.7° E	349.7

4-16 (B) and (C)							
T	340	032	152	319	000	296	259
V	15W	15W	15W	15W	15W	15W	15W
M	355	047	167	334	015	311	274
D	6.2E	16.8E	3.9E	0.9E	17.2E	6.0W	10.6W
C	349	030	163	335	032	317	285

(D) We guess steel because the deviations on opposite headings are not equal and opposite, which imply a more complex disturbance to the magnetic field common on steels vessels.

CHAPTER 5 – DEAD RECKONING

5-1. (A) 3.33h (B) 12.9h (C) 2.3h (D) 0.63h (E) 1.08h (F) 2hr 27m (G) 12h 47.4m (H) 2h 5.4m (I) 0h 22.8m (J) 1h 43.8m (K) 12h 12m (L) 18h 40m (M) 0307 tomorrow (N) 1342 today (O) 1453 yesterday (P) 0507 tomorrow

5-2. (A) 8.3 kts (B) 24 + 10.4 = 34.4h enroute at 5 kts = 172 nmi.

5-3. 15 kts / 24h = 0.625 kts.

5-4. (37 × 60) / 4 = 555m = 9h 15m.

5-5. (A) 22.0 hr, (B) 24h 9m.

5-6. 55 / 9 = 6.11 kts.

5-7. 3h 40m = 220m; (12 × 60) / 220 = 3.27 kts.

5-8. 4.14 kts.

5-9. (A) 8.57m = 8m 34 sec (B) 1.32 kts error (C) Indicated speed is 23% higher than actual. Actual is 19% lower than indicated. (D) 3.24 kts

5-10. (A) 5.25 kts (B) If 1 sec fast, then speed = 7 kts; if 1 sec slow, then speed = 4.2 kts.

5-11. Time = 3h 38m.

5-12. Total tacking distance = 18 × 1.5 = 27 nmi; at 6 kts = TTE 4h 30m.

5-13. Upwind leg total tacking distance = 4 × 1.5 = 6 nmi; at 6 kts = 1h enroute; plus 8 nmi at 6 kts = 1h 20m. TTG is 2h 20m.

5-14. (A) D 12.3, C 241 M, 1h 54m, (B) D 7.8, C 291 M, 1h 34m, (C) D 15.6, C 075 M, 2h 10m, (D) D 3.1, C 103 M, 0h 39m, (E) 1801.

5-15. (A) 28.4, 298 T, (B) 4h 03m, (C) Stbd tack 25.0 + port tack 13.4 = total distance 38.4 nmi. Time = 5h 32m. Using shortcut: 1.5 × 28.4 = 42.6 (or 6h 05m), which is mathematically (42.6/38.4) about 11% over estimate, however in practice this will always be an underestimate, i.e. the factor of 1.5 is a good practical estimate. (D) Three tacks. Legs are 10.7 + 11.4 + 14.3 + 2.0 = Total distance 38.4 nmi. This distance is exactly the same as with minimal tacks; therefore the time would be identical. (E) The new wind lifts us to the mark, so the sooner we get into it the better. The layline to the mark once we get to pure northerlies crosses 71° 10'W at about 41° 15' N, so we would not waste time on a port tack, but take the lifting starboard tack to the west which would gradually lift us to the point where we would be on a tight reach to the mark by the time we hit the northerlies. In short, we get there on one starboard tack with speed increasing. Assuming we just make 7 kts the whole way at hull speed (ie do not gain much when falling off), we would sail about 8 west, get lifted to the layline over the next 8 or so miles, then reach 14 to the mark, for a total of roughly 30 miles. (F) Neglecting the wind forecast and staying on wrong tack the most time, we might sail west 1 mile to clear the island, then north 11 then west for 13.5 or so and then a final reach of about 10 miles in the new wind, for a total of 34.5. In practice it might be worse if we ignored the fact we were getting lifted as we did proceed west.

In summary, steady NW wind we had 38.4 miles, taking advantage of the wind we got this down to 30 miles, and not taking full advantage it was about 34.5 nmi. The time lost with poor tactics would be about 4.5/7 = about 36 min.

5-16. One approach: choose a minimum speed with good steerage, say 3 kts. Compute how far you would go in 10 minutes at 3 kts: d = 3 × 10/60 = 0.5 nmi; then consider this the circumference of the circle, and since c = pi × diameter, we get a circle diameter of 0.5/pi = 0.16 nmi = 0.16 × 6000 = 960 ft = 320 yd. So you would have to be some 400 yards into safe water in all directions to make the turn.

To execute something like this, we might divide 360 by 15 to get 24 steps around the compass, 000, 015, 030, 045, etc, and then say that we are going to hold each course for 10 min/24 = 0.417 min = 25 seconds. Then watching a stop watch, head off at 000 for 25 seconds, turn to 015 for 25 seconds, etc and you should trace out a circle of about 320 yards diameter, probably a bit larger, in about 10 minutes, maybe longer.

5-17. (A) C 204 M. (B) 5126.2. (C) 5137.0. (D) Bearing 098 M. (E) Course 288 M. (F) 5153.0.

5-18. Leg 1 is 26 minutes at 7 kts = 3 nmi, Leg 2 is 45m at 4.0 kts = 3.0 nmi. (A) Return course is 053 M. (B) ETA is 1146.

5-19. (A) 41° 25.1' N, 71° 09.1' W' (B) 2.2 nmi (C) 148 M (D) Set is 133 T, drift 0.6 kts. (E) No. For this to be the true current, even assuming that there were no other sources of error in the DR, it is unlikely the current was constant in speed and direction for 3 hours in this region. Looking at the shape of the coastline along this course, it is unlikely that this is true in this case. The current north and south of Martha's Vineyard is driven by a significant flow north of Long Island, but the current nearer the coast of Massachusetts and Rhode Island is considerably sheltered from the main flow. The effects of the real current in this exercise are cumulative, the final result from averaging the current speed and direction during the overall trip. This type of DR offset is often referred to as an "error current." (F) No, the recorded speeds are roughly and consistently about 4% higher than the corresponding SMGs. (ie 38m for 3.8 mi = 6.0; 34m for 3.7 mi = 6.5, 87m for 10.1 mi = 7.0 and 56m for 7.0 mil = 7.5). Normally the log and knotmeter have the same calibration, so if one is off the other is off by the same amount and we would not see any difference here. So either there is an offset in the knotmeter readout somehow, or we are simply overestimating the averages we recorded. We can't really blame the timekeeping, since the intervals are much different, but the offset is near constant. What we learn is we must when we can, get to a measured mile in light air and still water and study this more, and of course check the manual to see if this unit does have separate calibrations for log and knotmeter.

CHAPTER 6 – PILOTING

6-1. (A) 41° 28.6' N, 70° 52.6' W. (B) 41° 29.3' N, 70° 51.8' W. (C) This is a 0.6 nmi error.

6-2. (A) A fix. (B) 41° 23.3' N, 70° 50.6' W.

Exercise 8-53 Answers							
Current Tables		Table 3				50-90 Rule	
EST	Speed	Intervals	Cycle	Factor	Current	Current	Factor
0443	0.0				0.0	0.0	
0543		1h 00m	3h 34m	0.45	1.0	1.2	0.5
0630		1h 47m	3h 34m	0.75	1.7	1.6	0.7
0717		2h 34m	3h 34m	0.9	2.1	2.1	0.9
0817	2.3				2.3	2.3	
0917		2h 14m	3h 14m	0.9	2.1	2.1	0.9
0954		1h 37m	3h 14m	0.72	1.7	1.6	0.7
1031		1h 00m	3h 14m	0.6	1.4		0.5
1131	0.0				0.0	0.0	
1231		1h 41m	2h 41m	0.8	-1.4	-1.5	0.9
1251		1h 21m	2h 41m	0.7	-1.2	-1.2	0.7
1312		1h 00m	2h 41m	0.6	-1.0	-0.9	0.5
1412	-1.7				-1.7	-1.7	

6-3. A measurement on the navigation chart shows the west edges of the two islands form a range at 192 M at the same moment the helm compass indicated 180. Therefore, we conclude that your magnetic course was 192 M when your compass course was 180 C. Using the mnemonic "TVMDC add West" shows the 12° difference must be subtracted, and thus the deviation on a southerly heading 12° East.

6-4. (A) 41° 15.1' N, 71° 26.1' W; (B) Although the problem stated magnetic course 305, how accurately can this truly be known at the helm? Then there are a number of potential radar inaccuracies depending on how well aligned the radar is on your vessel, and there is an inaccuracy introduced because of the beam width of the radar. Lastly, just how precise can bearings taken with a hand bearing compass be?

6-5. (A) 41° 21.4' N, 71° 08.9' W. (B) Most westerly 'fix' 41° 20.2' N, 71° 17.1' W. (C) Most easterly 'fix' 41° 21.3' N, 71° 06.9' W. (D) The distance from most westerly to most easterly possible 'fix' is 6.28 nmi, hardly a precise solution. (E) First, that some hand bearing compasses do not allow precision measurement; it's also a good lesson to take bearing fixes, if using just two, at about 90° apart.

6-6. Your actual location in presumed safe water is 41° 20.0' N, 70° 52.5' W. With 1.9 miles to go at 8 knots, you will be wrecked on the charted rocks in less than 14 minutes.

6-7. (A) The 60 ft contour line offers safe water and a fairly steady track to the entrance. (B) If the sea is calm, the gong would not sound, as it is wave motion that activates the clappers. In wind, it might not be audible. (C) As you near the Passage entrance the sea bed smooths somewhat, so following a particular sounding will become less sure. And as the shore just NW of Beavertail Point nears, a very careful watch must be maintained.

6-8. 2 fathom = 12 feet, so depth at that location at low water would be 14 feet.

6-9. (A) 41° 13.7' N, 71° 33.2' W, about a half mile NE of Grove Point, Block Island. (B) On the rocks. (C) In about 6 minutes, or about 1412. (D) A close fit of the depth profile is fairly accurate; but for sure, if the depth continues to shoal to 30 feet, it is doubtless time to turn east toward safe water and come up with an alternate navigation strategy.

6-10. (A) No MORE than (B) 130 M.

6-11. About 9 miles. (6° is 10% = 4.5 nmi × 2 = 9 nmi).

6-12. The terminology 'from a DR position' in this context means simply that you don't know exactly where you are, but you have an approximate location only. And as this problem gives you only a single landmark, it must be a running fix problem. Plot the first bearing to the spire, then plot a 284° course line intersecting somewhere – literally anywhere - along that first bearing line. Plot the second bearing line. Measure off along the course line the distance run in the time between observations = 1 hour at 5 knots = 5 nmi. Then advance the first bearing line to the distance run. Your position is where the second bearing line intersects the advanced first bearing line. (A) 41° 16.8' N, 70° 46.4' W. (B) This is indeed a fix, an Rfix, at 1845.

6-13. (A) 42°. (B) 338° M. (C) Distance off the light = distance run when the angle has doubled = 1.7 nmi.

6-14. (A) 41° 24.2' N, 71° 21.9' W. (B) You could do a running fix as the questions states; on the other hand, you know that you are 1.7 nmi from the Brenton Reef Light when it bears 338 M. It's that simple.

6-15. (A) 205 M. (B) 2.8 nmi. (C) 41° 23.3' N, 70° 53.4' W. (D) Sow and Pigs Reef.

6-16. Per the Light List the height of Buzzards Bay light is now 67 feet. Distance off = target height in feet / (100 × Target Angle in degrees) = 67 / (100 × 1.25°) = 67 / 125 = .54 nmi.

6-17. Gay Head light as charted is 170 feet high. The angle 2° 45' converts to 2.75 decimal degrees; therefore 170 / (100 × 2.75) = 170 / 275 = 0.62 nmi.

6-18. (A) 347 M. (B) 2.0 nmi. (C) 41° 23.8' N, 70° 51.3' W.

6-19. 41° 11.3' N, 70° 47.9' W.

6-20. 41° 22.9' N, 70° 53.6' W.

6-21. Your 1532 RFix is 41° 23.6' N, 71° 22.2' W.

6-22. (A) 41° 22.1' N, 71° 00.2' W. (B) 41° 22.6' N, 71° 00.7' N.

6-23. 41° 22.4' N, 71° 00.5' W.

6-24. (A) 41° 32.0' N, 70° 53.6' W. (B) 1.2 nmi.

6-25. 41° 21.3' N, 71° 26.6' W.

6-26. 41° 20.4' N, 70° 56.9' W.

CHAPTER 7 – ELECTRONIC NAVIGATION

7-1. (A) You run into Sow and Pigs Reef. (B) First of all, do not use automatic waypoint advance. In most cases this is more dangerous than helpful. The waypoints are the very places where the navigator should touch base with the navigation. Secondly, add real observations to each leg of the route that will confirm where you are... bearings to an identifiable mark, etc. Keeping a ships log with entries at each hour and at each major course, speed and weather change would greatly aid situational awareness.

7-2. Set up a route from A to B, then navigate to A, and just watch the cross track error (XTE). This is precisely what you want, namely how far you are to the right or left of the course line. You can simultaneously watch VMG to Waypoint to learn which of the two tacks is favored.

7-3. (B) ± 20 ft

7-4. (C) Wide Area Augmentation System

7-5. (D) You have sailed into a region or moved the instrument in such a way that part of the sky is now blocked from view of its antenna.

7-6. (A) The cigarette lighter socket and wiring. (This question arises from personal experience.)

7-7. In this installation the chartplotter uses GPS-derived COG for its direction reference, not a magnetic-based reference; therefore, the chartplotter's direction will be affected by current.

7-8. (A) 41° 21.7' N, 71° 24.5' W. (B) 41° 24.2' N, 71° 17.6' W. (C) Set 147 T, Drift 0.7 kts.

7-9. 41° 18.9' N, 70° 54.2' W.

7-10. (A) 41° 17.1' N, 71° 25.4' W. (B) 41° 16.8' N, 71° 26.1' W. (C) 0.6 nmi in direction 205° T.

7-11. (B) One range and one bearing is fastest. It can be read directly from the radar screen in seconds.

7-12. (C) Two ranges is most accurate, because the largest uncertainty comes in the calibration of the heading used for bearings. This however is the slowest fix if done by manual plotting, but still relatively fast if solved by ECS.

7-13. You can use an ECS on a home computer to set up and fine tune your desired route taking into account tides and currents on the date of sailing, then print out a route plan to take on the boat. This shows all courses, distances, ETAs at assumed speeds, along with the Lat-Lons of your waypoints which can then be entered into the boat GPS you will use.

7-14. Set up range rings on the vessel icon that match the range rings on the radar display and then you can easily identify the land masses seen on the radar, regardless of your heading.

CHAPTER 8 – TIDES AND CURRENTS

8-1. At 2233 EST the high tide of the day is 3.7 ft.

8-2. Both low tides are the same that day. At 0015 and at 1216 EST the low tides of the day are -0.7 ft.

8-3. At 2039 EDT the tide is 5.0 ft. Did you remember to add one hour to convert from EST to EDT?

8-4. At 0522 the tide is chart datum, 0.0 ft.

8-5. The previous day's 2311 EST tide height of 3.8 ft converts to 0011 EDT. The highest tide this date, 3.8 ft, occurs at 0011.

8-6. You will be aground. Whatever else happens it won't be pretty, especially if there is any wave action in the anchorage.

8-7. Low at 1235 is -0.5 ft, high at 1939 is 5.0 ft; therefore the tide range that afternoon is 5.5 ft. The moon is full.

8-8. 41° 30.3' N, 71° 19.6' W.

Time of Tide Answers for 8-9 through 8-12: The following Table may help keep these kinds of problems sorted out. A little practice will allow you to construct such a Table when needed in your navigation exam. The answer sought by each problem is in BOLD. Did you remember to add 1 hour for answers that should be in Daylight Savings Time?

#	At Reference	High/Low	Time Diff	At Subordinate
8-9	4.8 at 2030	High	+1 15	2145 + 1h for EDT = **2245**
8-10	-0.2 at 0132	Low	-0 16	0116 + 1h for EDT = **0216**
8-11	4.7 at 2140	High	-0 13	2127 + 1h for EDT = **2227**
8-12	0.0 at 1217	Low	-0 13	1204 + 1h for EDT = **1304**

8-13. 1.5 nmi. Cuttyhunk's high and low tides occur more than an hour later than Penikese, most likely because ?

8-14. At 0107 EST the highest tide of the day is 24.6 ft.

8-15. At 0613 EST the lowest tide of the day is -0.3 ft.

8-16. Low at 0828 is 2.6 ft, high at 1438 is 24.6 ft; therefore the tide range is 22.0 ft.

Time of Tide Answers for 8-17 through 8-20: The answer sought by each problem is in BOLD. Did you remember to add 1 hour for answers that should be in Daylight Savings Time?

#	At Reference	High/Low	Time Diff	At Subordinate
8-17	25.6 ft at 0055	High	-0 38	0017 + 1h for EDT = **0117**
8-18	2.3 ft at 1816	Low	-2 07	1609 + 1h for EDT = **1709**
8-19	28.2 ft at 2334	High	+1 06	0040 + 1h for EDT = **0140**
8-20	1.6 ft at 0541	Low	+0 26	0607 + 1h for EDT = **0707**

Height of Tide Answers for 8-21 through 8-26: The answer sought by each problem is in BOLD.

#	At Reference	Height Difference or *Ratio	At Subordinate
8-21	4.0 ft at 2218	*1.20	**4.8 ft**
8-22	-0.4 ft at 0001	*0.97	**-0.39 ft**
8-23	28.2 ft at 0043	-6.5	**21.7 ft**
8-24	0.3 ft at 0504	-0.7	**-0.4 ft**
8-25	27.9 ft at 0024	*1.90	**53.01 ft**
8-26	3.6 ft at 0615	*0.42	**1.5 ft**

8-27. The concern is not the bridge, but rather the power cables that have an authorized clearance of 95 ft.

8-28. Vertical clearances are stated relative to Mean High Water. To find MHW at Anthony Point, add half the Mean Range to the Mean Tide Level. Anthony Point has a Mean Range of 3.75; therefore 3.75 / 2 = 1.875, plus 2.05 Mean Tide Level, indicates that the charted clearance is based on a sea level of 3.925 ft above chart datum. If sea level rises above 3.925 feet, any excess amount subtracts from the charted 65 ft clearance. At 2100 on April 18, the tide level at that location is calculated as Newport's 5.1 ft × the Anthony Point high water ratio *1.09, which gives a tide height of 5.559 ft. The available clearance is thus reduced by the overage amount 5.559 ft - 3.925 ft = 1.634 ft. The clearance is then = 65 ft less 1.634 ft = 63.366 ft. Subtracting the desired 2 ft margin leaves a net clearance of 61.366 ft. So yes, your 61 ft mast complies with the authorized clearance at that date and time. 8-29. Max flood 2.4 kts is at 0634, plus 1h = 0734 EDT.

8-30. Max ebb 1.8 kts is at 0132, plus 1h = 0232 EDT.

8-31. 2154 plus 1h = 2254.

8-32. 0336 plus 1h = 0436 EDT.

8-33. Pollock Rip Channel floods toward 035° T. The Channel ebbs toward 225° T.

Time of Max Velocity Answers for 8-34 through 8-38: The answer sought by each problem is in BOLD. Did you remember to add 1 hour for answers that should be in Daylight Savings Time?

#	At Reference	Flood/Ebb	Time Diff	At Subordinate
8-34	2.3F at 0543	Flood	-0 34	**0509 EST**
8-35	2.4F at 0733	Flood	+0 08	0741 + 1h for EDT = **0841**
8-36	1.8F at 0121	Ebb	-0 58	0023 + 1h for EDT = **0123**
8-37	2.0F at 0800	Flood	-3 34	0426 + 1h for EDT = **0526**
8-38	1.8E at 0132	Ebb	-0 57	0035 + 1h for EDT = **0135**

#	At Reference	Flood/Ebb	Speed Ratio	At Subordinate	Direction
8-39	2.4F at 0733	Flood	0.4	**0.96 kts**	310°
8-40	1.8E at 0208	Ebb	0.4	**0.72 kts**	170°
8-41	2.2F at 0827	Flood	0.6	**1.32 kts**	001°
8-42	1.6E at 1710	Ebb	0.2	**0.32 kts**	217°

8-43. 0003 EST

8-44. 1250 + 1h = 1350 EDT

8-45. 1137 + 1h = 1237 EDT

8-46. 0642 + 1h = 0742 EDT

Time of Slack Answers for 8-47 through 8-50: The answer sought by each problem is in BOLD. Did you remember to add 1 hour for answers that should be in Daylight Savings Time?

#	At Reference	Before Flood/Ebb	Time Diff	At Subordinate
8-47	1501	Flood	-2 54	**1207 EST**
8-48	1250	Ebb	-1 18	1132 + 1h for EDT = **1232**
8-49	0146	Flood	-1 13	0033 + 1h for EDT = **0133**
8-50	2320	Ebb	-1 10	2210 + 1h for EDT = **2310**

8-51 (A) MHW equals half the mean range plus the mean tide level = 3.47 / 2 + 1.87 = 1.735 + 1.87 = 3.605 MHW, according to the 2011 tables we are using. (B) The table on the 1210 Tr chart from 1990 says MHW is 3.5 ft. (C) This is almost certainly global warming influence on mean sea level, which raises all tide values. The sea level rise in this area 2.58 mm/yr (±0.19), so 1990 to 2011 = 21 y × 2.58 mm = 54.2 mm = 2.1" = 0.18 ft, which is well within the uncertainties to account for this (see tidesandcurrents.noaa.gov for links to sea-level data). (D) The Tidal Information table states Woods Hole MHW is 1.8 ft. According to Tide Tables, Woods Hole Oceanographic Institution mean tide range is 1.8 ft, and its mean tide level is 1.0; therefore 1.8 / 2 + 1.0 = 0.9 + 1.0 = MHW at Woods Hole is 1.9 ft. Again we see a rise over the years.

8-52. The charted clearance is 11 ft, which is defined as height above MHW, so the first step is find MHW. This is often on the chart, but if not we compute it from tide table data: MHW=Mean Tide Level + (Mean Range)/2. Onset area tides are a secondary station (No. 967) referenced to Newport. Low occurs 1h 25m later at about the same height. At Onset mean tide is 1.97 and half of mean range is 1.75, so MHW = 3.7 ft.

On May 16, Newport low water for May 16 is -0.5 ft at 1246 EDT. The Low at station 967 is +1h 25m later, or 1411 EDT. So at 1411 the clearance is 11 + 3.7 + 0.5 = 15.2 ft. At that time you have a vessel clearance of 15.2 - 12 = 3.2 ft.

We can approximate the time span available to us from the Rules of Twelfths. The range either side of low is about 4.5 ft, so in the first hour the change is 4.5(1/12) = 0.4 ft and the second hour it is about 4.5 (2/12) = 0.75, so in 2h the rise is 0.4 + 0.75 =1.2 ft. So the 15.2 clearance drops to 14.2 ft which is our safety limit. Answer 1411 EDT ± 2h.

8-53. The table below compares predicting currents at intermediate times from Table 3 and the 50-90 Rule.

8-54. (A)

Rotary Current SW of Cuttyhunk Is.				
EDT	+H past Flood	Average Drift	Corrected Drift*	Set
0551	0	0.4	0.6	356
0651	1	0.3	0.4	15
0751	2	0.2	0.3	80
0851	3	0.3	0.4	123
0951	4	0.5	0.7	146
1051	5	0.5	0.7	158
1151	6	0.4	0.6	173
1251	7	0.3	0.4	208

* May 16 is day after Perigee and day before full moon, calling for max correction of × 1.4.

(B) A plot of the rotary currents is shown on the next page.

CHAPTER 9 – NAVIGATION IN CURRENTS

9-1. (A) 2/6 × 60° = 20°. CMG is about 200 + 20 = 220 M. (B) Larger. (C) CMG = 218.4, SMG = 6.32.

9-2. 2/6 of 40° = 13V. CMG is about 200 -13 = 187 M. The factor of 40° is used because the current is not on the beam, but quartering.

9-3. 1.5/5 × 60° = 0.3 × 60 = 18°. Head in about 18 or 20°.

Current Tables		Table 3				50-90 Rule	
EST	Current	Intervals	Cycle	Factor	Current	Current	Factor
0443	0.0				0.0	0.0	
0543		1h 00m	3h 34m	0.45	1.0	1.2	0.5
0630		1h 47m	3h 34m	0.75	1.7	1.6	0.7
0717		2h 34m	3h 34m	0.9	2.1	2.1	0.9
0817	2.3				2.3	2.3	
0917		2h 14m	3h 14m	0.9	2.1	2.1	0.9
0954		1h 37m	3h 14m	0.72	1.7	1.6	0.7
1031		1h 00m	3h 14m	0.6	1.4		0.5
1131	0.0				0.0	0.0	
1231		1h 41m	2h 41m	0.8	-1.4	-1.5	0.9
1251		1h 21m	2h 41m	0.7	-1.2	-1.2	0.7
1312		1h 00m	2h 41m	0.6	-1.0	-0.9	0.5
1412	-1.7				-1.7	-1.7	

88   Navigation Workbook 1210Tr

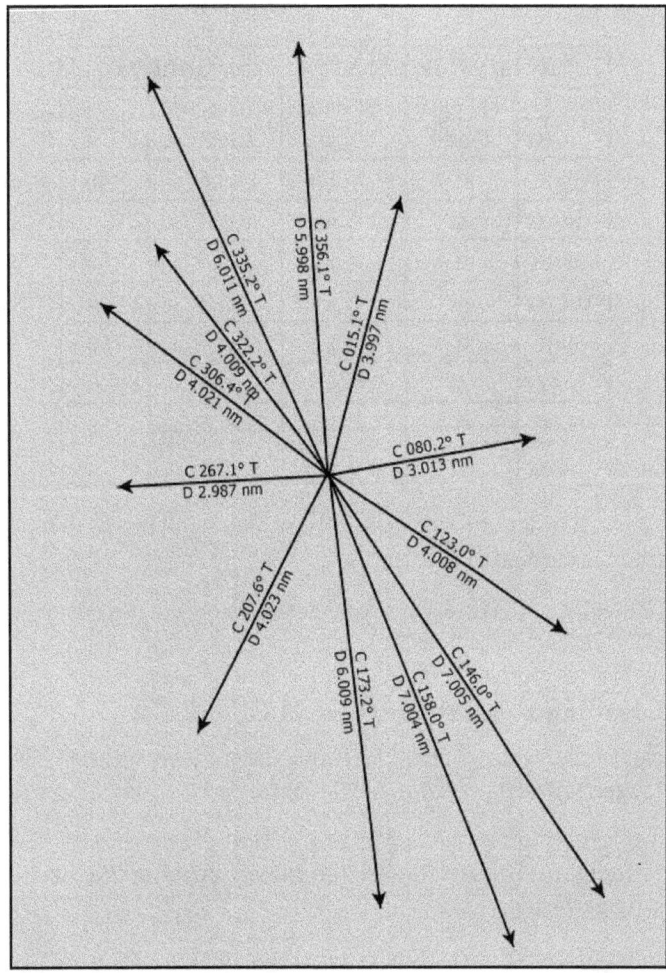

One way to plot rotary currents. Example from Cuttyhunk Is. Exercise 8-53(B). The labels mark hours past maximum flood at Pollock Rip. This was made with the range and bearing tool from an echart program, which accounts for non-exact values plotted.

9-4. (A) Beating in a southerly the wind is on your bow. Current set is 2/6 × 40° = about 13°. With a leeway of 10° you slip another 10° to leeward for a total of about 23 or say 25°. If your compass reads 205, you are actually making good a course more like 205 + 25 or 230 M. (B) With no current set or leeway slip, you would look at your compass of 205, know you tack through 90°, and reasonably guess your compass should read 205 − 90 = 115 after you come about to starboard tack. And if you did indeed tack through 90° (which you would know if you have tacked very often in these conditions and watched the compass), this would be right and that is what the compass would read. But we also know (or reasonably estimate) that we are slipping 25° downwind, so even when our compass reads 115 we are actually making good 115 − 25 or about 090. Hence we wait till the buoy bears about 090 then tack. When we tack the compass will read 115, and it will look like we are sailing well to weather of the buoy, as if we went too far tacking. But the wind and current will set us down the same 25° and we will make good a course straight toward the buoy.

Generally in these circumstances it is good practice to throw in another 5° for safety. In this case wait till the buoy bears 085 then tack. If you are too high, as soon as you notice it you can fall off. But if you underestimate it, you may not be able to pinch up enough to get around it. If you don't make it you have to tack twice more to get around.

9-5. Selecting two distant objects (such as the tree and a peak behind it) establishes a natural range, and as you walk across the field you maintain the range relationship to make progress on a straight range line. This is the same way you cross a current to check that you are not being set.

9-6. The back bearing shifted from 160 to 135 so you are being set left by about 25°. Sketch a diagram with these headings to see how this comes about. Hence point to the right about 25° or come to course 340 + 25 = 005 M. Then continue to watch the back bearings for a while to see if your correction was about right.

9-7. You can expect the current to be different, sometimes dramatically so, upon crossing a tide rip. However, if you are in a low powered boat, you can usually assume there is indeed a current flowing *through it* so you will, if being pulled in, get pushed out the other side.

9-8. (A) The nearest subordinate station is 1.4 nmi southwest of Brenton Point, which ebbs in direction 170 T, has a max ebb 1h 04m before Pollock Rip Channel, and an ebb speed ratio 0.4 that of Pollock Rip Channel. The reference station's max ebb that afternoon is 1.7 kts at 1252 EST, or 1352 EDT. Therefore the sub station's current is 1.7 × 0.4 = 0.68 kts in direction 170T. (B) Plot the 1h current vector, then plot one hour of boat speed from there. Read magnetic course as 103 M. (C) 111 M CMG. (D) SMG is 4.6 kts. (E) Distance is 16.1 nmi at 4.6 kts = (60 × 16.1) / 4.6 = 966 / 4.6 = 210m = 3h 30m.

9-9. Set was 053° T, and drift was (1.7 nmi in 90 min) 1.13 kts.

9-10. (A) With no current considered, your 1552 DR is 41° 21.1' N, 71° 21.5' W, which gives a range and true bearing to Point Judith Light as 5.6 nmi at 290 M. (B) CMG 075 M, SMG 4.8 kts. (C) After correcting for set and drift, your 1552 EP is 41° 21.2' N, 71° 25.0' W, which gives a range and true bearing to Point Judith Light as 3.0 nmi at 294 M. (D) CMG 067 M, SMG 3.9 kts, .

9-11. Some answers (shaded numbers) are given to the tenth for best comparison with solutions obtained, but in practice we are lucky to get these answers to within a few tenths, primarily because we do not know the input data well enough. In fact, it is rare to need more than we can get from the simple 40-60 approximation. In practical work we steer by COG from the GPS, but it is nevertheless beneficial to check that the current prediction are correct for future planning.

9-11. Answers

#	S	H	Set*	Drift	CMG	SMG	Set**	40-60
1	6.0	200	150	2.0	188	7.4	11.9	13.3
2	5.0	100	315	1.5	087	3.9	12.9	12.0
3	7.5	350	260	1.8	337	7.7	13.5	14.4
4	6.0	215	150	2.0	200	7.1	14.8	13.3
5	5.0	110	315	1.5	100	3.7	9.9	12.0
6	7.5	364	260	1.8	350	7.3	13.9	14.4
7	7.4	180	293	3.1	205	6.8	25.0	25.4
8	6.2	130	014	2.1	110	5.6	20.0	20.6
9	6.2	130	049	2.4	110	7.0	20.0	23.4

*The direction the current flows towards

**Difference between H and CMG

9-12. (A) Slack to slack (A to G in the Resources diagram) gives 63% of the peak, or average is 0.63 × 1.7 = 1.1 kts Flood. (B) E to G in the diagram is 48%, or 0.48 × 1.7 = 0.8 kts Flood. (C) F to G gives 25% or 0.25 × 1.7 = 0.4 Flood for about 1h and then A to C for 48%, or 0.48 × 1.4 = 0.7 kts Ebb for 3h. Then we can say that in 1h we went +0.4 miles in the flood direction, then we went 0.7 × 3h = -2.1 miles in the ebb direction, or a net of 0.21-0.4 = 1.7 miles in ebb direction over 4 hours, so the net current was 1.7/4 = 0.4 kts Ebb as the average current.

CHAPTER 10 – NAVIGATION RULES

Answer followed by Rules that apply.

Parts A & B. Definitions and Right of Way

10-1.	(D)	Rule 15, 17b.
10-2.	(A)	Rule 6b, 7b.
10-3.	(D)	Rule 6.
10-4.	(C)	Rule 13a.
10-5.	(D)	Rule 3a.
10-6.	(D)	Rule 12a.
10-7.	(B)	Rule 3f.
10-8.	(A)	Rule 3g.
10-9.	(B)	Rule 7d.
10-10.	(D)	Rule 13a.
10-11.	(B)	Rule 15a, 18a.
10-12.	(C)	Rule 17a.
10-13.	(B)	Rule 15.
10-14.	(A)	Rule 14.
10-15.	(C)	Rule 3d.
10-16.	(C)	Rule 17b.
10-17.	(B)	Rule 6a.
10-18.	(D)	Rule 18d.
10-19.	(B)	Rule 13b.
10-20.	(D)	Rule 15, 16, 17c.
10-21.	(A)	Rule 18a.
10-22.	(C)	Rule 18a.
10-23.	(C)	Rule 13c.
10-24.	(D)	Rule 19a.
10-25.	(D)	Rule 6, 7, 8, 19, Annex I & IV.
10-26.	(C)	Rule 17b.
10-27.	(A)	Rule 12a.
10-28.	(C)	Rule 18a.
10-29.	(B)	Rule 9a.
10-30.	(B)	Rule 19b.
10-31.	(B)	Rule 3j.
10-32.	(A)	Rule 12a.
10-33.	(B)	Rule 16, 18a.
10-34.	(A)	Rule 18b.
10-35.	(C)	Rule 15a.
10-36.	(A)	Rule 9c.
10-37.	(B)	Rule 13.
10-38.	(D)	Rule 3c.
10-39.	(D)	Rule 5.
10-40.	(A)	Rule 8a.
10-41.	(C)	Rule 3g.
10-42.	(C)	Rule 3h.
10-43.	(B)	Rule 19c.
10-44.	(C)	Rule 17a(ii).

Part C. Lights and Dayshapes

10-45.	(C)	Rule 24e.
10-46.	(B)	Annex IV.

10-47.	(C)	Rule 29.		10-83.	(D)	Rule 26, Rule 24a.
10-48.	(A)	Rule 27.		10-84.	(D)	Rule 24e.
10-49.	(D)	Rule 30.				
10-50.	(A)	Rule 26.				**Part D. Sound Signals**
10-51.	(D)	Rule 34.		10-85.	(C)	Rule 35a.
10-52.	(D)	Rule 27.		10-86.	(B)	Rule 37, Annex IV.
10-53.	(A)	Rule Annex II.		10-87.	(C)	Rule 34e.
10-54.	(A)	Rule 25.		10-88.	(C)	Rule 34d.
10-55.	(B)	Rule 24.		10-89.	(D)	Rule 35d.
10-56.	(A)	Rule 24.		10-90.	(B)	Rule 35b.
10-57.	(B)	Rule 24.		10-91.	(D)	Rule 37, Annex IV.
10-58.	(D)	Rule 21b.		10-92.	(C)	Rule 35c.
10-59.	(A)	Rule 13a, 21b.		10-93.	(B)	Rule 37, Annex IV.
10-60.	(B)	Rule 26b.		10-94.	(B)	Rule 32c.
10-61.	(A)	Rule 20.		10-95.	(D)	Rule 35f.
10-62.	(A)	Rule 23a.		10-96.	(C)	Rule 35i.
10-63.	(A)	Rule 23a.		10-97.	(B)	Rule 35f.
10-64.	(A)	Rule 30.		10-98.	(D)	Rule 37, Annex IV.
10-65.	(B)	Rule 24a.		10-99.	(B)	Rule 35f.
10-66.	(D)	Rule 26a.		10-100.	(D)	Rule 35c.
10-67.	(C)	Rule 21f.		10-101.	(C)	Rule 37, Annex IV.
10-68.	(B)	Rule 1, note 1 (Morse "S").		10-102.	(D)	Rule 35d.
10-69.	(B)	Rule 27d.		10-103.	(C)	Rule 8, 15, 16, 34a.
10-70.	(B)	Rule 26.		10-104.	(D)	Rule 19, 35b.
10-71.	(C)	Rule 27a.		10-105.	(A)	Rule 35.
10-72.	(A)	Rule 36, 37.		10-106.	(D)	Rule 33b.
10-73.	(A)	Rule 25b.		10-107.	(D)	Rule 33b.
10-74.	(D)	Rule 26.		10-108.	(A)	Rule 34d.
10-75.	(D)	Rule 27e.		10-109.	(B)	Rule 37, Annex IV.
10-76.	(C)	Rule 27a.		10-110.	(C)	Rule 34d.
10-77.	(A)	Rule 24a.		10-111.	(C)	Rule 35j.
10-78.	(D)	Rule 24e.		10-112.	(C)	Rule 37, Annex IV.
10-79.	(C)	Rule 24g.		10-113.	(C)	Rule 34b.
10-80.	(C)	Rule 21a.		10-114.	(C)	Rule 33a (for *both* inland & international).
10-81.	(D)	Rule 24.		10-115.	(A)	Rule 35d.
10-82.	(D)	Rule 36.		10-116.	(D)	Rule 34b, 34d.

10-117. (A) Rule 32, 34a.

10-118. (A) Rule 35f.

10-119. (B) Rule 35c.

10-120. (B) Rule 37, Annex IV.

10-121. (C) Rule 19e.

10-122. (A) Rule 34a.

10-123. (B) Rule 35c.

10-124. (A) Rule 34e.

10-125. (D) Rule 35a.

10-126. (A) Rule 34d.

10-127. (D) Rule 37, Annex IV.

CHAPTER 11 – NAVIGATION PLANNING AND PRACTICE

Trip 1.

11-1. (A) The eye height given does not matter to this question. Using 1210 Tr charted nominal range of 22 nmi, the luminous range at 5.5 nmi visibility is about 15 nmi. (B) The light on 1210 Tr was 101 ft high with nominal range of 22 nmi. It is now 67 ft high with a nominal range of 16 nmi. The light and horn characteristics have not changed.

11-2. (A) 13219. (B) 1:15,000. (C) Large scale.

11-3. (C) Underwater cable area.

11-4. (A) Brenton Reef Lt. (B) 4.5 nmi.

11-5. (A) Hard.

11-6. (A) 41° 13.6' N, 70° 43.3' W. (B) 70° 46.7'W.

11-7. 7.7 nmi at 279 T.

11-8. T = 035, var = 15 W, M = 050, dev = 4.5W, C = 054.5, ie 054 or 055 is correct.

11-9. (A) 292 R.

11-10. Schuyler Ledge.

11-11. 16 ft.

11-12. (B) When Gooseberry Neck Lt bears 317 T.

11-13. (A) 093 T. (B) 15.8 nmi. (C) 5.0 kts.

11-14. Correcting for current calls for 168 T, and correcting then for leeway takes this to 165 T.

11-15 through 11-19 are reserved.

Trip 2.

11-20. (A) 221 T at 8.8 nmi. (B) 238 T at 38.1 nmi. (C) 1522.

11-21. (A) 0.3 nmi (600 yards), (B) bearing 030 T.

11-22. 0745. (B) 1522.

11-23. (A) No. (B). It should have passed about 0.4 nmi off your port beam.

11-24. You have steered 221 T at a steady knotmeter speed of 5.0 and you are right at Buoy 10, which means made good a distance of 5.3 nmi in 1h 02m, for an SMG = 5.1, and your CMG has been 217. Thus the average current has been about 0.4 kts at 145 T.

11-25. The course to Buoy BB from Buoy 10 is 228 T, but you have been set over the last hour by about 4° to the left, so you might try pointing about 4° to the right of 228, which would be 232 T.

11-26. You have covered 8.8 nmi in 1h 42m, for an SMG = 5.2 kts. (Note that 8.40/1.7 = 4.9 is not correct for SMG)

11-27. (A)

Buoy	Run	Time
8	3.1	0819
6	5.6	0849
4	7.8	0915
2	9.1	0931

(B) Halfway between R2 and R4 to starboard. Other piloting clues include a bearing 317 T to Gooseberry Neck Light, and being able to see Gay Head to the Southeast.

11-28. (A) Fix at 41° 24.8'N, 71° 02.3'W. (B) Can do a standard running fix or note that the two bearings double the bow angle for a fix at distance off equal distance run (1.0 nmi). The knotmeter read 5.0, but we have noted that our average SMG has been 5.2, so likely better off to use 5.2 for distance run between 0937 and 0949.

11-29. (A) Cuttyhunk Island, 3.25 mi SW (i.e. near Buoy VS), and Browns Ledge, both of which are rotary currents with data and proposed corrections in Table 5.

(B)

Time		Cuttyhunk Is			Browns Ledge		
EDT	+H	Drift	x 1.4	Set	Set	x 1.4	Drift
0551	0	0.4	0.6	356	330	0.4	0.3
0651	1	0.3	0.4	015	012	0.4	0.3
0751	2	0.2	0.3	080	028	0.4	0.3
0851	3	0.3	0.4	123	104	0.6	0.4
0951	4	0.5	0.7	146	118	0.6	0.4
1051	5	0.5	0.7	158	123	0.6	0.4
1151	6	0.4	0.6	173	168	0.4	0.3
1251	7	0.3	0.4	208	205	0.3	0.2
1351	8	0.2	0.3	267	201	0.4	0.3
1451	9	0.3	0.4	306	270	0.4	0.3
1551	10	0.3	0.4	322	282	0.6	0.4
1651	11	0.4	0.6	335	318	0.7	0.5

Except for a difference in set of at most 30° off the average, these two stations have about the same speeds within ± 20%. The rotations are slightly out of phase, but not much. For practical purposes, without a lot more work, we can assume these predictions are about the same for these two relatively close stations in relatively open water, so this is not surprising.

11-30. (A) 27.2 nmi at 239T. (B) TTG at 5.0 kts = 5h 26m. (C) A quick look at the table or plot gives shows an average current of about 0.5 kts at about 200T, with some 20% and 20° uncertainty.

11-31. We assume the current is 0.5 kts at 200 T, with S = 5.0 and CMG desired to be 239T, then course to steer (CTS) = 243 T, and SMG = 5.4.

11-32. (A) Doing all DR with SMG = 5.4 and CMG = 239, we get an Rfix at 1015 at 41° 23.5', 71° 04.9'W. (B) The corresponding DR position is 41° 23.6' N, 71° 05.0'W. The Rfix is 0.15 nmi off the DR in direction 155 T. This is essentially in agreement with the uncertainties we have.

11-33. (A) Fix at 1108 = 41° 20.9'N, 71° 10.0'W.

(B) Using the small-angle rule (namely 6° right triangle has sides in the ratio 1:10), we have 2° which is one third of that, so sides are in the ratio 1:30. So the bearing is offset to each side by 1/30th of the range to the lights. Brenton Reef is 12.8 mi or ± 12.8/30 = ± 0.43 nmi, and Buzzards is 7.3 mil off for an uncertainty of ± 7.3/30 = ± 0.24 nmi. Thus we know our Lon a bit better than our Lat, but that is the ball park. Note too that bearing accuracies to ±2° is very good navigation. The problem is both targets are a long way off. As we get closer to the lights on Block Island we can do better.

(C) DR at 1108 is 41° 21.0'N, 71° 10.4'W. The fix is 0.3 mi off in direction 108 T. This means we are still getting set to the S-SE, so our corrections are not quite right. But we have lights for fixes now, which will help the navigation. This type of trip is better off at night or in light fog that turns on the lights as we can see the lights better than we can see the land... again we are doing this navigation exercise without GPS and radar. Either one of these would make this navigation very much easier.

(D) 240T at 20.2 nmi. Still about 4h out at 5 kts.

11-34. From 1015 to 1053 at 5.4 SMG we covered about 3.4 miles, and from there back to the light is about 5.5 nmi, which would be our estimate of the visibility... i.e. this is defined as the farthest we can see unlighted objects in daylight. It is not a very precise definition, and the value is rarely the same in all directions and even can vary notably with the angle we are looking, because the fog can increase in density with elevation... or vice versa. We will use a working visibility of 5 to 6 mi for the rest of the exercise.

11-35. Many of these lights have changed names and specifications as you would see in the Light List. We are using only the charted information for this exercise.

Light	Nominal Range	Height	Luminous range at vis 5.5	geo range at HE=10
1A	8	33	5.4	8.9
BI SE	21	201	12.6	17.3
Benton Reef	25	87	14.8	12.5
Buzzards	22	101	13.1	13.2
Pt. Judith	16	65	9.8	11.2
Sandy Pt 13	36			

11-36. (A) DR ar 1208 = 41° 18.4'N, 71° 15.7'W. (B) Fix at 1208 = 41° 17.7' N, 71° 15.5'N. (C) DR to Fix = 0.6 nmi at 163 T (D) We ran 1h so this is the current, namely 0.6 kts setting toward 163 T. (E) Making the astronomical correction to the data for a x 1.4 factor, the tables show 1051 EDT of 0.6 at 123 T sand then at 1151 0.4 kts toward 168 T. Considering all the uncertainties in the data and comparison, this has to be considered good agreement, meaning good enough that we can fairly assume the current for the next couple hours might be as forecast.... however, we are getting farther and farther from the Brown's Ledge location, so this is by no means certain. (F) New course is 242 T at 15.1 nmi.

11-37. (A) Yes, this is about the average we would expect. (B) To make good 242 T with your knotmeter reading 5.0 sailing in a current of 0.4 kts toward 225, you should steer 243 T and you will make good 5.4 kts.

11-38. Looking ahead along track 242 T, you see deepest water about 2.0 miles ahead. The track crosses between a 120 ft contour and a 130 ft sounding, so we can estimate the charted depth at 125 ft. At 5.4 kts, you will reach this point from the 1208 position in 22m or at 1230. (B) The charted depth is 125 ft below zero tide, but your depth sounder is 2 ft into the water, so the displayed depth without tide would be 123 ft. To estimate the tide height, note we are roughly in between the three stations Block Island, Pt Judith, and Nomans Land. These stations are all about the same so we can use their average. The height is then about 0.85 times the value at Newport, and the low water at these stations are all about 20m later than Newport. Newport has -0.5 at 1246 EDT going to +5.0 at 1949 EDT, thus low water at our location is 1306 at -0.85*0.5 = about -0.4 ft, and the tide is rising, so we would expect very near zero tide. Thus we anticipate seeing our sounder peak out at about 123 ft in 22m. Watching for this adds more control to our navigation, which would be more important in denser fog with fewer lights to work with.

11-39. (A) 1354 fix = 41° 14.0'N, 71° 26.4'W. (B) New course is 237 T at 6.2 mi off. (C) 1354 DR = 41° 13.3'N, 71° 26.6'W. (D) DR to Fix = 0.8 nmi at 015 T. (E) We assumed a current of 0.4 toward 225, and then get set as if there were an additional current of about 0.4 kts (0.8 nmi /1h 46m) in direction 015. This is a disappointment, but we cannot really hope to predict these currents very precisely in these conditions. This means our original current estimate was wrong by about 0.2 to 300 T, which is not out of the uncertainties in this data. It implies the current rotated faster than predicted or maybe there was some other factor... not to mention that we are rather far from the reference station. (F) The main lesson to learn at this point is although the currents are not large, we see that they do indeed shift our position notably, namely in this case some 0.8 nmi in 1h 46m—even after we made an effort to correct for them. The message is we have plenty of lights to see and we should be taking fixes more frequently. We know there is light fog now and it could get worse, so more frequent fixes would be best.

11-40. You left the 1208 position steering 243 T at knotmeter reading of 5.0. At the 1354 fix you see that you made good 246 T covering 9.0 mi in 1h 46m for an SMG of 5.1. From this we can figure that the effective current over this leg was 0.3 kts at 314 T. With the new course to the mark 237 T at knotmeter 5.0 this current calls for a heading of 234 T with a subsequent SMG of 5.1, which is what we will steer for the last leg of the trip.

11-41. (A) We assume we are making good 5.1 kts (our computed SMG), and from the estimated ominous range of 5.4 nmi, we see this is just 0.8 nmi off. Within uncertainties, we might be seeing it now, but if not we expect it soon and theoretically in 0.8 nmi which at 5.1 kts will take us about 9m or at 1403 EDT. (B) At this time the bearing to the BI SE light should be about 225 T.

11-42. Old Harbor in on Newport tides, with the HW 13m earlier at *0.82 and LW +15m at *0.86. LW at Newport on May 16 is 1246 EDT at -0.5ft and HW is 1949 EDT at 5.0. These translate to Old Harbor as LW 1213 at -0.4 ft and HW at 2004 at 4.3 ft. Based on our 1354 position and a SMG of 5.1, we expect to cover this last 6.2 mi in 1h 13m or at about 1507. Interpolating the tides this would give us a tide height of 1.0 ft at 1507.

11-43 (A) We have a contour at 90 ft, which is a distance off the 1354 fix of about 5.3 miles. Thus we know it is about an hour later or roughly 1454 or say 1500 EDT. This is about same time we computed earlier for a 1 ft tide, and the sounder is only 2 ft below the water, so within uncertainties the sounder draft and tide cancel each other and we are anticipating 90 ft displayed at about 1500.

11-44. Various reasons you would not hear a bell buoy: (i) The bell could be ringing but if it is downwind, you might not hear it till very close. (ii) Maybe there is no longer a bell on the buoy. Normally you would check that in the Light List, but for these exercises using this old chart we cannot do that because so many of the aids have changed. In actual navigation, it is always crucial to check the Light List and LNM on any aid you will be depending upon. (iii) The most likely reason in calm water is the bell is just not ringing. These bell and gong buoys are activated by wave action, and if the water is flat they are silent.

11-45. These astro corrections are already included in the reversing current predictions. To see this, compare current speeds for any standard (reversing current) location on days when the astro effects added 40% to rotary averages at the same location when astro effects reduced the average rotary predictions by 40%. Note we rarely know perigee and apogee to fine tune this, but we do know full moon and new moon and these are at least 20% effects.

11-46 through 11-49 are reserved.

Trip 3.

11-50. (A) 13226 and 13221. (B) Plus use satellite maps or Google Earth. Some echart programs let you navigate right on the sat images, or use electronic charts from your ECS. (C) RNC numbers are the same as the paper charts. (D) The ENC numbers are US5RI25M and US5RI20M.

11-51.

Waypoint Number	Waypoint Name	Reason for selection
1	Almy Point	Origin of trip, nearby landmark
2	Tiverton Groin	Important narrows
3	Gould Island	Nearest major mark to turn
4	Red 12	Passing
5	Red 10	Passing
6	Red 8	Important turn to stbd
7	Red 6	Important turn to port
8	Green 5	Important turn to stbd
9	Old Bull ROCK	Significant hazard
10	Sakonnet Harbor	Destination

11-52. (A) total distance 10.27 nmi. (B) Total time to go 2h 03m.

11-53. Current velocity getting through the groin at Tiverton, plus timing for help from the ebb along the way.

11-54. Stone Bridge near our departure at Tiverton, and Black Point about half way to destination.

11-55. Because it is not for our Gould Island, but for a different Gould Island. Plot the subordinate station Lat-Lon.

11-56. The Stone Bridge subordinate station's min before ebb occurs 2h 26m before slack at Pollock Rip Channel. On April 20, Pollock Rip Channel's morning slack before ebb occurs at 1050 EST, 1150 EDT. Subtracting 2h 26m = 0924 EDT min before ebb at Stone Bridge the morning of April 20.

11-57. Stone Bridge's max ebb occurs 3h 06m before max ebb at Pollock Rip Channel and runs at ratio of 1.6 x Pollock Rip Channel's max ebb. On April 20, Pollock Rip Channel's first max ebb of the day occurs at 0100 EST, 0200 EST, and runs at 2.1 kts. Applying the time correction would put the max ebb at Stone Bridge into a previous day, which is not what the question asked for. So the next max ebb at Pollock Rip Channel occurs at 1332 EST, 1432 EDT, and runs at 2.0 kts. Applying time correction 1432 – 3h 06m = Stone Bridge first max ebb of the day at 1126 EDT. Applying the factor, 2.0 kts x 1.6 = max flood at Stone Bridge 3.2 kts.

11-58.

Departure = 1107				
Leg	Course T	Distance nmi	Time Leg	ETA
1	191.4 T	0.25	3m	1110
2	177.7 T	0.575	7m	1117
3	184.1 T	0.757	9m	1126
4	185.8 T	0.366	4m	1130
5	185.0 T	1.194	14m	1144
6	195.9 T	1.517	18m	1202
7	141.2 T	0.618	7m	1209
8	176.0 T	3.256	39m	1248
9	146.9 T	1.737	21m	1309

11-59. (A) A circle with radius 0.2 nmi centered on Old Bull Rock yields a hand compass bearing to Sakonnet of 169* M (154 T + 15 W variation = 169 M) to clear that circle. (B) To remain clear of the hazardous side of the bear the compass should read NO MORE than 169* M. (C) A 085 M hand bearing compass to the spire is an alert to monitor the danger bearing, and (D) a bearing to the spire of 068 M means you can leave the concern behind you.

11-60. You arrive as planned at about 1300 and anchor in 9 feet depth. Our depth sounder has been calibrated to surface level. Your concern will be with both the low tide during the next day to make sure we don't go aground at low water, but also with the high tide to make sure we maintain sufficient scope for our overnighter.

Sakonnet subordinate station high water occurs 0h 09m before Newport, and the low occurs 0h 13m after Newport. High water ratio is *0.91 of Newport, and the low is *0.86 of Newport. On April 20 and 21, Newport's high over the next 24 hours will be 4.7 ft at 2140 EST, 2240 EDT. Newport's low will be -0.5 ft at 1435 EST, 1535 EDT. After corrections are applied, Sakonnet's high water will be 4.2 ft (4.6 x *0.91 = 4.186 ft) at 2231 EDT (2240 – 09m = 2231) this evening. And after corrections, Sakonnet's low water will be -0.43 ft (-0.5 x *0.86 = -0.43 ft) at 1548 EDT (1535 + 0 13 = 1548).

We have not answered the question yet, because we don't know the state of the tide when we anchored. Using the Rule of Twelfths, we will find the state of the tide at 1300 on April 20.

Sakonnet high and low water prior to and after our arrival occur at...

Newport EDT	High or Low	Time Diff	Sakonnet EDT
1014	High	-0 09	1005
1535	Low	+0 13	1548

And at a height of...

Newport High Height	Difference	Sakonnet High Height
4.0	*0.91	3.64

Newport Low Height	Difference	Sakonnet Low Height
-0.5	*0.86	-0.43

Creating a Rule of Twelfths diagram results in a total range of 4.07 ft = .34 ft per twelfth.

Sakonnet Time			Sakonnet Height
1005	3.64	3.64	3.64
1102	-1/12	0.34	3.30
1159	-2/12	0.68	2.62
1256	-3/12	1.02	1.60
1353	-3/12	1.02	0.58
1450	-2/12	0.68	-0.10
1548	-1/12	0.34	-0.43

Our arrival and anchoring occurred at about 1300, or about a tide level of 1.6 ft above chart datum. The tide level will still lower from 1.6 ft down to -0.43 feet, or another 2 ft. The tide level will still rise from 1.60 ft to 3.64 ft, or another 2 ft. So one of the answers is that we've anchored in 9 ft, and we have another 2 ft to lose, so at low water we should have 1 ft clearance. The other answer is that if we anchored in 9 ft with, say, 3:1 scope, and assuming we have a 3 ft freeboard, we now have 36 ft of rode out. A rise of water level of 2 ft will reduce scope to 2.4. Perhaps a little weak depending on bottom and anchor type and weight. Should probably let out some more rode.

CHAPTER 12 – IN DEPTH...

12-1. The *Navigation Rules*. If you learn and obey the Rules you will avoid collisions with both other vessels and also with other objects, such as land. Rules for Safe Speed and Proper Watch alone will accomplish most of this.

12-2. Radar, GPS, and depth sounder.

12-3(A) (a) Natural range, (B) depth contour

12-4. The expected ocean DR uncertainty is about 5% of distance run plus the set of an unknown current of about 0.5 kts, as an optimistic estimate and 7% and 0.7 kts as a conservative estimate. (A) This gives 6.0 mile plus 12.0, which add as the sum of the squares to get 13.4 mi. (At 7% and 0.7 kts, we get 18.7 mi) (B) 14.4 from the run, and 12.0 from the current, yields 18.7 mi uncertainty with 5% and 0.5 kts. (At 7% and 0.7 kts, we get 26.3 mi.)

12-5. Parallel rulers and dividers.

12-6. ScotchBlue Painter's Tape.

12-7. (A) Use Tacking distance = 1.5 × Upwind distance. (B) 1.5 × 2 = 3, then 3/6 = 30m. That is, going direct it would be 2/6 = 20 min, but tacking takes about 1.5 times longer, so 20 + 10 = 30m.

12-8. About 2.5% of the wind speed.

12-9. Equal and opposite, or 5° W.

12-10. Geomag (see starpath.com/navpubs).

12-11. 9m23s=9.383m=0.1564h. S=1/0.1564= 6.39. Then 6.39/6 = 1.065. (A) Knotmeter is low (B) by 6.5% (ie multiply what you read by 1.065 to get the right speed). Note we knew immediately it was low because it should have taken us 10m at 6 kts and it took less.

12-12. (A) 10 min/mile, (B) 6 min/mile, (C) 100 ft/min

12-13. ECDIS is the IMO sanctioned echart system using a specific format of vector charts only, and the viewers must have identical controls. ECS is any form of echarting, using vector or raster charts, or even navigation on satellite images, using any of hundreds of echart software or firmware programs. Put another way, the merchant marine and navy uses ECDIS; everyone else uses ECS.

12-14. (A) True, (B) True. We do not correct for leeway influence on speed as it is included in what we read on the knotmeter. (C) True. (D) False. Leeway is motion through the water so it is logged by however we are measuring this. (E) True. (F) True. Leeway depends on the wind direction. (G) False. Current changes CMG to differ from H, and SMG to differ from S; leeway change in speed is measured and accounted for in the knotmeter speed S. (H) False. A given current will move you a given distance in a given time, regardless of your heading. (I) True. Fall off close hauled and leeway drops quickly. (J) True. With calibrated knotmeter and compass, we can solve the vector problem to get set and drift from CMG and SMG. (K) False. We can estimate it under specific conditions, but it is tricky to measure accurately, because it changes with wind speed and wind angle, sails set, trim, etc. (L) False. Although leeway increases with wind speed, leeway is also large in very light air. It goes up in both wind speed directions from the optimum wind speed the boat and sail plan is designed to. (M) True. Tidal currents go often go from minimum to maximum in 3 hours.

12-15. VMG as SMG to windward, and SMG in the direction of the active waypoint.

12-16. Waypoint Closing Velocity, also called VMG to Waypoint.

12-17. Channels 67 and 72.

12-18. (A). They cost less; they are more durable, and they are always up to date. (B) We have less stores now that stock charts that we can look at in real size before purchasing (though all are online to see in as much detail as desired.) Second, some POD papers are still not quite as good as the lithographic charts for erasing pencil lines... though this is improving with time.

12-19. (A) 20% and 20 min, or 2.7 ±0.5 and 1220 ±20m. (B) The honest, most general answer is you have no idea. The current could be running the opposite way at that time. Current predictions apply only to the stations themselves and to nearby open water, uninfluenced by land or bathymetry.

12-20. It sees around corners that radar cannot see; it tells you directly the course, speed, and name of the target vessel; it identifies the class of the vessel (tanker, tug, etc).

12-21. (A) Set = 115.4, Drift = 1.2. (B) Course to Steer = 034.1, SMG = 6.3. (C) Guess = 035, best = 034.1, error = 0.9°. Note this comparison varies with different configurations, but the assumption of equal is a good, quick working guideline.

12-22. Reference to all is Rule 19d. (A) No one. There is no right of way in the fog. (B) Large turn to the right. (C) Large turn to the right. (D) Large turn to the right. (E) Large turn to the left.

12-23. (D) Any of the above reasons can be used to justify your maneuver.

12-24. (A) is true by law, (D) is true by common sense. The other two are wrong by law.

12-25. (D) None. It is illegal and you will be fined.

12-26. 100 yards... due to Federal Protection and Security Zones.

12-27. (A) There is a specific optimum way to fold them (inside out, with the chart name and number hand lettered onto the back side at the double-fold corner.)

12-28. 1907-1525 = 3h 42m = 3.7h, and 3.7 × 7.4 = 27.4 nmi.

12-29. (A) 50 to 90 ft, (B) 150 to 500 ft. A poor fix means the unit got just enough signals to compute a fix, but it is a poor one. Both of these answers are transient, and best learned by direct measurement, ie out with a broad open view of the horizon for (A), and through one window of your house or deep fjord underway for (B).

12-30. One your instrument must be WAAS capable, and two you must have one of the specific (geostationary) WAAS satellites in view and in use in your fix.

12-31. First the easy parts: Your masthead wind instruments might not be perfectly aligned with the centerline, or your sail trim is not the same on each tack. More complex to consider is the effect of a current, which can only be addressed after the first two items have been ruled out by tests in guaranteed still water and modest air... ie not too strong and not too weak.

If current is present, the effect on VMG depends on how you compute the true wind direction that you are using as a reference. In other words, when the electronics solve for the true wind direction they have to use a course and speed input. This can be S from knotmeter and C from compass, or it could be SOG and COG. This topic is beyond the scope of this book, but we can appreciate the issue by imagining tacking into a north wind, with an west flowing current. The starboard tack would have a higher apparent wind speed than the port tack. Then there is also the issue to consider that wind angle is measured relative to the centerline, but your actual COG is not aligned with the centerline in notable current. Do an Internet search on "true wind versus water wind" for an extended discussion of this complex topic.

APPENDIX

A1. Using Electronic Charts

If you intend to use electronic charting on your vessel, it will be excellent practice to solve many of these practice exercises using electronic charts in addition to the traditional solutions using paper charts. In principle you can get more accurate results with the echarts, once you have mastered the special tools available. A few tips and tricks are outlined below.

Electronic charts of US waters made by NOAA are free Internet downloads. We maintain a portal to these that is easy to remember

starpath.com/getcharts

You will see multiple options for various formats, including the new pdf versions in both booklet or full chart formats. The pdf charts are convenient for study and they will open in almost any computer or mobile device, but they do not serve well as a base chart for navigation, and they will not open in any standard echart reader. To use echarts in an electronic charting system (ECS) you must choose between one of two formats, either RNC (raster navigation chart) or ENC (electronic navigation chart)—this is not a tidy nomenclature, but it is now standard.

RNC echarts are graphic images of the actual paper chart, as opposed to ENC which are vector charts. A vector chart is essentially a mathematical prescription for drawing the chart as it is displayed. ENC are smaller files, and in principle they can include much more data, as they have layers of information that can be displayed, often with user selected formatting. But the final product does look different than the corresponding printed chart, so many users new to ECS find it more suitable to start with the RNC, and then they are looking at charts they are familiar with.

Furthermore, the RNC are by definition "right" in that they are direct copies of the printed chart, whereas ENC might include discrepancies with the printed chart. Both chart formats should be updated weekly, just as the new print on demand (POD) paper charts are now.

So we recommend starting with the RNC and later experiment with the ENC. Eventually all charts will be ENC, simply because in principle they have more options and can include more information, but this will take a while.

The chart numbers used for the RNC are the same as used for the corresponding paper chart. The corresponding ENC, on the other hand, use a more obscure nomenclature. You cannot guess the later number from the former. To find the equivalent chart number, proceed as if downloading an ENC, then choose the list of individual charts, and one of the columns will be the corresponding paper chart number. There is not always a one to one correspondence, because some ENC incorporate several RNC.

The main challenge to the echart navigator is what software program should be used to view the charts. We are referring here to programs or apps you run in your own, stand-alone computer or tablet, in contrast to navigation instruments that include their own proprietary software using also proprietary ENC charts (ie C-Map).

There are many options. The software is generically called *navigation software*, or sometimes just *echart viewer*. The distinction between these two types is often that the latter lets you do everything with the echart except display a live GPS vessel position. To work exercises from this workbook and to learn the ropes of chart navigation with ECS, a simple viewer is all you need. This can also be accomplished with the free or demo versions of commercial software that must be purchased in order to add live GPS tracking.

An open source option for PC or Mac is found at opencpn.org. Another that we have used for classroom echart viewer for many years is at memory-map.com. The memory-map viewer includes a GPS simulator with optional set and drift, which is a convenient aid to navigation training. NOAA has an extended list of echart viewers online. We provide a link to the NOAA list and to related resources at starpath.com/1210tr. This link also tells how you can download a free copy of the 1210 Tr (RNC) echart for use with this workbook.

The plotting and measurement tools used in echart software are often unique to the product, but there are common factors and procedures that are easy to adapt to any version. Examples of the use of these functions to solve typical charting exercises are covered below. Most programs have good Help files linked from their menu bars

(1) Set-up

The first step with any program is check the set up. You have a choice in all units, bearings, and Lat-Lon format. Generally you want nautical miles, feet, true bearings, and dd mm.mm format for angles. Then you have optional displays. You want a planning mode rather than a navigation mode that takes a GPS input, and you want an easy way to show the Lat-Lon at the cursor. Don't forget the right click. Many programs have convenient options with a right click

Next is learn how they load the charts. Generally you download the charts to a known place on your computer, then choose a menu option for installing or registering charts. Usually after that the chart outline shows on the background (maybe another option).

(2) Read Lat-Lon of a Point

Ideally this is a simple display option. Sometimes it shows right at the cursor, sometimes in a panel that you have to set up and position. Maybe it shown in a status bar at the top or bottom of the screen. Often the position will be given to 0.001' but it would be very rare that this last digit is accurate enough to justify its use (ie ± 6 ft or so).

(3) Put a Mark or Waypoint on the Chart

Some programs distinguish between marks and waypoints, others do not. To place one to a place on the chart of choice, just click the tool, then click the chart. To put a mark at a specific Lat-Lon, just place it in the approximately right spot, then right click it, and in the Properties assign it the precise Lat-Lon you want. You can also give it a name, and lock it if desired so it cannot be accidentally moved.

(4) Range and Bearing Between Two Points

This common application can be done with a dedicated Range and Bearing Tool, or with the Route Tool. Use the Route option by making a one-leg route from Point A to Point B. A typical sequence might be to left click the Route button, single left click point A, then double left click point B mark the point and end the route. Then you can right click the line to view Properties, ie range and bearing between them. If you end up with too many points, i.e. you single clicked the second point not double clicked, it does not matter. Just double click at some point to finish the route and then delete the extra waypoints. The procedure will be mastered with little practice. A dedicated Range and Bearing tool does this in one step, which is more convenient.

Often we must distinguish between range and bearing from a Point A to a Point B, versus from the boat icon (your position) to Point B. The latter tool will not make sense in a planning mode.

With echart options we can read very accurate range and bearing by zooming in on the chart before point selection. Remember that buoys and lights are located at the positions of the small circles associated with their symbols.

Dedicated Range and Bearing tools work differently in different software, and some programs to not have any and we must use the Route Tool. A nice feature is one that lets you draw in the line at the desired orientation anywhere on the chart and then click and move the entire line without changing its orientation. (Coastal Explorer is a commercial ECS program that has this feature.) These tools are effectively acting like parallel rulers. Some even let you digitally set the precise orientation and length from its properties window once you have made an approximate one.

(5) Plot a Circle of Position

Suppose you measured distance off of a place called Mead's Peak and found you were 0.21 nmi off the peak. Place a waypoint on the peak and then go to waypoint properties and make an alarm ring. In some software you can do this in any distance units you choose; in others you will have to convert to or from nmi. Circles of position are a powerful tool in ECS chart navigation.

For more Help

Reference books and resources are listed at starpath.com/1210tr.

A2. Interpolation

It is common in marine navigation to need an interpolated value from a table. We each need a way we are comfortable with to solve this. Here are a couple suggestions.

Suppose we know that the deviation of a compass is 20°E at compass heading 000 and it is 6.5°E at compass heading 045. What is the deviation at heading 030.

Procedure 1. Make a custom table.

(1) Write down what you know:

$$000C = 20E$$

$$045C = 6.5E$$

(2) Figure how many equal steps it takes to make a table that has your value in it. We can do this example in 3 steps, namely 000, 015, 030, 045.

(3) Figure the increment per step based on the values known: That is, $(20 - 6.5)/3 = 4.5°$ per step.

(4) Now we can make a table with our desired answer in it by just adding the increments at each step:

Compass heading		Deviation
000 =	20 =	20
015 =	20 - 4.5 =	15.5
030 =	15.5 - 4.5 =	11.0
045 =	11.0 - 4.5 =	6.5

And from this we see immediately that the deviation at 030 C is 11° E. In many, if not most, interpolation cases, it will be easy to choose the steps and make such a table. The next procedure is more systematic, which may appeal to some.

Procedure 2. Compute proportions

Consider this table of the known and unknown.

Compass heading	Deviation
A = 000 C	C = 20.0°
X = given = 30	Y = unknown
B = 045 C	D = 6.5°

We want to know Y, which we can get from proportions, namely:

$(X - A) / (B - A) = (Y - C) / (D - C)$, or

$(D - C) \times (X - A) / (B - A) = (Y - C)$.

Solving for Y and regrouping we get:

$Y = C + (X - A) \times [(D - C) / (B - A)]$.

In the last example,

$Y = 20 + (30 - 00) \times (6.5 - 20)/(45 - 00)$

$= 20 + 30 \times (-13.5/45) = 20 - 9 = 11.0$

To use this method, fill in the table below and use a calculator to get the answer. For the formula to work as given, the desired unknown must be in variable 2, as shown.

Variable 1	Variable 2
A =	C =
X (given) =	Y (desired) =
B =	D =
$Y = C + (X - A) \times [(D - C) / (B - A)]$	

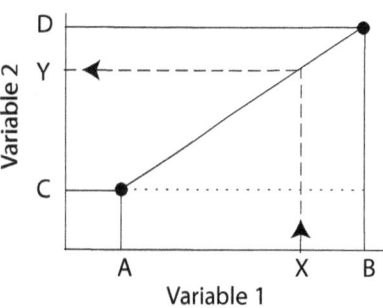

Example 1. Heading 310, dev = 8W, heading 290, dev 2E, what is the deviation at heading 305? It does not matter how we label E or W, but one has to be + and the other -. So call E -, then: A = 310, B = 290, X = 305, C = 8, D = -2. And we can find Y = 8 + (305 - 310) × ((-2 - 8)/(290 - 310)) = 8 - 5 × (-10/-20) = 8 - 2.5 = 5.5, which is + so it must be 5.5 W.

Example 2. At 40N, sunset is at 1706 and at 45N, sunset is at 1658. What is the time of sun set at latitude 43° 15'N? First we have to get things into nice units: 1658 = 16h 58m, and 1706 = 16h 66m. Likewise, 43° 15' = 43+(15/60) = 43.25°.

So we have 40° = 66m and at 45° we have 58m, and we wish to know what is sun set minutes at lat 43.25°. We can choose A = 40, X = 43.25, B = 45, and C = 66m and D = 58m. Then Y = 66 + (43.25 - 40) × ((58 - 66)/45 - 40)) = 66 + 3.25x(-8/5) = 66 - 5.2 = 60.8m = 60m 48s, and the answer is 16h + 60m 48s = 17h 00m 48s.

 *A very convenient 99¢ iOS app for navigation interpolation is called Interp Plus; see mintaka-research.com. The Help file for this app includes varied applications, including times, angles, temperatures.*

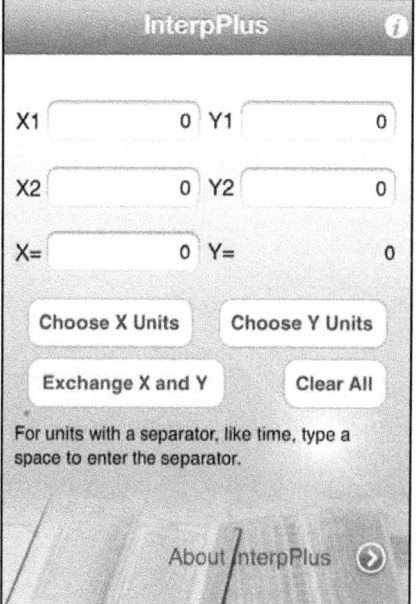

A3. Sources for 1210 Tr Printed Charts

For this particular chart there are two options, either the now standard Print on Demand (POD) or a bulk printed paper chart. The POD versions come in several paper options; the standard printed charts are on a durable heavy paper, but not quite as heavy as the historic NOAA lithographic charts.

These dealers are also the source for any NOAA chart and some stock international charts as well.

Sample Sources for 1210 Tr	
Outlet	**Location**
Blue Water Books and Charts	Ft. Lauderdale, FL
Captains Nautical Supply	Seattle, WA
Landfall Navigation	Stamford, CT
Maryland Nautical Supply	Baltimore, MD
Safe Navigation	Long Beach, CA

www.ingramcontent.com/pod-product-compliance
Lightning Source LLC
Chambersburg PA
CBHW080521110426
42742CB00017B/3193